[*The Voice of the Martyrs*]

Hearts of Fire

VOM
BOOKS

Published by VOM Books, P.O. Box 443, Bartlesville, OK 74005-0443.

Previously published by Thomas Nelson (ISBN 978-0-8499-4422-2).

Unless otherwise indicated, Scripture quotations used in this book are from The New King James Version (NKJV), copyright © 1979, 1980, 1982, Thomas Nelson, Publishers.

Other Scripture references are from the King James Version of the Bible (KJV).

"Because He Lives" Words by William J. and Gloria Gaither. Music by William J. Gaither. Copyright © 1971 William J. Gaither, Inc. All rights controlled by Gaither Copyright Management. Used by permission.

Many of the names and places in this book's testimonies have been changed to protect the identities of those represented. It was also necessary to omit details concerning ministry activities that continue within these nations to protect the lives of those involved. Some court transcripts and other quoted materials have been edited for brevity and clarity.

Library of Congress Cataloging-in-Publication Data

Hearts of Fire / by The Voice of the Martyrs.

p. cm.

ISBN 978-0-88264-150-8 (softcover)

1. Christian women—Developing countries—Biography. 2. Persecution—Developing countries—History. 3. Christian biography—developing countries. I. Voice of the Martyrs (Organization). II. Title.

BR1608.5.H43   2003
272'.9'0922—dc22

Printed in the United States of America

[*Contents*]

Dedicated to

Sabina Wurmbrand,

a voice for martyrs

Foreword

I am humbled to be asked to write a foreword for such a book as this. I would not begin to group myself with these stalwart women of the faith.

As I read their incredible stories of God-given courage, I could relate to many of their feelings. During the year (May 2001 – June 2002) that my husband, Martin, and I spent in captivity with Abu Sayyaf terrorists in the Philippine jungle, I, too, felt hopeless, wanting to die. I was homeless and starving . . . but for me, I knew that as soon as my release came, I would return to my life of relative ease. Now here I sit in America with a beautiful home, plenty to eat, and a support group—while these women continue to endure hardness as good soldiers of Christ.

So when I'm taking a nice hot bath, I pray. When I'm putting on make-up and fixing my hair to get ready to go speak, I pray. When I'm running errands for my kids, I pray. When I pass an encouraging sign outside a church, I pray for all those who don't have the "infrastructure" I have. For those who are suffering because they believe in Jesus. For those who think they are all alone, yet remain true to their faith.

I pray for them the same thing I prayed for myself in the jungle: "Lord, let them feel You close to them. Help them remain faithful as this situation just keeps going from bad to worse. Show them a glimpse of Your goodness so they know they are not alone. And at the end, I know You'll be there."

Oh, that each of us reading this book would readily commit ourselves anew to letting God use us however He sees fit—even if it means giving up freedom and comfort. The day may come when we are beaten or even killed for being a Christ-follower. Let us take courage from these simple women.

God will not test us above what we are able. He will, with the testing, make a way to escape (provide everything we need) so that we will be able to bear it. I choose to believe that God does all things well. Man does not. We have made a mess of this beautiful world. If there is anything good in this life, it is from God. He has a plan, and He is sovereign. We wait patiently for His timing when He will make all things new.

Until then, may He give us the grace to live for Him, as these women are doing. He is worthy.

—Gracia Burnham
New Tribes Mission
Author, *In the Presence of My Enemies*

Acknowledgments

When we first undertook this project on behalf of The Voice of the Martyrs, we knew it would take quite a team. First we needed Christian women who would be willing to share their testimonies. Without them, there would be no book, and to them we express our heartfelt appreciation.

Each chapter (with the exception of Sabina Wurmbrand's) also required a number of field personnel, and some required translators. In more than half the stories, secret locations had to be arranged and safety protocols implemented. Needless to say, we could not have undertaken this project without the support of VOM field staff and coworkers. Due to current risks, most of these workers cannot be named. But we wish to extend our thanks to all who helped in each of the countries where we traveled.

Assisting with writing and editing are Todd Nettleton (also on staff with VOM) and Sue Ann Jones. You were both a tremendous help. Thank you.

It is not always easy to get behind projects that deal with persecution and some of the more harsh realities of our faith. But Greg Daniel and the team at W Publishing Group (who originally

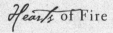

published this book) have proven their commitment in bringing these incredible stories of tenacity and courage to the forefront. Thanks for making *Hearts of Fire* come alive.

And a special thanks to our children, Jordan and Elena, who graciously "gave up" Mom and Dad many nights and weekends, and during our trips overseas. We pray these stories will become part of your own foundation of faith.

—Steve & Ginny Cleary

Hearts Ablaze with
Courage and Conviction

*K*idnapped. *Beaten. Imprisoned.* In many parts of the world today these words are synonymous with being a Christian. And for Christian women in these areas, another challenge exists: the social stigma of being looked upon as lower class, unfit for leadership, and belonging under the control and guidance of men.

Hearts of Fire is the stories of eight women who, despite such circumstances, have shown incredible courage, conviction, and love for Jesus Christ and His church. In the harshest settings, they have become leaders who have exercised extraordinary boldness and tenacity, refusing to shrink from the needs and opportunities that challenged them. Ironically, only in suffering have they had equal rights with their male counterparts; in some instances, they have suffered even worse.

When we first considered a book of testimonies about Christian women persecuted for their faith, we faced a number of challenges. First and foremost, we wanted the testimonies to be as contemporary as possible. This required that we travel to each nation where these women currently reside and in many cases still face grave danger. We also wanted to present examples of women who had not only faced times of personal suffering but who had also displayed leadership qualities in ministry. Finally, beyond the dramatic stories of pain and torment, we wanted to portray inspiring examples of steadfast hope and how these women, even in the darkest places, found ways to let Christ's love shine through.

It is important to note that the women highlighted in *Hearts of Fire* are but a small example of the countless women around the world who face similar situations. We chose women who would represent a variety of regions where Christians are persecuted, and we selected those with whom we could arrange to meet individually. Those we interviewed usually told us they thought others would be better candidates with more dramatic stories. None wanted to call attention to herself as a unique example of Christian heroism.

The stories comprise an amazing diversity. While some of the women served years in captivity, others served no time at all but endured other hardships. Their ages vary widely, and many different backgrounds are represented, from Christian to Islam, Hinduism, or atheism. Even more amazing were the similarities: a deep drive and a strong conviction that pushed each woman beyond human expectation and human frailties.

It is our prayer that you come away from reading *Hearts of Fire* with a deeper conviction and steadier direction for handling life's difficulties. If you are only amazed at these incredible testimonies, we have failed. If you can find in your own life similarities with one or more of these testimonies, and if you can gain strength from these examples of extraordinary courage, we have succeeded, and so have these women who have so graciously offered to share their stories with you.

[Introduction: Hearts Ablaze with Courage and Conviction]

When we first undertook this project we planned to include a short devotional thought at the conclusion of each chapter. However, after compiling the stories, we realized none were needed. Embedded within each testimony are precious gems of faith and fortitude. We trust these qualities will kindle a spark in your own life as you experience *Hearts of Fire*.

—The Voice of the Martyrs

Adel:
Amid the Horror . . . Hope

Indonesia
5:00 p.m., Monday, January 10, 2000

*U*nder the shadow of swaying palm trees, Adel gathered the children together, about fifty of them. Her voice rose as she began to sing "Onward, Christian Soldiers." She could see the fear in the children's eyes as they joined in the song.

"I don't want to die!" one of the children called out. He was not yet ten years old.

"We're not going to die. Come, clap your hands with us." Adel leaned toward him, speaking directly into his ear to be heard above the children's voices.

The scared boy reluctantly joined in. They sang another song, again clapping their trembling hands together. Adel was attempting to drown out the shouting—the screams and the terror—drifting up the hillside from less than a mile below.

She knew she had to keep the children from crying, especially the older ones. If one of them started wailing, there would be mass hysteria. Adel admired their bravery. Even the other parents who

5

were clustered in small groups around the children seemed to gain strength from their spirited youngsters.

As the singing continued, Adel gazed over the assembled youth and spotted her own two children. Christina was already nine, and Christiano, seven. Adel could be brave, she reassured herself; she could be brave for her children—all the children. Her trust was firmly rooted in Christ. She worried about them, though—especially Christiano, her little "Anto." He was so young, and small for his age.

Adel silently prayed for God's protection and again was thankful she'd grabbed her Bible before fleeing her home. She opened it now, carefully turning the worn pages to a familiar passage, and read aloud: "I can do all things through Christ who strengthens me."[1] Then Adel flipped to the back of her Bible, where numerous songs were printed, and she led the children in another chorus.

While they were singing, some of the children began complaining that they were hungry and thirsty. They had been on the hill since noon, and now the setting sun cast a vivid, tawny glow over the sky. Sunsets could be so spectacular here on their small Indonesian island of Dodi. But today the twilight was an ominous prelude to the darkness about to fall on their village.

Suddenly Methu's shouts pierced through the children's singing. "Run! Adel, run!" Adel rushed to the edge of the hill and struggled to see in the waning sunlight. She could barely make out the silhouettes of men scrambling up the steep trail. Again Methu's voice rang out. "Take the children, Adel! Hurry! You must run into the jungle."

Instead, Adel froze, paralyzed by the crackling sounds of fire now drifting up the hillside as smoke ascended into the darkening sky. *They have set the entire village ablaze.* Every house would be consumed, she knew, including her own.

She agonized over the choice she must make. Should she help Methu as he made his way up the rocky embankment, or should she run to her children? It was all happening too fast. In the same way a person's life can pass through her memory in an instant, Adel's past and future now collided in her mind. Two wonderful children . . . a loving husband . . . life had been good.

She turned toward the children, then glanced one last time at Methu. And in that instant, she remembered an uninvited, audacious seventeen-year-old who had stubbornly seated himself on her mother's couch . . .

"Only God Can Separate You Now"

July 1989

"Mom, he looks like a monkey!" Adel hissed, peeking out from the kitchen door toward the young man waiting in the living room.

Her mother was not impressed. Adel might be too young to get married, but she could still show a little respect and appreciation for the young man's relentless determination.

He arrived at their house at approximately the same time each day. Adel didn't know if she was more flattered or annoyed as, each day, Methu confidently settled himself on the couch and repeated the same request. Actually, Adel had answered him numerous times, but Methu was either refusing to accept her answer or just pretending not to hear her.

"I don't want to get married. I'm too young. And even if I did want to get married, I don't want to marry *you!*" Adel persisted. She was seventeen too, and her beauty had recently blossomed. But she had no interest in starting a relationship—although she certainly had plenty of opportunities.

Methu offered no argument nor took offense at her impetuous

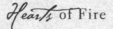

remarks. He just sat there and patiently explained again to Adel that she was to be his wife. "It is God's plan. Even if you think I look like a monkey."

Adel chuckled as she caught the hint of her mother's smile. Undeterred, Methu once more made his request: "So, will you marry me?"

She knew there was no logic in answering, so Adel just sat there, wondering when he would go away. Finally Methu got up to leave, but before departing he removed his outer shirt, folded it neatly, and placed it on her lap. "There," he said, "you won't answer me, so my shirt will wait in my absence."

Adel couldn't help being flattered by his youthful yet sincere gesture. Maybe he wasn't so bad after all . . .

Three months later, Adel and Methu were married.

It was a traditional wedding according to local customs. It started early on a bright October afternoon and went long into the night. Two complete meals were served to the entire village that came out to witness the joyous event. It all seemed to go by in a flash as Adel fought off intermittent waves of anxiety, worrying again that she was too young and marriage was a terrible mistake. She was the first among seven siblings to marry; how could she possibly comprehend her new obligations as a wife? Only the words of the pastor after the ceremony brought the new bride comfort. "Adel," he had told her, "only God can separate you and Methu now."

Adel became pregnant a month after the wedding, and although she carried the baby full term, the child was stillborn after a long and intensive labor. Adel and Methu were devastated.

But five months later, Adel was pregnant again. This time the baby was born three months early and wasn't expected to live. Friends who came to visit comforted Adel and encouraged her to "be strong when the baby dies."

"My baby's not going to die!" Adel answered obstinately. Her heart was entirely convinced, and she refused to be swayed by the opinion of her family or neighbors. She would *not* lose another child.

Adel gently laid her newborn daughter on a pillow and softly spoke to the tiny girl, praying to God at the same time. "Why are you here, Christina?" she whispered. "You didn't reach your full time in my womb, but here you are. And even though you are so small, Methu and I love you so much. And I know God is going to protect you."

To the amazement of her family and the villagers, Christina developed into a healthy toddler and was joined two and a half years later by her brother, Christiano.

Adel and Methu couldn't have been happier. Soon after Christiano was born they moved into their own home. It was a simple three-room house made mostly from bamboo, and it had a dirt floor. It was humble, but it was theirs. Perhaps when the children were older they could afford a better, larger house. That would be something to look forward to. For now, though, they were happy just to be out from under the roof of Methu's parents.

Nearly all the families of Adel's village were Christian, and she enthusiastically assisted with the church's youth programs. There were more than fifty children close in age to Christina and Christiano, and Adel loved to read them the same exciting Bible stories her grandfather had once read to her. It seemed fitting that she was now doing the same work as her grandfather—preaching the gospel—even if it was to neighborhood children.

THE IMPENDING JIHAD

Life passed with little trouble for Adel and those in her village, until the neighboring Muslims paid their first "official" visit.

Although she wouldn't realize it at the time, the nightmare actually started at 3:00 p.m. on September 9, 1999—a day that, looking back, Adel will never forget. At the sound of a nearby commotion she hurried outside and immediately caught sight of the banner. On it only two words were printed in large block letters: "*Cinti Damai*," meaning "Love Peace." Clustered around the banner were thirty men, women, and children from a Muslim village named Dahma.

"People of Dodi," a dark-skinned, middle-aged man proclaimed, "we are your neighbors, and we should commit to each other to live in peace." There was no sound system, but his booming voice flowed easily through the crowd. He stood tall and lean on the old wooden platform of the meeting house. There should be no misunderstandings or fighting between the Muslim and Christian villages, he said. They should all live in peace.

Adel and the others who had crowded around the platform thought this was peculiar considering there hadn't been any previous confrontations, but they extended a hand of friendship to their visitors, who stayed the remainder of the afternoon.

Later that evening, after Methu had returned from work in the local mines, Adel related the events. "But what about the rumor?" Methu questioned.

A strange piece of gossip had been circulating that the ninth day of the ninth month of 1999 would be a dark day for Christians on the island of Dodi. However, Methu and Adel had dismissed the rumor as just that. Now they considered the Muslims' visit and agreed there seemed to be no apparent threat. Actually it had been a jovial atmosphere as their children played together.

Nearly four months passed without an incident or cause for suspicion, and the Dodi residents assumed the rumor was unfounded—until just after Christmas, when Yulpius, a young merchant, returned to the village after a failed attempt to leave the island. Seeing him again so soon after he had left, the villagers asked him why he had returned so quickly.

"They wouldn't let me leave," Yulpius announced.

"Who? Why not?" one man asked as others pressed forward with increasing anxiety.

Yulpius continued, "A number of Muslim men stopped me, and I don't know why. At first they simply told me not to travel right now, that it was too dangerous. I protested and told them I needed to leave the island to get more supplies, but they didn't seem to care. They got really aggravated and seemed offended that I was a Christian. I recognized some of the men as ones who were part of the group that visited us to proclaim the so-called peace. I didn't want any further trouble, so I turned around and came back home."

Adel, Methu, and many others started to mull over Yulpius's story, rethinking the events of September 9. But with no proof of imminent danger, there was little they could do. Then, on January 10, their worst fears swept through their village like a rampant storm.

Adel was resting with an ailing Christiano around noon when they were awakened by the sounds of an upheaval developing among the neighbors. Adel ran out her front door and gasped at the sight of large columns of smoke rising in the distance. A nearby village—a Christian village—was burning. Then came the rising shouts of panic. They must flee their homes. Three thousand armed Muslims were on their way, and there was little hope of stopping the impending jihad.[2]

Adel ran back inside, yelling for Christina and Anto. But no one answered. The pounding in Adel's heart grew louder as she frantically searched for her children, running back outside and screaming their names. Finally someone told her they had been seen already making their way up the hill behind the village. Adel ran back inside once more to hurriedly grab a few things. As she headed again for the door she spotted her Bible on the table. She grabbed it . . . and fled.

"Mom, Are We Going to Die?"

6:00 p.m., Monday, January 10, 2000

Methu and the other village men had held off the Muslim attackers for nearly four hours, but there were simply too many of them, and they were well armed with machetes, torches, and firearms.

Now the entire village was ablaze, and the mob's shouts of *"Allah Akbar! Allah Akbar!"*[3] filled the air. Methu and the other men frantically fled up the slippery embankment, hoping the jihad warriors would be satisfied with the destruction of their village. Instead a sadistic rage seemed to spread among them, and soon they were also scrambling up the hill, wildly firing their rifles in the direction of the assembled Christians.

Methu and Adel swiftly gathered their children and their mothers as everyone began fleeing in different directions. Hoping to avoid the rampant gunfire, they threw themselves into the deep grass and proceeded to crawl as quickly as possible into the jungle. But the strenuous journey on their hands and knees proved more difficult as a heavy rain began to fall, turning the bare ground into a continuous pool of mud.

After crawling for almost two hours through the dense jungle, they came to an abandoned shed on the edge of a coconut plantation. Constructed of wood with three sides and a roof, it had been used by farmers as a respite from the sweltering afternoon heat during harvesttime. Hopefully, tonight it would serve as a sanctuary for the weary family. They were too exhausted to travel any farther.

Christina and Christiano fell asleep almost immediately as Adel laid them down on a bamboo mat they found in the deserted building. Like the rest of the family, the children were soaking wet and covered with mud. And while the deteriorating structure provided some shelter, the roof was full of gaping holes allowing steady trickles of rain to fall on the children.

Adel couldn't hold it in any longer. Like the rain, the tears poured down her face as she wept aloud.

When she had regained control, she and Methu huddled together for a brief and somber time of prayer, then they quietly sat together with each of their mothers throughout the fearful night. As dawn broke, Christina and her brother awoke, slowly coming to understand that the horrific nightmare they thought they had dreamed was, in fact, reality. For some time they sat silently, staring at the adults. Their wide eyes begged for a few words of comfort, but a deathly silence overshadowed the frightened family and no one knew what to say.

Finally Christiano whimpered, "Mommy, I'm hungry."

Adel's eyes swelled closed again as she tried to hold back the tears, but by the time she could bring her young son into her lap, she was weeping uncontrollably.

"Please don't cry like that, Adel," Methu pleaded. "I'll go look for food." He tried to reassure his wife, but he knew she had reached her limit. Adel's heart was being ripped apart as she helplessly witnessed the suffering of her precious children.

Methu was going back to the destroyed village to look for food. Adel begged him not to go, but she knew they had to do something. They couldn't remain in the shed without food or water.

Time seemed to pass in slow motion after Methu left. A deep sense of fear continued to grip Adel. Unable to fight the anxiety, she led her family back into the jungle. They eventually came upon others from their village who were hiding along the edge of a cornfield. Adel led Christina and Anto and the mothers through the neat rows of corn, and they began picking the dried ears. At least they would have something to eat.

A few hours later Methu rejoined his family carrying twelve cans of Coca-Cola. It was all he could find. But as the children reached for the tabs to open the cans, gunshots rang out, echoing like rolling thunder throughout the field. No one knew which direction the shots were coming from, so they threw themselves to the ground, having no clear thought of where to run. Finally Christina looked up at Adel and asked, "Mom, are we going to die?"

Yes, we are, was the thought that ripped through Adel's mind, but she knew she had to be brave for her children. She pulled both of them together and told them everything would be OK. But Adel knew her words of comfort couldn't replace the dreadful reality of their situation. She knew what she had to do. It would be the most difficult conversation she would ever have with her children, but Adel had no choice. She had to tell them . . .

"Christina and Anto, please look at me and listen very carefully. If we are caught by those of the jihad, they will ask you if you want to become a Muslim. If you say no, they may kill you." Adel looked directly into the children's eyes. She knew there was only one right answer, but how could children so young be expected to be so brave?

Both her children answered simply, "We want to follow Jesus."

Without a second thought, Adel opened the Bible she had brought with her and turned to the one passage that had continually run through her mind since she had fled her home. Adel's grandfather had read it to her so many times as a child it was practically etched into her heart: Psalm 23. She instructed her two children to repeat after her and began reciting the words, "The LORD is my shepherd; I shall not want. . . . Yea, though I walk through the valley of the shadow of death, I will fear no evil;

for You are with me . . ." She continued until both of them had committed the psalm to memory. They both appeared so brave, but Adel wondered if they truly comprehended the gravity of the situation.

Feeling the tears forming again in the corner of her eyes, she hastily wiped them away with the back of her hand and asked, "Christina, aren't you afraid they may kill you if you say you are a Christian?"

Christina brought her face close to her mother's, looked straight into her eyes, and softly answered, "Mom, please don't worry. I'm not afraid to die."

After the gunshots ceased, those in the cornfields eventually scattered. Adel, Methu, and their family made their way back into the opaque jungle, where they traveled wearily for another two days. They walked well into the darkness of night and slept only a few hours before rising again at dawn. At one point Methu had met others from their village and learned from them that some Christians had already been killed. Worried for his loved ones, he just pushed them deeper into the jungle.

Everyone was exhausted, and finally Methu and Adel realized they could not push the children any farther. Although they had a small amount of fresh coconut milk, the hunger pains were growing worse, and Adel cried each time one of the children asked for food. They had also met up with Methu's father and brother.

They came to what Methu believed would be a safe place to rest, and he gathered some dry palm leaves for the children to sit on. Hearing the rippling sounds of a stream below the ravine, he and his brother decided to venture down to see if they could find something to eat.

At such a tender age, Anto didn't understand why they hadn't had any food in the last few days and bluntly asked if he could have some rice and fish. "Your father will be right back, and

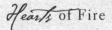

maybe he will have some fish. Then we can eat," Adel told him, attempting to offer some encouragement. But she knew it wasn't likely that Methu would find food for them, and she pulled Anto close, softly humming a chorus and gently rocking him.

THE ALL-POWERFUL BLOOD OF JESUS

Less than ten minutes had passed when she heard Methu scream. At first Adel thought he was crazy to yell like that, knowing the jihad warriors could be close by. Then she realized Methu had already been surrounded, and he was yelling for Adel and the rest of the family to flee. Again she heard the words that had chilled her heart just a few days earlier. "Run, Adel! Run!"

Before Methu could cry out again, Adel heard the rapid crackle of an automatic weapon. She immediately pushed herself up but with Anto's arms still wrapped around her neck, she stumbled. She turned just in time to catch a glimpse of Christina running in the direction of Methu's cries. Adel drew a breath to yell at her to stop, but it was too late. They were surrounded by men in long white robes.

Anto was lying on the ground where Adel had dropped him. When he tried to get up, one of the men swung his machete and caught him across the back with the broad side of the blade. Adel screamed at the top of her lungs and threw herself on her son to protect his small body from another blow. She could see her son's face turning white with fear as he slipped into shock, but her attempts to help Anto proved useless as one of the Muslim men grabbed her long black hair and easily lifted her into the air.

A bloodstained machete was pressed against Adel's neck as the men forced her toward a pair of bamboo trees. She knew their intentions as they began tearing at her clothing. She was still clutching her Bible, but it fell to the ground as easily as her clothes. Adel closed her eyes, silently praying for her family and begging God to save her from being raped.

Adel then heard the screams of her mother, her mother-in-law, and her precious Anto, and she knew they were being massacred by the vicious thugs who had driven them from their home. It was too much to bear. On the edge of fainting, she fell to her knees as she saw those who had attacked her family turn and come toward her. Blood dripped from the edges of their machetes. Anto's blood.

"Oh, God!" Adel cried. She didn't know how she could go on. One of the men took off his sweaty turban and tied it around Adel's head. On it was written, "Allah Akbar." With her last bit of strength Adel shouted, "The blood of Jesus is all powerful!"

"She is a Christian! A pig! A stinking pig! Let's just rape her and get it over with," a voice sneered. A larger number of enraged Muslims now surrounded Adel, discussing what to do with her. They were speaking in their local dialect, not realizing Adel could understand everything they were saying.

Attempting to conceal her tears, Adel quietly prayed in her heart, *Lord, please help them realize what they are doing. It is so evil . . . please make them understand. They cannot know what they are doing. It isn't humanly possible.* As she continued to pray, from the commotion in front of her a hushed, soft voice whispered, "Adel, is that you?" She looked up to discover a man they had captured from her village. His name was Hans.

Hans had also been stripped naked and was bleeding severely. Her heart fell deeper into despair; she was certain he would not survive the day. She asked him if he had seen Methu or Christina. He shook his head no.

One of the men bundled up Adel's clothing, shoving it into her arms. She was not allowed to put it on. She looked down at her Bible, which had been torn to shreds.

The two captives were marched up a steep mountain trail with machetes prodding the most vulnerable parts of their beaten bodies. As the trail narrowed, Adel looked down over the ridge, realizing how high she was and how easy it might be to jump. She knew she would probably be killed if she jumped, but that was OK. *Help me, Lord! Please, help me*, she continually pleaded. Resisting the temptation to jump, she finally came to the top of the mountain, where well over a thousand jihad warriors were gathered. They were of all different ages, some barely teenagers, but each was dressed exactly the same in a long white robe with a tightly wound turban on his head.

At gunpoint, one of the soldiers forced Adel and Hans to stand one behind the other. The soldier was middle-aged with broad shoulders. He laid his rifle by his side and slowly removed a long machete from its sheath. Adel looked around, realizing she and Hans were the only two Christians in a sea of white robes. She closed her eyes, believing, even hoping, it would finally be over.

Within seconds, she felt the warm flow of blood running down her face and body. "The blood of Jesus is all powerful!" she screamed again and again. Hans was screaming too. And she could hear the angry voices of other men yelling and chanting in the distance. She dared not open her eyes. If she just kept them closed long enough, she thought, she could open them on the other side, in heaven. But after waiting for what seemed like hours, she couldn't help but lift her eyelids. In front of her was the mutilated body of Hans.

SEVEN SIMPLE WORDS

Adel was covered with blood but couldn't tell if it was hers or Hans's. She was in severe pain from the repeated blows of the Muslim men, but there didn't appear to be any open wounds on her body. Her voice was getting weak now, but she managed to repeat the words: "The blood of Jesus is all powerful." Somehow she knew God was protecting her. She should have died many times by now. Over five hours had passed since they had stripped her of her clothing and started beating her. She already knew Anto, her mother, Methu's mother, and Hans were dead, and she suspected the others were too. But she was still alive, and there had to be a reason why. Amid the horrible assaults, Adel somehow felt an amazing glimmer of hope.

The band of jihad warriors gathered their weapons and told Adel it was time to leave. She would be their guide, they said. They shoved her to the front of the forming line, and she led them down a winding road on the opposite side of the mountain. Adel had no thought of where they were going. She simply walked in a state of semiconsciousness and tried to shake the sounds of Hans's brutal execution and the sight of his mutilated body from her mind. Not satisfied with cutting him to pieces, the men had covered his body with palm leaves from the surrounding coconut trees, poured gasoline over the pile, and lit his corpse on fire.

When they reached the bottom of the mountain, Adel was no longer needed as a guide. The men pushed her in the direction of Dahma, their village, continually pulling her long hair, taunting her, and smacking her naked body with the sides of their machetes. At each attack Adel continued to shout, "The blood of Jesus is all powerful! The blood of Jesus is all powerful!" Sometimes one of the men would run from behind and swing the flat of his machete blade wildly at the back of her head. She would fall to the ground like a rag doll and cup her head in the palms of her hands. It felt like a thousand needles had been driven into her skull, but when she pulled her hands back, she was astonished to discover she was not bleeding.

FIGHTING THE HATRED WITHIN

Adel's courage increased as she again realized God was miraculously sparing her life. But why? She couldn't comprehend why she was still breathing after so many others had been cruelly murdered. Even her captors had a confused look on their faces, and she wondered if they were also questioning how such a defenseless woman had been able to survive their repeated attacks. They were even more infuriated that she kept calling out about the blood of Jesus.

Finally one of them stopped her, lit a handful of tobacco leaves on fire, and forced them into her mouth. Adel's eyes grew wide as she saw the burning leaves coming toward her. She tried to resist, but there was no way she could overpower his strong arms. Convinced he had finally quieted the "infidel," the man smiled in satisfaction to the others. But after he removed his hands from Adel's mouth, she spat out the smoldering leaves and said confidently, "The blood of Jesus is all powerful." The seven simple words had become more and more real as Adel's hellish nightmare continued.

The sun set, and the light from a nearly full moon lit their path as they continued on toward Dahma. Adel could see the lights from the homes and the silhouettes of children running and playing. She envisioned her own village and sadly remembered how the children there had played in the evenings just like these children were doing.

The group stopped and Adel was ordered to put her clothes back on. Two young men—they couldn't have been older than twenty—were left with pistols to guard Adel as the others proceeded into the village. Adel asked the two young men if they knew what had happened to her daughter.

"Yeah, we killed her," one of them scoffed.

Adel sensed they were lying, but she could see the hatred in their eyes. She also felt the hatred arising within herself, and she prayed to God to take it away.

A little while later Adel was taken into the village, where she was again subjected to mockery and torture. The warriors were brutal, but she was strong. If it was her time to die—even at the hands of jihad soldiers—she was ready. Once more Adel realized she was the only hostage in sight. She didn't dare imagine how many of the others had been killed. At that moment she didn't know which was worse—to be dead or to be held captive by these vicious madmen. In spite of the torment, she continued to proclaim loudly, "The blood of Jesus is all powerful" each time a soldier unleashed his terror on her frail body.

At the jihad command post, Adel was stripped again. Three women led her into a back room where she was bathed in cold water in a rusted metal tub. "Please let me wash myself," Adel pleaded. But they refused, and after Adel asked again, the women beat her with large wooden spoons. After the cold bath she was given an old T-shirt and a pair of shorts that were full of holes. Her own clothing belonged to a "filthy pig," the women told her, and it would be burned.

"Where Are the Christians Hiding?"

Eleven men were assigned to interrogate Adel as another thirty or forty milled around them. She recognized a number of the leaders as men who had come with their banner to her village on September 9 chanting, "Peace to the island of Dodi." The man who led the interrogation was the same one who had spoken so confidently from the platform that day. Again Adel could feel her hatred growing as she realized that the very people who had come to make a covenant of "peace" had come back to attack her village

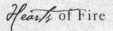

and kill her friends and family, including her precious Anto. Now, as they firmly sat her on a wooden chair in the center of the room, she wondered what their definition of *peace* really was.

"Where are the other Christians hiding?" the tall, lean man calmly asked.

"I cannot tell you. Even if you kill me, I will not answer." Adel knew where many of them were probably hiding—and also knew what would happen to them if she told.

"Come on. We won't hurt them. We just want to know where they are. Don't you want to go home?" Adel sat silent, refusing to answer their questions. The interrogation went on for another thirty minutes, ending with Adel being slapped across the face. A plate of food was placed in front of her, but she refused to eat. Undeterred, two of the men pried her mouth open and began forcing the food in. Adel spat it out, even though she hadn't eaten anything in three days.

Word of Adel's refusal to eat or speak traveled quickly through Dahma, and many people gathered outside the command center, crying out, "Hand her over to us! We will cut her into pieces and drive her into the ground!"

Hearing the angry voices, Adel was flooded with hate and fear at the same time. Finally an elderly man known as Saboom Sabar walked into the room. He didn't appear to be driven by the same rage that had possessed the others. Kneeling down next to where Adel was seated, he asked her if she could tell them where the other Christians were hiding.

"No, I can't," she answered as fear won out and the tears began to flow. Sabar got up and said to the commander. "It is better if this child comes with me. If she stays here any longer, she will be killed."

A group of men continued screaming at Adel and threatening to kill her as she was escorted to Sabar's home. They promised to wait outside for the opportune moment when they could attack her. But Sabar told her, "You will be safe here. You can sleep in my spare room."

Walking into the sparsely furnished bedroom, Adel quickly closed the door behind her. Then she sat down on the bed—a thatched mat—and let the tears fall as she thought of her precious Anto.

"Do You Think He Can Save You from *This*?"

The following day a group of uniformed soldiers entered the village; they were immediately brought to Sabar's home to meet with Adel. They had the same question as the others: "Where are the other Christians hiding?"

Again Adel refused to answer. She was allowed to return to her room but could hear the men's conversation through the thin walls. The determined soldiers had only one objective—to find the other Christians—and they had decided that Adel should go with them as their "guide." Adel was horrified. She committed in her heart that she would die first.

Later that afternoon three of the village wives brought Adel some food, but again she refused to eat. As the women began talking among themselves, Adel realized she had known them previously. They were from another village and were Christian by birth. However, they had married Muslim men and had been persuaded to convert. One of the wives, Umi, began maliciously criticizing Adel. "It's your fault that your son and mother are dead," she scolded. "You refused to convert to Islam, but now you are experiencing it firsthand. You want to believe in Jesus, but do you think He can save you from *this*?"

"Shut up, Umi! Stop speaking like that," one of the other women commanded. "What do you think? Do you think

Mohammed will save *us*?" Adel could see the tenderness in the woman's eyes, and before she departed Adel reached up and hugged her. The woman started crying and whispered in her ear, "Maybe one day I can return to Christ."

Adel couldn't tell if she was making a statement or asking if it was possible. She looked at her sorrowful face and answered softly, "If you really want to return to the Lord, He will make a way."

As evening approached, the soldiers returned. It had been decided that all the Christians on the island had to be rounded up and that Adel would be the best person to help find them. Once they were gathered, they would all be burned, every one of them. None should be left alive. Adel knew there was nothing she could do to stop their evil plan, so she remained locked in her room and prayed for strength. If they took her as a guide, she knew her refusal to cooperate would mean certain death.

Some men started cheering outside Sabar's home, and Adel crawled to the outside wall to peek through the cracks so she could see what the commotion was. The warriors had caught another Christian family. The husband had been killed, and the wife and three children were on their way to Dahma. She heard them say the woman's name was Rose. Adel's heart sank as she returned to her mat. She knew the family well. One of the children was Anto's age and had played in their home almost every day.

Nearing midnight, Sabar returned to the room. His face was long. "Adel, what are we to do? The military has demanded that you go with them."

Adel was amazed that he had said *we.* Sabar almost seemed to identify with her suffering. His kindness offered a little island of comfort in the surrounding hatred. But Adel knew she had no choice. "Tell them they can shoot me right here on the spot. I am not going with them."

"Why are you so afraid of them?" Sabar asked.

"Because I know their plans. I overheard them talking, and I will have no part in helping them kill anyone," she answered.

Sabar left the room. Another sleepless night, and Adel had still refused to eat. In the predawn hours, more reports came in. Another family killed . . . more women and children captured . . . a young girl found. Adel kept wondering if she would hear of Christina, if she had been one of the new captives. Adel thought if they had killed Christina, it might be better. It was an appalling thought, but she dreaded what the vile soldiers would do to her sweet, innocent daughter.

CHRISTINA

At four o'clock in the morning, Adel was crying out to God. "Why won't You let me die?" The tears kept coming, one after the other, steadily rolling down her face as she repeated the plaguing question, "Why?"

The unrelenting threats continued outside her room. One man almost succeeded in stabbing her by pushing his machete through the outside wall into her room. Two of the wives who had visited Adel the previous day also returned, begging her to eat. But she refused. She remained in her room, managing to get a little sleep in the stillness of the morning, but the majority of the time she huddled against the wall and wept. She continued to pray for Methu and her in-laws—but mostly she prayed for Christina.

Then the news came.

"Adel! Adel!" Sabar called as he rushed into her room. "Some men are outside. They say they captured your daughter, Christina."

It was a risk . . . a big risk, but Adel had to know. Could Christina really be alive? Or was it just a cruel deception to lure her away from Sabar's home? There was only one way to find out.

They traveled by boat to the village of Salubi: six jihad soldiers, Adel, Sabar (who at Adel's request had agreed to go along), and a young captive named Maksi. Another friend of Anto's, Maksi was only seven. Adel grabbed the young girl and hugged her tightly. She wept as she brushed Maksi's matted hair away from her face. It was a familiar face, a friend of the family.

Adel sat next to Maksi, tightly holding her and caressing her head on the short journey to Salubi. Maksi reminded Adel so much of Anto. But the peaceful moment quickly vanished as Adel saw the armed soldiers waiting on the shoreline. They yanked Adel out of the boat, and their brutal treatment, still fresh in her memory, returned.

Maksi was terrified as she watched the vicious attacks on Adel. She screamed loudly, and her body went into an uncontrollable convolution. Hearing her young friend's cries, Adel again proclaimed, "The blood of Jesus is all powerful!" She now feared the trip to Salubi had nothing to do with Christina. Hope was quickly fading as the beatings continued. Sabar began yelling at the men, begging them to stop. Managing to break Adel from their grasp, he helped her into a large home just beyond the shoreline, where other captives were being held. Then he told her he had to leave. "There is nothing more I can do for you. If I interfere any more, they will kill me, too. I'm sorry."

There were other women in the house, trembling as the horrid chanting of the men outside continued. Adel had buried her face deep in her hands to weep when she heard footsteps running toward her. Looking up, Adel saw her. It was Christina!

Christina threw herself into her mother's arms and cried, "Mommy, Mommy!" They held each other tight, and Christina continued struggling to get the words out. "I'm so sorry, Mommy

. . . I'm so sorry. They killed Grandmamma. And I saw his body, Mommy, I saw Anto . . . they killed him, too. Oh, Mommy!"

"I know Christina . . . I know they killed them." The memory was still too much, and Adel began to cry uncontrollably. Christina didn't know what to say, so she just kissed her mother . . . again and again, she kissed her mother.

SEEKING AN ANSWER THAT WOULD NOT COME

On the evening of the sixth day of her captivity, Adel and sixty other captives were gathered together and told that they had to convert to Islam the following morning.

"I will never become a Muslim," Adel responded.

"That's fine. You don't have to. But if you don't, if any one of you refuses, we will kill all of you," the commander countered. "And their blood will be on your head."

A meeting was convened that evening among the Christian captives. It was the first time they had been allowed to meet as a group since the attacks. They hugged one another, and tears were shed. The Christians knew they had to decide what to do: Would they agree to convert, or would they join the ranks of Christian martyrs? "We can repeat the words; we can say their prayers. God knows our hearts; He will not judge us," one man finally offered.

"How can we? We have resisted this long. Was it all in vain?"

"What about our children? Are we willing to see them executed before our eyes?"

"Does God want us all to die here in this Muslim village?"

The arguments continued, seemingly fading into the distance as Adel contemplated their dire situation. For herself, she could easily refuse to convert; she knew her faith would carry her through to the end. But was it fair for her actions to determine the fate of the others, including Christina? The dilemma plagued

27

Adel as she cried out to God for an answer. None came.

The next morning the Christians were assembled in the court-yard. "Have you made your decision? Will you convert—or will you die?" a jihad warrior questioned.

No one dared to be the first to answer. Even the younger children refused to speak, frozen in a state of fear and an inner struggle to remain true to their faith. The commander was growing increasingly agitated at their obstinate silence and barked orders to his subordinates in his native language. The soldiers returned with a dozen spoons, and in a bizarre ritual they began mixing mud and forcing the Christians to eat it. The commander slapped Adel across the face when she spat it out. "Eat it! Eat it now!" he shouted at her.

Adel refused.

A hose was then brought out and each of the captives was sprayed in an "Islamic baptism" as the Muslims began chanting verses from the Koran. When they finished, they danced like drunken men and fired their rifles into the air, celebrating their alleged victory of converting the Christians to Islam. The Christians, standing silently together, looked on in confusion as they watched the soldiers continue their futile celebration.

But their hearts dropped when they spotted soldiers carrying cans of gasoline toward the assembled group. A well-dressed, distinguished-looking officer walked ahead of the others. Adel recognized him as a leader from the island of Java. Without an ounce of misgiving, he calmly ordered his officers to lock the Christians in one of the houses and douse it with the gasoline.

Shoved inside a nearby hut, the terrorized Christians began to scream as they huddled around the small children. They were not afraid to die for Christ. Each of them had proved that again and again during their captivity. But the thought of being burned alive and of watching their little children go up in flames, was too much to endure. In unison they knelt down, crying out to God to save them from such a horrific death.

As they were praying, an argument broke out among the soldiers outside. They were debating whether they should burn the Christians. One of them contended that the prisoners had now converted to Islam and could be useful in the jihad. Quickly it was agreed. If the captives were willing to participate in the jihad, it would confirm their commitment to Allah and result in their being spared.

THE PRICE OF REBELLION

Hearing the arguments outside, Adel and the others remained in a state of shock. It was not the answer they were looking for. But a decision would have to be made. If the older captives agreed to go out with the soldiers in the next Jihad, all would be spared. Otherwise the gasoline would be poured on the hut, and the Christians would be burned. The trembling captives froze on their knees, once more looking at one another for courage and wondering who would dare speak first. The commander stormed into the hut, announcing their good news: "If you are old enough to carry a machete, come join us in the jihad. It will be fun!"

The anger in Adel surged as she listened to the sickening mockery of the captives. Feeling a rush of courage, she stood up. The commander smiled, thinking he had his first volunteer. Instead she addressed the others. "Don't any of you go with them. If they are going to kill us, it is better for them to kill us here. At least we will all be together."

The commander, infuriated by her defiance, grabbed her by the arm. "What did you say?"

Adel repeated, "We will not be joining the jihad. Now please get out." The commander squeezed Adel's arm tightly, looking straight into her eyes. He didn't have to speak; his eyes communicated his fury perfectly. But Adel believed God would spare them. She also believed her outright rebellion would come with a price. As the commander quickly turned his back and left the room, the others, while admiring Adel's tenacity, wondered if she had just sealed all of their fates.

Miraculously, the soldiers left too, and the captives were taken out of the hut.

Two weeks went by, and Adel was under constant threat. The Muslims knew she had influenced the other prisoners and thought she should be eliminated. Her physical strength was now coming back as she slowly began to eat at the insistence of Christina.

Military leaders were traveling back and forth to the small village almost daily to discuss what should be done with the captives. They doubted the Christians' conversion to Islam was sincere, and they argued that they should have burned them in the hut as previously planned, keeping their village from any further defilement. As a last effort to confirm the conversion of the hostages, they decided all the women should be circumcised.

Some of the women were horrified and began crying hysterically. Their opposition confirmed the suspicions of the village commander, and again he insisted they be executed. Others still thought the Christians would be useful if kept alive, so it was agreed among the Muslims that, for now, they would live. However, they took all the girls who had not reached adolescence, including Christina, and crudely cut them. The pain was excruciating, and Christina cried incessantly. Adel's anger fumed, and she again tried to control the familiar rage boiling inside her. Her own ordeal was difficult beyond imagination, but watching her daughter's suffering was exceedingly worse. Adel felt hatred for every one of the Muslims except Sabar. She knew hatred was a cancer of the soul and that forgiveness would be the only antidote. But forgiveness seemed far off, an impossibility. All she could do was pray.

Six weeks went by without another direct threat of execution, but Adel remained deeply troubled. She could see the way the Muslim men looked at her, and a group of them had already tried to rape her. She could sense their lust increasing as the days went on, and she wondered how long she could fend them off. Even the village commander had made inappropriate advances. She longed for Methu's comfort, wondering if he was even alive.

METHU

Unexpectedly one morning a small conclave of government officials came by boat to Salubi. The officials were investigating allegations that Christians were being held hostage in the village, a charge the Muslim soldiers vehemently denied. However, Nahor, the man who owned the boat, was a Christian and had heard that a woman named Adel was being held captive. After dropping off his passengers, he immediately set out looking for her.

"Are you Adel?" Nahor quietly asked after someone pointed her out.

"Who are you?" Adel responded suspiciously. She had barely gotten the words out when Nahor swept her into a hug and started weeping. "I have heard all about you and your situation here," he said.

"What? How do you know me?"

"Methu told me."

Adel couldn't believe her ears. Methu was alive! For the first time in more than six weeks, she felt a surge of joy and actually smiled. "Methu's alive?" she asked, making sure she hadn't heard him wrong.

"Yes, of course he is. Would you like to write him a letter?" Nahor asked.

The thought of writing Methu quickly went through Adel's mind. How she longed to make contact with him! But she knew there were more pressing matters. "Yes, I would love to write to Methu. But I have something I must do first. Quickly! Give me a pen and paper."

Adel sat down and began furiously writing down the names of all the captives. She was still working on the list when she saw the commander approaching. "Quick, take these with you, Nahor. And please be careful!" Adel gave Nahor a quick hug and slipped away, regretting that she hadn't been able to write Methu. How she longed to tell him everything . . . how much she loved and missed him . . . how Christina was being so brave. But there just wasn't enough time, and she was compelled to get out word of the other captives. Unquestionably, their families would be worried too. Now she just hoped nobody had seen her talking with Nahor.

"What were you writing down?" The commander was furious when he learned that Adel had not only spoken to the owner of the boat but that she had also passed him a piece of paper. "Did you send out a letter?"

"No, I didn't write a letter," Adel answered.

"What did you write down?" His words came in angry, measured tones as he held a knife to Adel's neck.

Steadily, Adel told him, "I simply wrote down the names of those you are holding prisoner here."

"You did what?!" The commander was fuming. Adel thought for sure he was going to plunge the knife into her neck, but for the first time, she was not afraid. She had accomplished what she believed had to be done, and she knew Methu was alive. Today was a good day. A day even the heartless commander couldn't ruin.

"I just assured the government officials that no one was being held here against their will. I signed an agreement. Now you give them a list of 'prisoners'! You pig! You'll pay for this."

The commander was true to his word. Adel was brutally beaten that afternoon and many afternoons to follow.

In less than two months the village of Salubi again came under investigation. Adel's list had been circulated through government offices and among the captives' families, including Methu. Word now reached Adel that "Methu is coming with government officials to collect you and Christina."

Adel was ecstatic. She and her daughter had survived a nightmare that had been hellish beyond imagination, and now they were going home. Her spirits were lifted, and she even found herself smiling again. But Christina didn't seem convinced. "Are we really going home?" she asked skeptically. "Will we get to leave with Daddy? What if they don't let us go?"

Adel could hear the anxiety in Christina's voice and knew her questions were valid. She hugged her brave daughter and wondered what ploy their captors might use to prevent their release. The next day she found out.

"I Cannot Go with You"

Adel and Christina were made to stand in front of all the assembled captives. The commander, addressing the Christians, said, "We will soon take Christina and Adel over to Dahma to meet with her Christian husband." With great anticipation the news of Methu's coming had already spread among the captives. They knew Adel. If she was allowed to go, she would not rest a moment until all the other captives were released too. Adel would be their lifeline to freedom.

Then the commander continued with a now-familiar threat:

"Adel and Christina will be asked if they want to remain here with you or leave with Methu. If either one of them chooses to go with Methu, we will kill every one of you." As the commander walked away, he crouched down in front of a young girl no more than five. Removing his knife from its scabbard, he pressed it against the trembling girl's throat and maliciously added, "even you."

The Christians stood and stared at Adel. How could she make such a decision? they wondered. And they also pondered what they would do if they were in her shoes. Adel knew that none would blame her or Christina if they chose to go with Methu. But before she could offer any kind of response, the commander said, "Let's go."

Now? Adel had no idea Methu was already waiting for them. Everything was happening too fast. She needed time to pray and to consider if the commander would really kill all of them or if it was just a bluff. How could she possibly turn her back on Methu? But how could she make a choice that might mean the death of the other captives?

Before she knew it, she was being led into the room where Methu was seated alongside military officers. As they entered, the commander whispered in Adel's ear, "Remember: If either of you goes back with him, I'll kill every prisoner. Not only them, I'll kill Methu, too. I swear, I'll kill him, too." His icy words sent chills down the back of Adel's neck, driving out any thought that he might be bluffing.

Adel could see the anguish in Methu's eyes. How he longed to be back with his wife and daughter! The last three months must have seemed like a lifetime to him, but he was hopeful now. He also was determined, and Adel knew he already would have committed in his heart that he wouldn't leave the room without them. All she could do was pray for strength.

An officer introduced himself as Mr. Said and without hesitation asked, "Adel, do you want to leave with Methu or remain in

Salubi?" Adel knew this was going to be the question, word for word. She had been instructed exactly how she was to answer. She tried to speak, but her lips moved soundlessly. Mr. Said repeated the question a little louder. "Adel, do you want to go with Methu or remain in Salubi?"

Adel looked directly at Methu, who was now wondering why she was taking so long to answer. "Methu . . ." Tears rolled down her face as she choked on the words. "I cannot go with you."

Methu was ready to jump from his chair, to run to Adel and ask her why, but Said held him back, refusing to let him respond. Immediately, Said pressed the same question to Christina. Adel was still crying as she looked at her daughter, unsure how she would answer. She hadn't had time to confer with Christina and was now convinced they would kill all the captives and Methu, if either of them agreed to go back with Methu. But how could her nine-year-old daughter possibly grasp the severity of agreeing to go with her father?

"I cannot go with you, Daddy. I'm so sorry . . . ," Christina sobbed, desperately trying to apologize to her father and explain the situation.

Mr. Said rudely interrupted, "There. We are finished. We will not have another word about the matter. Understand?"

Adel and Christina were given five minutes with Methu under strict supervision and instructions not to whisper to one another. Ignoring their orders, Adel spoke softly, praying they would not overhear her. "Methu, I had to answer this way. They threatened to kill the others if we go with you. Please don't hate me. As long as I live I will never give up hope. I know, one day, we will be together again."

Methu looked at his beautiful wife, seeing the pain in her eyes and even admiring her courage. There was nothing left to say. He just looked at his family and replied simply, "I understand."

CLINGING TO HOPE

As quickly as the meeting had started it was over, and Adel and Christina were led from the room. Adel began to turn around to get a final look at Methu, but the commander caught her first, jabbing his fist into her side. "Don't you look back at him," he hissed. "He is just a child of Jesus. He is a pig!" With her hopes shattered, Adel could only wonder what the future now held. All she could do was cry.

For the next few weeks Adel clung to the hope of someday being reunited with Methu. It helped ease the infinite pain of her captivity and gave her something to hold on to, even if it was a distant dream.

Then, on April 10, her dream turned into a nightmare . . .

"Adel," the commander began, "I have decided what to do with you. You have caused me a lot of grief and are obviously a troublemaker. I have decided to let one of the men marry you. Perhaps he will be able to control you."

Adel couldn't believe it. "I can't marry anyone! I'm already married to Methu!"

"I told you. Methu is not a man. He is a pig, and I do not recognize his marriage to you. If you refuse to marry the man I choose for you, I will let them *all* have you." The commander accepted no further argument, and Adel knew by the unyielding look on his face that he was serious. There would be no escape.

Adel went to the other women captives and begged them to help her. She knew there was little they could do but hoped they would at least stand with her in protest of the forced marriage. But the others remained silent, fearing for their own lives. Finally one of them told her, "If you don't marry one of them, they may rape and kill us all."

Adel was devastated. She had tried so hard to stand with these women, and now she felt betrayed. She began to sob, "How can you turn me into some kind of commodity and sell me off just to save yourselves?"

The others could only apologize as they clung together and wept. They knew it would not be the last time one of them would be forced to marry.

When she and Christina were forced to move in with Almin, her new husband, Adel believed the situation couldn't get any worse. But the situation *did* get worse. A few months later, Adel became pregnant.

A New Life

By October Adel's emotional state had come crashing down. She felt as if she were uncontrollably spiraling downward through an endless pit. These monsters had killed her son and mother, and they had beaten her mercilessly more times than she could count. Now she believed they had even taken away her hope of being reunited with Methu. The hatred that had begun that horrible day she was captured was growing faster than the new life inside her. She cried as she searched for hope but found none. She couldn't even love the innocent baby in her womb. To Adel, it was just a reminder of all they had taken from her.

"I won't let them take any more," she decided.

She waited until she was alone. Then she took the knife off the kitchen counter. It was hard to believe things had progressed this far. Adel questioned why she had been spared only to experience such despair. She knew God had saved her, but she no longer felt she could live. Slowly putting the knife to her womb, she closed her eyes and prayed God would forgive her.

"Mom, stop!" Christina yelled as she came running into the room and grabbed the knife from her mother's grasp. Adel burst into tears and crumbled to the floor. Christina was now crying alongside her mother. "Mom, what are you doing? You can't do this to yourself. And this baby has done nothing wrong. It is innocent."

Adel was broken. For hours she cried as Christina's words echoed through her heart and soul. She begged God to forgive her as she confessed her hatred for those who held her hostage. She began to realize how her rage had nearly destroyed an innocent life, just as the jihad warriors had done to her. It was a sobering reality, and although she didn't feel immediate forgiveness for those who had hurt her, she knew she had to be willing to let God's grace work. Her hatred had blocked the healing power of God's love that she now began to experience.

Adel began caressing her womb and speaking to the young life inside her. Believing it was a girl, she named the baby Sarah. "Sarah, please forgive me. Please forgive the sins of your mother. You have done nothing wrong. You are the good that can come from such a bad situation. I love you."

A dark cloud seemed to lift as she continued to pray and speak to Sarah. Previously Adel had considered the unborn baby another enemy, the child of her own son's killer. Now she realized it was *her* baby and one of God's creations. An instant bond formed as she hugged both her daughters.

The next day Adel grabbed a sheet of paper, knowing she had to communicate with Methu. She had to tell him all that had happened and beg his forgiveness. Even if he didn't consider her his wife any longer, she understood, and she would not hold anything against him. She loved him and longed for their reunion. As she wrote, her tears mixed with the ink, making a mess of the letter. She wondered if he would even be able to read it. By the time she finished she had written six pages. For Adel, it was the most painful and important love letter ever written. She carefully folded it up and hid it away, praying for an opportunity to get it to Methu.

On December 24, all the captives were forced to work in the coconut plantation. It was difficult work, especially for Adel, who was now six months pregnant. But the prisoners also realized it was the day before Christmas, and each savored past holiday memories. That evening when Adel started to softly hum the tune of "Silent Night," the others joined in. Soon they all began singing the lyrics as the stern-faced guards listened suspiciously. Each one knew the dangers in singing the traditional Christmas song about Christ. They would probably be beaten, but no one seemed to care. The joy of singing would be worth the punishment.

Late into the evening they sang and reminisced about their families. Their bodies remained captive, but their souls were set free as they continued to sing into the heavens. The next morning they cried tears of sorrow and joy, mourning their imprisonment but looking forward to happier times. They would never forget the Christmas they spent together in the fields.

On March 18 Sarah was born.

Now that the baby had come, Christina felt it was time to tell her mother, "You must try to escape, just you and Sarah. You must leave. If you don't leave, we will all die here."

"I can't leave you, Christina. I will never leave you," Adel assured her daughter.

"Mom, listen to me. You *have* to leave," the tenacious ten-year-old pleaded. "Almin will never let us all leave together. But if you and Sarah go, he will think you will surely come back. But you can't. You must get to Daddy. He will come back for me. It is our only hope."

Adel knew her daughter was right, but she didn't know how she could possibly implement such an idea. She didn't know if Methu would even take her back. And now there was Sarah. Adel

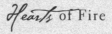

simply didn't have the courage to plan their escape with so many questions still lingering.

Then, in April, her answer came. Adel had been carrying the letter to Methu for over six months, hoping and praying for an opportunity to send it out. One afternoon, as some children were visiting their village, the occasion came. Adel knew one of the children and quietly made her way to where they were playing. She quickly passed the letter to the one she knew and asked her to make sure it got to her husband Methu. The child simply took the letter and nodded in agreement.

Adel walked back home, praying the letter would reach Methu . . . praying he would forgive her . . . praying he still loved her. And each day Adel peered across the village, anxiously waiting for the child to come back for a visit. A few days later her wait was over.

"Did you see Methu? Did you give him my letter?" she promptly questioned the child she had given the letter to.

"Yes, I did give it to Methu. And at the same time I handed it to him, he handed me this."

Adel was astonished when the girl handed her the letter. Methu had written to her before he had even received her letter. She could tell by the discolored envelope and its frayed edges that he had carried it for a while, just as she had carried the letter she'd written to him.

She considered reading it on the spot but quickly changed her mind. What if Methu hated her? What if he had married another woman? Adel's emotions were on a roller coaster as she ran back to her home, tearing open the letter. Her heart skipped a beat as her eyes fell on the words.

Adel, you could have ten children by ten men, and you would still be my wife. Don't you remember what

the pastor told you? Only God can separate us now. I
love you.

Methu

Adel had her answer. She would plan her escape.

ESCAPE AND RESCUE

Barely two months later, on June 18, Almin gave his permission
for Adel to visit some relatives on a neighboring island. Holding
Sarah tightly, Adel reached for Christina as she proceeded to
board the small ferryboat. But Almin pulled Christina back.
"She's staying here."

Adel begged Almin to let Christina go, but he refused. "I'm
not going without Christina," she insisted. But Almin wouldn't
budge. He knew his "wife" would run if Christina went along.

But it was just as Christina had planned. She hugged her
mother and whispered in her ear, "Please, Mom! Please promise
me you and Sarah will go to Daddy. Please, I'm begging you. I'll
be OK." Adel held Christina tighter, wondering how she could
ever leave her alone. But Christina's plea seemed to cut directly
into her heart. Wondering how her daughter could be so brave,
Adel kissed her and said good-bye. She knew it might be the last
time she saw her for a while. Or maybe forever.

Adel stood against the boat's railing, slowly watching
Christina fade into the distance. She hugged Sarah and began to
cry once more as she asked herself again if she was making the
right decision. She had no intention of visiting her distant
relatives. She would quickly make her way to Methu before
Almin realized she had escaped. Then, somehow, they had to get
Christina back.

It took Adel a week to reach the place where Methu was staying.

The journey had been long and difficult, and Adel had avoided making contact with Methu up to this point, fearing Almin would find out what she was up to. She sat on a bed, quietly holding Sarah in the back room of the guesthouse, anxiously waiting. *Will Methu really want me?* she kept asking herself. *And what about Sarah?*

Even though Adel was now free, she still felt captive. Worse, she felt like a traitor. She had married another man and left her daughter Christina behind. How could Methu ever forgive her? Over and over she questioned her decisions as she cried herself to sleep.

Adel awoke abruptly to the sounds of Methu entering the house. She sat up in the bed, trembling; then she grabbed Sarah, who was still sleeping, and stood up. Suddenly convinced she had made a terrible mistake, Adel gave in to an urge to run from the house. She didn't think about where she would go; she would just run. She couldn't face Methu.

But before she could get to the door, Methu walked in. Without pausing even an instant, he crossed the room and swept up his wife in a joyful embrace. Then he looked down at the baby girl Adel held in her arms, and he smiled. "So this is our new daughter," he said. Adel cried—happy tears now—cherishing their long-awaited reunion. Adel wanted to hold on to Methu forever, to relish the security of his strong arms around her. But she knew Methu had to leave. She knew he wouldn't rest until he had rescued Christina.

Adel nervously waited day after day, not hearing a word from Methu or Christina. *What if they have already killed Christina? What if Methu is dead? Is it all my fault?* She tried to fight the agonizing questions relentlessly pounding through her mind by crying out to God for reassurance.

Adel found comfort in the familiar passages of Scripture she had desperately missed during her eighteen months of captivity. She remembered how the jihad soldiers had hacked her Bible to pieces in the jungle. Adel turned again to Philippians 4:13 and as was her habit, she read the words aloud: "I can do all things through Christ who strengthens me." She remembered the last time she had read these words. It was on the hill behind her village the very day of the attack. A lifetime had passed since then, and she had traveled to hell and back. She knew her nightmare was far from over, and she couldn't stop thinking of Christina, wondering if she had betrayed her own daughter.

Methu had been gone more than two weeks before Adel finally got word that he was with Christina and she should come join them at once. They would finally be reunited, a family again. Tears of joy rolled down her face as she thanked God that Methu was able to rescue Christina. But now she wondered . . . how far would Almin go to get them back?

Epilogue

When we interviewed Adel, she and Methu were studying in a secret Bible school, learning to be evangelists. Even though several months had passed since she escaped, Adel and her family continued to be constantly on the run to elude Almin, who, with the help of many Muslims he had enlisted, continued to hunt them down. On more than two occasions, Adel was nearly captured.

Adel had to deal with two significant issues upon her release. The first was something that, at first, she thought she could never do. As a Christian, she knew she had to forgive the jihad soldiers. The difficult process had actually begun with her pregnancy, when Christina reminded her that the baby growing inside her had done nothing wrong, that baby Sarah was innocent. Adel knew she could say the words "I forgive" but that they needed to penetrate her heart, where real forgiveness takes place. During the months following her escape, Adel spent much time in prayer. She prayed for the salvation of those who had hurt her and her family. She believed this prayer was a key to being able to forgive them in her heart.

The second issue was equally challenging. Adel had to forgive herself. Because of her forced marriage to Almin, she often thought of herself as a traitor. Unfortunately, other Christians confirmed this self-accusation, and the idea continually plagued her soul, bringing her much anxiety, especially during her escape. At times she believed that Methu and other Christian friends would "put her out" because of her forced marriage. At times this inner turmoil was more difficult to handle than the physical abuse she had endured.

When Adel came out of captivity, she was debriefed by a Christian missionary couple who had befriended Methu and had worked both nationally and internationally to help her cause. When Adel approached the husband, the Lord quickened his spirit, and the very first words that came out of his mouth were, "Adel, you are *not* a traitor."

Hearing his words, Adel broke down and wept, and on that day, she began to forgive herself.

Adel and Methu have continued to work to secure the release of those who were held captive with her. It continually weighs on her spirit that some of the individuals mentioned in these pages are still held captive today.

She asks for our prayers.

Purnima:
A Child Imprisoned, a Soul Set Free

Bhutan
March 1, 1993

It was especially cold and late in the evening when the police once again rounded up the group of believers and hauled them to the district administrator's office. Thirteen-year-old Purnima shivered as she and the others were forced to stand out in the open courtyard while the interrogation droned on. The officers bombarded them with the same questions they always asked: "Why do you want to be a Christian?" "Where does your support come from?" "This is a Buddhist country, and you have dishonored us by accepting this foreign religion. Why do you want to turn your people against you?"

One by one the thirty-five believers were questioned throughout the long, cold night. There were about twenty officers, most of them big and intimidating. Purnima cringed as one of them slapped a Christian brother near her. Some in the group cried; others tried to preach. Young Purnima stood before the men who

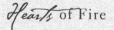

towered over her, praying for enough courage to face the impending questions.

"Who gave you permission to celebrate Christmas in the village of Purtah? This is Bhutan. You are not allowed to celebrate Christmas in Bhutan! This is your last choice: You either return to Buddhism, or you leave Bhutan." The officer was speaking directly to Purnima now, and she felt the impact of his ultimatum. "Do you understand? You are not permitted to stay here and practice this foreign religion. What will it be?"

Purnima didn't doubt for a minute the officer was serious. It was a matter of honor to either get the Christians to recant or to publicly denounce them as traitors and force them out of the country. She had already been kicked out of her home and her village. She had no idea where she would go, but she knew what she must do.

"I will not deny Christ! I do not wish to leave my country, and I will not leave Christ. He is the only One who can save me—or you." Purnima could feel her body shake as she spoke defiantly to the red-faced officer, but her heart was fixed, and in that moment she knew her fate was sealed. She and the others were officially given five days to leave Bhutan. They were told to go to Nepal.

Five days.

Purnima had less than a week left of the life she had always known. Word of the officers' threat had quickly spread throughout the area, and her sister and brother-in-law had already left, fearing for their lives. Now that the Christians were officially labeled traitors, some of the more outspoken villagers took that as a license to attack them.

Before Purnima could leave there was one thing she had to do. She needed to see her mom. A little more than a year had passed since her parents had forced her out of their home. Now she found herself sneaking back. Confident that word had already reached them about her imminent departure, she softly prayed her parents would be willing to see their little girl one last time. Under the covering of nightfall, Purnima made her way back to the house she grew up in, the home she had been forced to leave at the tender age of twelve . . .

A Miraculous Recovery

Purnima had grown up in a small Buddhist village in the green hills of eastern Bhutan. Her father was the local witch doctor and often led rituals and performed animal sacrifices to drive out evil spirits that threatened to harm their community. Their family of eight was neither rich nor poor by local standards, but they had a large home and a close relationship. Sival, who was married to Purnima's older sister Maya, also lived with them. Purnima probably would have grown up like any other kid in her village if the ailing Maya hadn't recovered so miraculously.

For three years Purnima had watched again and again as her father sacrificed chickens on his makeshift altar, beating a homemade drum and calling on the spirits to heal his daughter. Afterward, Purnima would sit by Maya's bed, expecting her to get better, but Maya didn't improve. She had good days and bad days, but the incessant pain in her stomach and severe headaches often kept her in bed for days at a time. Watching her sister suffer, Purnima had frequently asked her mom, "Why are the spirits so mad? Why aren't the sacrifices working?" But there were never any answers.

Now, after the painful years of illness, Maya was up and about. No more pain . . . no more ringing in her head. Purnima's mother and father were glad their daughter was feeling so much better, but they were not pleased about Maya's new claim that Jesus had healed her.

"How can you say such things? How can you bring such a dishonor on our home and community?" their father exclaimed. "We are Buddhists, and I will not hear another word about this foreign god. Do you understand? Not another word!" He was furious. Worse, he was fearful of what the local villagers would think if they found out. In fact, he was afraid for his own life.

But Maya and Sival couldn't deny their newfound faith. When one of Sival's friends had learned of Maya's illness, he had confessed to being a secret Christian and had given Sival a Bible. He also told Sival he believed Jesus could heal Maya. And He had. After that, their faith had grown quickly as they read their new Bible together.

"If you insist on being Christian, you can no longer stay here," Purnima's father had declared to Sival and Maya that final evening. "The villagers will never allow it. They will drive us out too, and your new religion will bring disgrace and calamity on the whole family."

Purnima was heartbroken to see her sister and brother-in-law driven from the family home. However, even at the tender age of ten, she understood all too well that what her father was saying was true. She knew the villagers would never accept this new religion, and yet she couldn't help but secretly be in awe of Maya's restored health and the new look that brightened her whole face, even as Maya packed her meager belongings to leave the only home she had ever known. Adding to the pain was the fact that Maya was six months pregnant.

After they left, the home felt as if a death had occurred. Purnima's mother was depressed, and her father seemed full of bewilderment over what had happened to his family. Purnima wanted to talk to her mother about Maya, but no one was allowed to even mention her name. And no one was allowed to visit the couple in their place of exile, a tiny bamboo hut a few miles outside a neighboring village.

But when Purnima heard that Maya had given birth to a baby boy, she couldn't take the loss anymore. She marveled at the fact that her sister had given birth to a healthy baby, and she still wasn't able to shake the curiosity that made her continually think about her sister's amazing healing. She imagined what the baby must look like.

Powerful questions relentlessly invaded her thoughts: *What kind of God would heal without asking anything in return? What did Maya and Sival find in this religion that gave them the courage to stand against their families and society—even to the point of being expelled from their home?*

These questions caused Purnima to boldly sneak to her sister's home for that first wary visit. Cutting across fields and keeping out of sight in the trees, she quickly covered the distance that had separated her from her sister for so many weeks. When Maya opened the door of her pathetic little hut to find Purnima trembling on the doorstep, her startled demeanor quickly melted into a barrage of tears and hugs as she enveloped her little sister in her arms.

Purnima began to sneak out regularly to visit Maya. She could never stay long, sometimes leaving after only fifteen minutes. But each time she came, Maya would read Purnima a story from the Bible, and she listened intently, absorbing every detail. She was most fascinated by the story of Moses. Not so much by the wondrous powers God worked through him, but by the fact that he was forced to leave his home and eventually became the mouthpiece of God, even though he had difficulty speaking. If she was a Christian, she imagined, she would want to be like Moses.

The following year Maya gave birth to another child, Esther, and Purnima's visits came more frequently. To young Purnima, it had become an adventure to secretly slip along the footpaths of the village to visit her exiled sister and her young niece and nephew. Even if she was caught, she reasoned, she wouldn't get in too much trouble. After all, she was just a kid.

But Purnima's mother didn't see it that way. "Purnima, we both know what you're doing," she told her one day. "I've already lost one daughter; I don't want to lose another. Do you understand?" Purnima nodded in agreement as her mother went on to explain that Christianity was a foreign religion and for a lower class of people. "It is not for our village or our country. Maya has been duped by Sival and his friend," her mother concluded.

INEXPLICABLY DRAWN TO GOD

But Purnima loved the time she spent with her sister, and the secret visits continued. On Christmas Day, Maya and Sival permitted Purnima to join them in the small fellowship that had been formed over the past eighteen months. The many visits to her sister had firmly planted seeds of faith in Purnima's heart, and as she listened to the sermon about the birth of Christ—how He was born of a virgin and came to bring salvation—she felt herself being inexplicably drawn to call out to God in her heart.

For days she told no one of her decision to accept Christ until she sneaked another visit to Maya and told her she wished to be baptized. Maya was overjoyed at her sister's decision, but inwardly she worried how Purnima would handle telling her parents the news. About three weeks later, on a bright Sunday morning, Purnima was baptized. She emerged from the water overcome with conviction. "Maya, I know what I must do now. I must tell Mommy and Daddy the news. I can't hide it any longer. I want everyone to know that I now live for Christ—and I don't care what they say or do!"

"But Purnima, you are so young; you're only twelve, and you know what they will do. Are you really ready for that? I had Sival, so it was a little easier for me to leave home. Perhaps you should just wait to tell them the news—and keep praying."

Purnima was unwavering. "I can't do that, Maya. Now I understand all the things I have been hearing, all the things you told me from the Bible. I have never felt this way before, and I know it is real, like you said. How will I ever be able to hide it down inside and not tell Mommy and Daddy? Besides, I have you . . ."

Maya melted at that remark and embraced her sister. "Of course you always have me. Do you want me to come with you?"

"No," Purnima answered. "It's too dangerous for you to come near the village. Don't worry. It'll be OK."

Maya watched with mixed emotions as her little sister ran off toward home. She couldn't believe the youngster's audacity, and though she was afraid of her parents' reaction, she felt tremendous pride toward Purnima for her boldness. *Perhaps the Lord has special plans for her,* she mused.

In her twelve-year-old innocence, Purnima simply came home and blurted out the news. "Mom, I'm a Christian." Her mother froze at the words.

"Surely you're joking," she said apprehensively. "You're too young to be a Christian. And besides, I told you I wasn't going to lose another daughter."

But Purnima confidently confirmed her decision. "Mom, I don't want to have to leave like Maya did. I want to stay. But I have decided to become a Christian, and nothing can change my mind."

She was forced to leave that same evening. As she made her way down the now-familiar path to Maya's home with her meager possessions, behind her she could hear her mother crying. She knew her mother loved both her daughters, but her parents were afraid of what the village would do to them. Earlier, Purnima had been afraid too. But as she walked in the darkness, she decided she would not be afraid any longer.

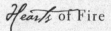

She had lived with Maya and Sival since then, and while she enjoyed being with her sister's family, conditions there were cramped, and they all struggled to survive. Then the arrests started on Christmas Day 1992, exactly one year after Purnima's conversion to Christianity.

The village police had grown increasingly fearful of the growing number of Christians in the area and had stepped up their pressure on the believers. The Christians had endured ten interrogations in as many weeks, and each time the authorities had tried to persuade or coerce them to deny Christ and return to their Buddhist roots. The men had been slapped and beaten; some of them had been held for a week or more in a large detention center, where they were beaten even more severely. The detained women were humiliated and accused of prostitution. In response, some members of her group had agreed to deny Christ, but young Purnima only grew more obstinate.

Now, to Purnima, her older sister, Maya, her brother-in-law, Sival, and the friends from neighboring villages who regularly fellowshipped with them, the authorities' latest directive was simple but heartrending: "Leave Bhutan."

"How Can You Be So Brave?"

Continuing through the fields, Purnima saw the lights shining through the windows of her parents' home—what used to be *her* home. She wondered what she would tell her mother. She wondered if her mother would even let her in. They had not spoken or even seen each other since the night Purnima had been sent away. Now, forced to leave Bhutan, she also wondered if she would ever see her mother again.

As she quietly approached the front door, she decided to simply let herself in. "Mom? Mom, it's me."

"Purnima!" Her mother grabbed her daughter tightly. "Please tell me you're home to stay. Please tell me you're not a Christian any longer." Purnima remained silent for a few minutes. She could see how sad her mother was; the tears were already flowing. She didn't want to cause her mother any more misery, but she had to tell her. "Mom, I have to leave Bhutan. The police won't let me live here. I'm sorry."

Her mother looked at her young daughter and envied her bravery. But she was still so young, so innocent. "Purnima, you are not yet fourteen. How can you be so brave? How can you forsake your country?"

Purnima was now crying with her mother. "I'm not forsaking my country, Mom," she sobbed. "My country has forsaken me." She knew how much her mother loved her, and she knew she had never wanted to force her out of the house. But everyone was so afraid. Afraid of the Christians, afraid of Christmas, afraid of Christ. Purnima couldn't help but wonder what made them all so scary.

"Here. Take this." Purnima's father handed her a small wad of money. "And please be careful." He looked into his daughter's teary eyes, gave her a quick hug, and left the room.

Purnima remained with her mother for a few more minutes, trying to memorize every feature of her dear face, the tone of her voice, the way her eyes sparkled when she smiled. Her mother was so beautiful, and she didn't know when, or if, she would ever see her again. One last hug, and then Purnima disappeared through the fields one last time.

The following morning she joined eight other Christians from her fellowship who were also being forced out of Bhutan. The government had provided a bus to take them from their village of Purtah to the border of India. From there, they would be on their own.

"Who will be our guide?" they kidded among themselves,

attempting to relieve the anxiety. None of them had ever ventured out of their surrounding community, and none had any knowledge of the place they were going.

A short distance past the border, the bus stopped, and the nine refugees got off. They watched through a wall of gray exhaust fumes as the bus turned around and pulled away. It was their last contact with Bhutan, and now it was gone. They had been told simply to walk "that way" through the hills of India into Nepal.

HAUNTED BY DREAMS

The Christians journeyed three days by foot without incident but grew increasingly exhausted from crossing the mountainous terrain. Coming to an unusually large tree along the road, John, who had become their unofficial leader, suggested they camp out under the tree for a day or so to regain their strength. There was no rush, but the reality of their dilemma was beginning to set in, and Purnima was growing increasingly fearful. She didn't want the others to know, but she had been crying herself to sleep, and since leaving her village, vivid dreams of her mother had been haunting her sleep. This night would be no different . . .

March 8, Purnima's birthday. Purnima snuggled up to her mom, looking up into the clear night. They loved to gaze at the stars together, pointing out imaginary shapes. Being the younger daughter, Purnima was able to spend more time with her mom, and she never felt more secure than when the two of them were alone together.

"So, birthday girl, what are you going to do now that you're all grown up?" her mother jested.

"Grown up? What do you mean, grown up? I'm only fourteen,"

Purnima said, giggling. She often felt trapped between her youthful spirit and the looming responsibilities of being an adult, but tonight she was just her mother's little girl.

Purnima's joy was short-lived, abruptly ending when she spotted four officers coming out of the field toward them. She began to panic, realizing the men were coming for her. Curiously, her mother didn't seem to notice.

Before Purnima could escape, the four officers had surrounded her. One of them tightly grabbed her, driving his long fingers into her arm so hard her hand tingled from the restricted blood flow. "Let me go! You're hurting me!" she pleaded.

There was no answer. Slowly Purnima was being pulled away from her mother and away from her home. Both seemed to dissolve into the distance.

"Mom! Mom!" Purnima's voice echoed back toward home. "Please help me! Please make them stop!" But it was no use. Her mother sat silently on her chair as if nothing were happening . . .

Purnima awoke with a harsh jerk, taking a deep breath as her mind slowly came back to reality. She could taste the salt from the tears that had dried around her mouth. She wondered if she would ever get used to feeling so alone.

It was pitch black, and only a sliver of the moon was visible, casting a faint glow on the large branches above her. As her body began to shiver, she pulled her light jacket tighter around her shoulders. Bunching up the sweater that served as her pillow, Purnima's eyes peered through the darkness. She was amazed how frightening the silence of the night could be.

Is it really my birthday? she thought to herself. Purnima tried to figure out what day of the month it was, but it was no use. The events of the last few weeks had happened so fast she had lost track of the days. Not that it mattered now.

She wondered how she would survive the days, weeks, even years to come. All she knew for sure was that she was terribly homesick. As she drifted back to sleep, Purnima thought again of her mother's sweet face and the warmth of her touch.

Bruised, Bleeding, . . . and Broke

"Get up! Get up and hand over your money, and we will let you live!"

Purnima was rudely awakened by loud voices and the impact of a heavy boot slamming into her side.

"I said, get up!"

The pain ripped through her body as the unknown attacker kicked her again. She couldn't tell how many men were attacking them, but there were several of the bandits. Her small group offered no defense.

The vivid cries of her traveling companions told her they, too, were coming under the harsh blows of the thieves. Purnima tried to shield herself as she was repeatedly kicked and beaten. Paralyzing fear gripped her body, but suddenly a verse from the Bible flooded her mind—she thought it was from the Gospel of Matthew—"Do not fear those who kill the body."[1]

Kill the body, she repeated to herself, praying that wasn't to be her immediate fate. Her mind raced as she remembered the wad of money her father had given her. As the mob continued to rampage through the makeshift camp and plunder their meager possessions, Purnima struggled to grab the money hidden in her belongings before the thieves discovered it. Her hand found what it was looking for just before she received another painful blow that landed squarely in her back, knocking the wind out of her. She cried out to God as she brought her arms in to protect herself and attempted to roll away from the harsh boot that kept smashing into her body.

After the outlaws had sufficiently terrorized the weary refugees and confiscated all their possessions, the robbers lined up four of the Christians, including Purnima. None of the refugees dared to say a word as they stood facing their attackers. There were about twelve of them, each with a bandanna tied around his face. Purnima looked at the others standing beside her. Each was frozen in fear. She knew it would be nothing for the thieves to shoot them on the spot.

"You should not report this to the police" one of the men warned as he carelessly swung a pistol in front of them. "If you do, we will come back and kill you." His finger remained on the trigger, and he continued pointing the gun in each one's face to reinforce his words. Purnima closed her eyes and wondered if she would hear the gun go off. When she opened them, the thieves were gone.

The wounded victims gathered together as best they could and began surveying the damage. Although they were thankful to God for sparing their lives, all of them were bruised and bleeding, and all quickly realized they had nothing left. The thieves had taken everything, even their extra clothing. Never had they imagined that their journey to Nepal would harbor such dangers.

The next morning John managed to wave down a large farm truck that had a homemade wooden box behind its rusty cab. Learning the truck was heading toward Nepal, he pleaded with the driver as the others quickly gathered around. "Can you please take us with you? We cannot stay here. It is too dangerous."

"Do you have any money?" the elderly driver asked as he stepped out of the cab, assessing his opportunity to make a few extra dollars.

John explained how they had been robbed the previous night and had literally lost everything they owned. "Please," he continued, "some of our group can barely walk after the beatings they received." But even after he had seen their wounds, the driver of the truck refused to give them a ride. He was still focused on making a profit.

John and the others began to turn away, discouraged by their lost opportunity of a ride, when Purnima spoke up. "I have some money." The others looked at her in astonishment, wondering how she could possibly have any money after what they had been through. The robbers had been extremely thorough in their search.

"Let's just say I hid it carefully," Purnima said, smiling as she handed the money to the driver. The youngest of the nine refugees became their hero as they all hugged her and piled into the back of the truck. It wouldn't be the last time Purnima's clever and generous nature would come in useful.

The rising afternoon sun refreshed the small group of Christians and helped fight off the endless chills from sleeping on the cold, damp ground. And while most took the opportunity to get some sleep, Purnima again thought of her mother, and for the first time, she started questioning whether she had made the right decision. Perhaps she should have kept her faith a secret, as Maya had once suggested. She opened the Bible Sival had given her after her baptism and remembered to thank God that the thieves had found no use for it.

Turning the pages, Purnima quickly found her favorite passages. She had read them a hundred times and marked them so she could find them more easily. Ever since her early visits with Maya, she also had been fascinated by the adventurous stories in the Bible. She thought about Mary and Joseph fleeing to Egypt, about how David had run from the hands of King Saul, and she remembered her favorite Bible character, Moses, who had fled from Egypt. These stories fueled Purnima with courage to face another day. Clutching her Bible, she knew she was in good company.

REUNITED REFUGEES

As evening fell, the driver finally stopped in the Indian town of Ason and told his passengers he needed to refuel and pick up some supplies. They had a few hours before they would depart again, he said. Taking a much-needed opportunity to stretch their legs, Purnima and the others began walking through the town, eventually meeting a local pastor.

The pastor was originally from Bhutan, and he was amazed by their story and their willingness to leave all behind to follow Christ. He was especially taken by young Purnima. He pulled John aside and asked him how old she was.

"I'm not sure—either thirteen or fourteen," John replied.

"Is she traveling with any family members?" the pastor inquired.

"No. Her sister's family is also heading to Nepal, but they left ahead of us. We do not know where they are."

The pastor couldn't help but feel sorry for young Purnima. He asked John if he should invite Purnima to come live with his family. John agreed that it would be a good idea. He had worried about her, too. He encouraged the pastor to present the invitation directly to Purnima.

Purnima agreed to move in with the pastor and his wife. It was refreshing to be part of a family again. But it wasn't *her* family, and she continually prayed to be reunited with Maya. She didn't know how it could possibly happen; she just prayed that it would.

Three months had gone by when the pastor invited Purnima

to join them at a Christian conference they were preparing to attend outside Ason. She happily accepted, unaware that her brother-in-law, Sival, would also be attending.

She was thrilled to see Sival again and quickly decided to go back to Nepal with him, a decision that saddened the pastor and his wife. "Are you sure you want to leave, Purnima?" the pastor asked. "Do you know how difficult it will be for you in Nepal? You will be forced to live in a refugee camp."

Purnima listened to his gentle argument, knowing he was right. The pastor and his wife had treated her like their own daughter, and it *was* hard to leave them. But her mind was made up. "Yes, I'm sure," she answered. "I want to be with my own family. I appreciate all your kindness, but I believe this is God's will for me."

Purnima and Sival arrived at the refugee camp on the northern border of Nepal late on a cloudy evening, so she could not see the details of her new home right away. All that mattered at that moment was seeing Maya again. The sisters fell into each other's arms with shrieks of joy. Afterward, Purnima fell asleep quickly on one of the thin bamboo mats.

"Purnima, wake up!" Little Esther was running around Purnima's head, clapping her hands and laughing in the overcrowded hut. When Purnima opened her eyes the first thing she noticed was the rickety bamboo frame covered with thick plastic—the "roof" of their hut. As she sat up she heard what sounded like hundreds of people bustling about right outside the entrance of their hut. Quickly the camp's congested conditions and the utter poverty of the thousands of families living there became apparent to Purnima. The more she saw of the camp, the deeper she sank into despair.

Maya, happy to be together with her sister again, tried to bolster Purnima's spirits. "Listen, Purnima," she told her little sister. "I know this place stinks, but God's hand is always on us, no matter where we are. He must have work for us to do here. Just think of all the people here who have never heard about Christ. And you know how people are always drawn to you. They listen when you tell them about God—maybe because they are not used to seeing such a young and pretty preacher."

Purnima blushed and smiled. "I suppose so," she said. "But how long do you think we'll have to stay here? Is it really God's plan that we never get to go home again?"

Maya had no answer, but she pulled Purnima close and held her tight. She wanted to be strong for her little sister, but the truth was, she had often wondered the same things.

As the weeks wore on, Purnima slowly discovered the dos and don'ts of camp life. *Do* try and obtain an "out pass" when attempting to leave the camp and go out into the surrounding villages. *Don't* tell the authorities you're going out to preach the gospel and hand out tracts. *Don't* conduct big meetings with the other Christians in the camp; stick to small groups and "house church" meetings. *Do* take advantage of the language classes offered, and so on and so on. The refugee camp had a culture and life of its own that was unlike anything Purnima had expected.

A Passion for Sharing the Gospel

The high point of camp life for Purnima was the fervent growth of the church that was occurring among the thousands of refugees. She enjoyed the security of the family of Christ and the close friendships she had developed. Many times she and her friends would sneak out in small groups, undetected, to visit other Christians in neighboring camps and villages; they used these opportunities to practice their new language while preaching. Purnima felt most contented during these adventures as she continued to discover her gifts for music and her growing passion for the lost. Wrapped up in the passion of sharing the gospel, she could almost forget the wretchedness of camp life.

Purnima and her friends continued these gospel-sharing expeditions outside the camp until, the following year, they were caught. The group had set out in the early dawn of a brisk Sunday morning in August for the two-hour trip to Hona's place. Hona had heard about the spirited Christians in the refugee camps and had invited a group of them to fellowship in his home and evangelize in the local marketplace. Purnima and the others willingly accepted.

Quietly, in groups of two or three, eleven of them snuck out of the refugee camp and met up about a mile down the road. Carrying Bibles, a few gospel tracts, and a guitar, the Christians were excited at the prospect of preaching in a new village to people who might never have heard the gospel. But they knew they would have to move quickly to be back to the camp by nightfall.

They arrived at Hona's home by noon, and after fellowshipping for a few hours, they left for the marketplace. They had barely set up to sing a few songs when Purnima and the others were accosted by five police officers. "Come with us," they ordered.

The startled group had no choice but to follow the officers, and soon found themselves sitting before a stern-looking captain. "Where are you from?" he demanded. "Who permitted you to come out of the camp? Who gave you permission to spread your religion in Nepal?"

"You Have No Rights Here"

All day they waited in the dank, dark jail while the captain questioned them individually, the men first and then the women. Purnima was growing tired and, thinking this was just a misunderstanding, decided to challenge the officer. "We haven't done anything wrong. Why are you holding us here? Please let us go. We have to get back to the camp before it gets dark."

"No!" the captain shouted. "Tonight you will stay with us, and tomorrow you have an invitation from the district commander." Purnima cringed at how pleased the captain appeared to be for arresting and detaining them. She and the other three women were locked away in a tiny, filthy cell where they huddled together and fervently cried out to God throughout the night, asking for His protection. They had known it could be dangerous preaching in Nepal, but so many who had never heard the gospel were eagerly accepting it that the rewards seemed worth the risk.

The next morning the police gathered the eleven Christians back together. "If you have some money, you may buy something for lunch," one of the officers told them. "Now we are all taking a long walk."

Purnima exchanged a questioning glance with her friends but decided not to worry too much. Surely this would all get straightened out today at the district commander's office.

All day they trudged through the jungle, eleven Christians and nine policemen with guns. *I guess we must look pretty dangerous*, Purnima contemplated, eying the weapons. Her muscles stiffened, rebelling against the rough terrain. Because she and the others had no money, they had no food and no water except for when they crossed a stream.

It was dark when they finally arrived at the district office. Purnima was exhausted, cold, and hungry, but she still felt encouraged that God was with them and was confident they would be returning home soon. But her hopes were dashed as soon as the questioning began. Five officers sat behind a thick wooden table in the dimly lit interrogation room, and they barked questions at the Christians in a wave of anger: "Who gave you permission to preach in the Jhapa marketplace? Who is supporting you? Where did you get your materials? You are dirty refugees! You have no rights here."

Anyone who tried to answer the shouted onslaught was slapped or kicked, but the prisoners were also slapped and kicked when they *didn't* answer. For hours the questions—and the beatings—went on, until another officer stepped in and said, "Enough. No more tonight. Give them some food, and we will continue tomorrow."

The conditions in this cell were even worse than in the first jail. Purnima choked back the bile that rose in her throat as the retched smell hit her. The cement floor was cold, and there was not even a bucket for them to use as a toilet.

In the morning, Purnima and the other women waited in their cell with apprehension. The officers started taking the prisoners out one by one and questioning them. The district commander told Purnima they had proof that she and her friends had destroyed a Buddhist temple and insulted their gods.

"No, it's not true!" Purnima cried in disbelief. The officer slapped her hard across the face.

"You insolent little liar!" he screamed. "Just tell us the truth, and you will have a light sentence. If you continue to lie, you will go to the federal prison for a long, long time." Purnima was starting to panic, but she held her ground. Again and again she was slapped and kicked, and after a while she fell into a surreal state as the man's cruelty enveloped her. With the exception of the mugging that first dark night in India, she hadn't really known men could be so evil. But throughout the next twenty-eight days, she was to receive a harsh education. It was a difficult lesson for a fifteen-year-old.

The long days of interrogation dragged on as the officials continued their mission of wearing down the spirit of Purnima and her friends. The routine was always the same, except they never knew who would be called out first for the daily round of questioning and beating. *Question, wrong answer, slap. Another question, another wrong answer, another slap.* And on and on.

In their cell, Purnima and the other women sang softly and prayed long into the night, trying to encourage each other with hopeful words. "Just hang in there. It will all be over soon and we will be going home," they whispered in the darkness.

Home, Purnima thought ironically, *now there's a relative term.*

GLOWING WITH THE PEACE OF GOD

In the camp Purnima had continually thought of her parents and how much she missed her home in Bhutan. But now she missed her sister and the sordid little hut in the overcrowded refugee camp more than she would ever have thought possible. She wondered what her niece and nephew were doing and worried how Maya was holding up. Had she received any news at all of Prunima's whereabouts?

Oh, Maya, I am so sorry to cause you so many problems. You must be going crazy, Purnima thought.

In fact, some Christians in the refugee camp, including the fellowship pastor, *had* heard rumors of the group's arrest. They had even traveled to the detention center where Purnima and the others were being held, only to be severely beaten by the officers and then turned away. The eleven imprisoned Christians were made aware of what was happening, and they were devastated by the unprovoked assaults on their friends.

On day twenty-five of her incarceration, one of the guards came early for Purnima. The district commander was waiting for her in the familiar interrogation room, ready to inflict his cruelty. Once again the questions started: "Who told you to preach? You are so young. Perhaps it is not your fault. Surely someone has coerced you into this religion with the promise of money. Who sends you support? If you just tell me who it is, the beatings will stop. Maybe you can even go back to the camp."

For Purnima the next few minutes seemed an eternity. Tired and worn down physically from lack of food—the prisoners were fed rice twice a day—and dirty from being unable to bathe, she nevertheless felt the peace of God glowing inside her during these sessions. Losing herself in the presence of Christ helped her immensely as she prayed for God to forgive her tormentors and give her strength for whatever came next.

"Answer my questions!" the commander screamed.

Purnima summoned her courage as she braced for a slap. She knew he wouldn't like her answer. "I didn't accept Christ for the sake of money or support or anything else! I accepted Christ because my sister was sick for three years, and then she accepted Christ and was miraculously healed. I have seen many miracles, and I have peace and joy. There is no other reason."

Frustrated, the commander came within inches of her face. Smelling his breath and seeing the dark fury in his eyes scared her, but she tried not to recoil. "You lie!" he shouted in her face. "I know you are hiding something. You are not telling the truth. Now you will have to go to prison for a long time. Are you ready for that?" Before Purnima could reply, he slapped her hard, knocking her off her chair. "Take her back to her cell," he ordered.

Purnima's cellmates gasped when they saw her frail, bruised face, already starting to swell from the vicious slap. "Don't worry," Purnima lied as tears formed in her eyes. "It's not as painful as it probably looks."

The women knew otherwise, as they, too, had received their share of pain and humiliation from the heartless officers. They comforted Purnima as best they could, commiserating over the officials' unwillingness to believe their story. The policemen just couldn't seem to believe that Purnima and her friends were not receiving outside financial help from foreigners. They were convinced that the Bibles and tracts had to come from outside Nepal, because Christianity was a foreign religion. They refused to accept that it was spreading indigenously without compulsion or the promise of personal gain.

The next few days passed quietly as Purnima and the others wondered about their fate. Prayer and quiet singing helped ease their minds and pass the time, but Purnima had a sense of unease about the sudden lack of interaction with their captors. *What could they be doing? Why aren't they letting us go?* she wondered.

"HOW BLESSED I AM"

Finally, early on Tuesday morning, September 20, the group was again gathered in the district commander's office. Purnima knew something was up because, until then, the women prisoners had been separated from the men. Little was said as the refugees were unceremoniously lined up and handcuffed then marched across the village square to the tin-roofed courthouse. Purnima was so elated to be out in the sunshine, even for a brief moment, that she forgot to worry about what awaited them.

The room was full as the group was escorted to the front and seated next to their court-appointed lawyer. On the opposite side of the room, the government's lawyer indicated he was bringing official charges against the eleven. Ironically, as the contrived charges were read—a list that included lies involving the destruction of the Buddhist temples and the killing of sacred cows— Purnima actually began to feel hopeful. Perhaps this would be the day of their vindication, and they would go free. Surely the judge could see they were innocent.

Their lawyer argued convincingly enough, but the prosecutor obviously had a script to follow, and making an example of the Christians seemed to be his main goal as the day dragged on into the evening hours. It was nearly ten that night when the judge finally made his decision and the sentence was read to the weary group. Purnima stood as her name was called along with the other prisoners'. A shock jolted her body as the judge sternly announced that they were to be remanded to the federal prison for a term of three years.

Three years. The words rang through Purnima's mind.

Purnima had promised God she would be faithful no matter where He sent her: away from home . . . out of Bhutan . . . into a refugee camp. But *prison?* It was more than the fifteen-year-old could bear. She closed her eyes and again sought comfort in the Bible stories she had committed to memory. She imagined Jesus sitting on the mountaintop, instructing His disciples, and she felt her courage build as the familiar words swept through her mind: *Blessed are those who are persecuted . . . for theirs is the kingdom of heaven. Blessed are those who are persecuted . . . Blessed are those . . . * She stopped as she realized the truth. *Blessed am I . . . "*[2]

It was hard to think of a prison sentence as a blessing; Purnima's spirit and soul accepted the fact before her mind did. But in the days to come, this promise would become the source of the prisoners' bedrock of strength as they frequently repeated the words in unison.

Now they were shackled two by two and led from the courtroom to begin yet another arduous journey through the jungle. The prison was on a mountaintop several miles away. As Purnima's mind replayed the court hearing, she grew increasingly convinced of God's role in what was happening to them. They had been falsely accused and were going to prison because of the cause of Christ. This knowledge was comforting to

Purnima, and she felt privileged to be called to suffer for Christ. Looking at her ten friends as they trudged through the jungle, she knew again that she was in good company.

"Welcome to Hell"

They reached the prison gate at three in the morning. In the moonlight Purnima was able to make out the high wall surrounding the compound and the huge outer gates that gave an ominous creak as they opened for them. The place had a somber, imposing atmosphere and looked like it once might have been a grand fortress but now was in a serious state of disrepair. As they walked on through the open courtyard toward the inner buildings, Purnima stole one last glance over her shoulder as the grand gates closed behind them. The loud clang reverberated through the prison, her new home.

Purnima and the other women were handed a thin straw mat and led into their cell. It was almost pitch black, but gradually their eyes could make out the silhouettes of others sleeping on the floor. An eerie voice rose from the ground, "Welcome. Welcome to hell."

Purnima anxiously wondered who her cellmates were. What crimes had they committed? Were they violent? Would they like her? The unanswered questions threatened to unnerve her as she found a vacant spot along the outside wall and pulled her knees tight to her body. She was exhausted but felt too frightened to sleep.

Within a few hours a glimmer of sunlight came through the barred openings high up on the walls, allowing Purnima and her friends to observe their surroundings. The room was not large, but it was not overcrowded. There were five other prisoners in their cell, and each woman had apparently claimed her own space, clustering her meager belongings around her on the floor. The bathroom, if you could call it that, consisted of a raised cement pad adjacent to the outside wall. There was a rusted sink but no soap, no hot water, no door. A hole in the cement opened into a dug-out pit that Parnima suspected, judging by the smell, had apparently never been cleaned out. The stench from the pit filled the cell.

The prison's concrete walls were stained with layers of paint that had given way to years of grime. The floor was cold, damp, and filthy. A small interior window, about eye level, allowed the prisoners to see out into the courtyard and toward the much larger men's cell on the opposite side of it. Far above the courtyard was a railed catwalk from which the prison guards could keep watch, although Purnima had seen no guards there yet.

Tulasa was the self-appointed leader of the cell. "Why are you here?" she asked bluntly, looking directly at Purnima. "You're a little young to be locked up, don't you think?"

"I don't know if I'm too young," Purnima replied, "but we're here because we are Christians."

"Christians?" Tulasa almost spat out the word. "Why would they lock you up for being Christians? Stupidity isn't against the law." The others joined in her laughter. She introduced herself, but there was no warmth in her words. "They say I killed my mother-in-law," she snarled. "So I'm going to be here awhile, and I would appreciate it if you kept to yourself!"

Purnima couldn't help but stare at the woman, even though she felt intimidated by Tulasa's harsh words. Somehow Purnima suspected a gentle, caring soul existed behind the cold faccade, and from that moment on, she prayed that God would give her an opportunity to find it.

Tulasa returned to her corner of the cell, letting loose a stream of profanity as she went. Purnima noticed she had an ample supply of blankets and other personal effects, an indication that Tulasa had been there for a while and had received some items from friends or family members on the outside. The newcomers, on the other hand, had come with nothing except the clothing they wore. That first morning, they huddled together and prayed, committing to begin each day in prayer and to fast every Friday. The new inmates were given basic cooking utensils, and each day they received two meal rations, usually rice and potatoes. Occasionally they were given a small allotment of money so they could buy personal items.

The Christians soon discovered that adjusting to prison life was, in some ways, like adjusting to life in the refugee camp: Learn the rules, try to steer clear of trouble, and watch your back. The glaring difference, of course, was their complete lack of freedom and the guards' unwillingness to step in when trouble inevitably occurred.

But, Purnima thought, at least they didn't have to face daily interrogations and beatings here, and they could enjoy their quiet times of fellowship, despite the incessant mocking of the other inmates and the constant onslaught of filthy language. Purnima's greatest fear arose from the prison guards' sexual innuendos, which had started shortly after she arrived.

The first few months dragged by, and Purnima got little sleep. She quickly learned why the other inmates hadn't made their "home" along the outside wall: It was cold there. Her health was declining with the onset of winter, and she had neither warm clothing nor even a single blanket. Slowly her optimistic outlook was being replaced by an inner feeling of despair. Realizing what was happening, Purnima worried about her vulnerability and her declining faith. Again she wondered if she had made a terrible mistake. Her dreams of home, of her mother, had also returned, making the nights even more unbearable. She was ready to give up.

One afternoon Purnima heard screams coming from the men's block, followed by angry voices shouting, "Get him! Get him! Finish him off!" It wasn't unusual for fights to break out in the men's cell, but this time chills went up her spine when she heard a voice yell, "Just finish him off. A dead Christian can't pray *or* sing!"

Purnima knew the threats were real. Tulasa had told her someone had been murdered in the men's cell shortly before their group had arrived. Knowing it was one of her fellow Christians who was facing death at the hands of the other inmates, Purnima called frantically for a guard, but none came. Sobbing, she collapsed onto her mat and prayed. And in that moment she realized how much harder imprisonment was for her brothers crammed into a cell with more than two hundred other men, many of them violent criminals, than it was for her. She saw how absorbed she had become in her own self-pity—while, across the courtyard, one of her friends was being beaten, maybe even killed.

"Dear God," she prayed, "please don't let them kill him; please don't let him die."

Then she wept, and this time not just for herself, but for all of them.

A brother named Ashok had been the victim of the attack in the men's block; he had survived, but barely. Thankful for his recovery and determined to shift her focus off herself, Purnima looked for ways to be a witness to the other women in her cell. She knew she had to somehow remain active if she hoped to survive the three-year sentence. In the past weeks she had allowed not only her body to be imprisoned but her soul and spirit as well, and that situation had to change. "Show me what I can do, Lord," she prayed. "I am free to serve You, no matter the circumstance."

It occurred to her just then that it was almost Christmas . . .

The Christmas Gift

The man known only as "Uncle" had become a permanent fixture at the federal prison. He had been there so long and wandered around the prison so freely, new arrivals usually believed he was part of the staff, but he wasn't. Each week he made his rounds of the cells, asking the prisoners if they wanted him to buy them something at the market.

"Good morning, Purnima," he called to her this day. "What can I get for you today, or are you just going to keep all your money until you're released? Why do you save it anyway? What good is it if you don't spend it?"

Just as he spoke the words, the idea came to her. *That's it! That's what I'm going to do. Thank you, Uncle!*

She hurriedly pressed all the money she'd saved into Uncle's waiting hands and whispered her instructions through the bars of her cell. Watching as he ambled away from the women's cell, she prayed he would buy exactly what she had requested. Uncle had thought she'd gone crazy when he heard her request, but he replied sweetly, "How can I refuse such an innocent face?"

When he returned later that day, he delivered the package into Purnima's eager hands. "It's all there," Uncle assured her. "But I still think you're crazy. Prison will do that, you know."

Purnima smiled her thanks and reached through the bars to shake his hand. Then she began making her preparations as the others looked on. Finally unable to hide their curiosity, they came right out and asked what in the world she was doing, but Purnima just ignored them and kept on working. It took her the rest of the afternoon, but she was determined to get it right. Finally, when she was done, she turned to the others and made her announcement: "Since I have been here, God has put it on my heart to save my prison allowance. I didn't know why until this morning, and then I knew what to do. I asked Uncle to use the money to buy the best chickens and vegetables he could find. And now, I have cooked it all—for you."

Stunned into silence, the others looked on in amazement.

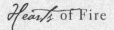

Tulasa eyed her suspiciously, waiting for the "catch," and wondering why Purnima, to whom she had never uttered a kind word, would do such a thing. "What are you talking about? What's the trick?" she asked sarcastically.

"I just want to share it with you, Tulasa—with all of you. There's no trick. It's my gift to you. So let's eat!"

That evening the inmates in the women's cell had the best meal they could remember. Even the guards were walking by and peering in. Word spread quickly through the prison: Purnima had prepared a feast!

The following evening, Tulasa left her corner to come sit by Purnima. "Why did you do this for us?" she asked, sincere and courteous for the first time in Purnima's presence. "We have done nothing but make fun of you and the others since you got here. And that was *your* money, all of it. You obviously could use it yourself, so why did you spend it on us?" Tulasa simply couldn't grasp such kindness. She thought Purnima was either very foolish or very wise, and she wanted to find out which one applied.

"Tulasa," Purnima began, a smile on her face, "have you ever heard of *Christmas* . . . ?"

In this way an unlikely friendship developed between a convicted murderer and a teenage preacher. Purnima told Tulasa the story of how she had accepted Christ during a Christmas service nearly three years earlier. In her gentle but enthusiastic manner, over the next few months Purnima spoke often to Tulasa about Christ, and incredibly, the two became close friends. In a small way, Tulasa reminded Purnima of her mother, and the girl felt comforted by the older woman's companionship. Although she didn't know what the future would hold, Purnima resolved to face it bravely. She recognized her weaknesses but refused to let them imprison her. She would rise to the challenge and leave the rest to God, just as Moses had done.

Epilogue

Purnima, along with the other Christians, was released from prison after fourteen months and six days. Word of their arrest had traveled back to the refugee camp and eventually spread around the world. An international collection of Christian leaders began to petition the Nepalese government for their release. "We know you are holding eleven Christians in the federal prison," they protested to the king of Nepal. "And one of them is only a child!"

Purnima and the others were later informed that their early release was more of a blessing than they realized. The prison authorities had intended to keep them locked up for seven years (the amended prison sentence for leading someone to convert to Christianity).

Immediately after their release, to the surprise of the officials, they requested a meeting with their former cellmates. After three months' imprisonment, the Christians had begun receiving help from their family members. Now they gave their cellmates the possessions they had collected, as well as the additional money Purnima had saved for another special occasion. And they reminded the others they had been persecuted because of their faith in Jesus Christ. Some of the other prisoners had become Christians and were encouraged to "keep the faith." The eleven promised to remember them, and all the other prisoners, in their prayers.

Remarkably, one of the men who had taken part in Ashok's beating came forward and said, "A bright light entered our prison. But now it is leaving."

Just before leaving, Purnima hugged Tulasa, now a Christian, one last time. (Tulasa was later released when her conviction was overturned. She is now an active leader in the church.)

From the first time Maya read her the Bible story, Purnima

had admired Moses. He was exiled from his land, and even though he felt inadequate in speaking, God used him in a powerful way. In a similar manner, Purnima, who often felt inadequate because of her age, has now become somewhat of a celebrity around Nepal. She is frequently invited to share her testimony in churches surrounding the refugee camp where she still lives with Maya, Sival, and her niece and nephew.

Her prayer is that she will someday return to Bhutan, her homeland, to see her mother and to preach the gospel.

Aida:
A Voice for the Voiceless

Russia
July 1968

She didn't want a lawyer. Aida Mikhailovna Skripnikova didn't need a mouthpiece, especially not one who was assigned by the Soviet government. She wanted to speak for herself, to lay out her case before the judge. Sitting at the defense table in the wood-paneled Soviet courtroom, she stared up past him into the stern portrait face of Lenin, the "father" of the system now holding her captive.

The prosecutor was against the idea. He didn't want the defendant speaking for herself; it meant giving her too much freedom. He pointed out that the defendant had spent time in a mental institution. How was she capable of conducting a criminal defense?

The judge finally sided with Aida, and her defense lawyer left the courtroom, leaving Aida responsible for her own case—and her punishment. It wasn't Aida's first time in a courtroom or her first time to be indicted for practicing her Christian faith. If the

77

judge found her guilty and sent her to a labor camp, it wouldn't be her first time there, either. No, all those things she had endured before. What was different this time was that she would not have a passive, government-approved defense. This would be the first time she could speak for herself, clearly articulating her case on behalf of people of faith in her homeland.

There were many charges, and the judge read each one with a loud, accusatory voice that could freeze the blood. Aida was accused of living in Leningrad without the proper residency permit (her permit had been rescinded). She was also charged with being a member of an unregistered church group and with distributing illegally printed Christian materials.

Slander Versus Truth

At the heart of the most significant charges against her was a single word: *slander*. Aida, the prosecution contended, had collected and distributed "false" information reporting how Christians had been arrested, tried, and imprisoned in the Soviet Union. More dastardly, in the government's eyes, was the charge that she had passed on the information to foreigners, allowing information damning to the Soviet Union to reach other countries.

Just as the prosecution would focus on a single word, so would Aida's defense. Hers would rest on the word *truth*. If the information she had passed on was true, she reasoned, it could not have been slanderous. And she planned to show the court that the information was most assuredly true.

As the list of charges was read, Aida learned for the first time how thorough the police surveillance of her had been. They knew about Miss Jursmar, the pretty Swede who had come into the country to receive Aida's information. They knew when and where the two had met. They had confiscated Miss Jursmar's notebook, which contained references to the meeting with Aida. The judge even listed each item and publication that Aida had passed to Miss Jursmar, a tone of sarcastic disdain creeping into his voice.

"Jursmar tried to take the literature she had received out of the country," the judge intoned, "but during the customs inspection the above-mentioned literature was discovered and promptly confiscated." He looked up from the indictment to glare at the defendant, a hint of a triumphant smile on his face.

They knew about David, another foreign Christian friend, and the copy of a Christian magazine, *Herald of Salvation*, Aida had sent to him. They knew she'd gone to another area to meet with her sister, to whom she had given magazines that were later passed on to Christians in the underground church. The police seemed to know everyone she'd met with and every piece of paper she'd given out.

Aida calmly wondered what other information they had intercepted and, as a result, which Christian prisoners were still unknown because her messages had been intercepted before reaching outside eyes.

Again and again as he read, a phrase rolled off the judge's tongue. According to the indictment, Aida had distributed "deliberately false statements slandering the Soviet State and social order."

A QUIET CONFIDENCE

Aida sat quiet and alone at the defense table, uncomfortable in the hard wooden chair. She'd thought she might feel nervous or unsettled. Instead she felt a quiet confidence, a sense of Christ's presence in the room. Jesus told His followers not to worry about what they would say when facing kings or judges, and she was not worried.

When police questioned her, the judge said, continuing to read

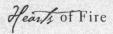

the indictment, she had not admitted her guilt, although she had admitted to sending and giving away Christian materials. Copies of many of the documents she had sent out were found in her apartment, police said, clearly tying her to the case. She told the police the materials did not contain slander but merely "accurately reflect the situation of the church in our country."

Finally the judge finished reading the indictment. Looking sternly at Aida, he asked, "Defendant, do you understand the charges against you?"

She looked back at him, confidently staring into his dark eyes. "Yes."

"Do you plead guilty?"

"No." Her voice was calm and firm.

The judge looked down at his notes then announced that the trial would begin immediately. The first witness, he declared, would be Aida herself.

A FAMILY RACKED BY GRIEF

When she began following Jesus Christ at the age of twenty-one, Aida had no idea that the path He would take her on would lead to a courtroom. She was born into a Christian family and had known from an early age who Jesus was. But her family was racked by grief when, in 1942, her father was arrested for refusing military service. He had been promised a certificate exempting him from military duty, but the certificate never came. Instead, he was executed, leaving two-year-old Aida without even memories of him.

Her mother was left to raise the family alone in a small Siberian community, and she did so through hard work and prayer. She read to the children regularly from the Scriptures. And in spite of the risk of arrest and prosecution, she took the children to gatherings of

Christians who met secretly in each other's homes. Sometimes her uncle would remain outside the meeting to watch for any signs that police or soldiers were on their way. Aida remembers clearly the Sunday the police raided a meeting at their home. When they left, they took her uncle and two other Christian men in handcuffs and filed criminal charges against them.

Sadly, when Aida was eleven, her mother died. One of the clearest memories Aida had of her mother was how she worried that her children might grow up and leave their faith in Christ. But despite her mother's efforts, Aida did leave her faith. It was not so much a deliberate back turning as a simple drifting away, a loss of interest. Aida was being raised by an older sister, and in moving around, the family stopped going to church meetings. In school they were taught that there is no God, and slowly even the mention of Him disappeared from their home.

FAITH REBORN

At age nineteen Aida moved to Leningrad (now St. Petersburg). Her brother Victor, five years her senior, had finished his naval service and settled there, and Aida moved there to be near him. One day, the subject of religion came up in their conversation.

Aida said, "I do not know whether there is a God or there isn't."

She was surprised by the intensity of her brother's reply: "What has come over you?" he demanded. "I have never even doubted it! I know there is a God."

Aida wished she could share her brother's certainty. But she needed proof.

Shortly after that conversation with her brother, Aida walked by an antique-books store, and she remembered hearing someone mention that the store sometimes sold Bibles. Almost on a whim, she went in and asked for one. The clerk told her Bibles were very rare and that the store didn't have any. Aida turned to leave when another shopper followed her outside and offered to sell her a New Testament for fifteen rubles.

It was almost all the money she had, but she gave it to the man in return for the old Book. Aida's brother was thrilled with her purchase, especially because it came at the time he needed it most. He had been diagnosed with cancer, and his doctors told him it would be fatal. Victor asked Aida to go to the prayer house to let his friends there know of his condition.

Aida did as he requested, and the friends came regularly to visit and encourage Victor. She watched as her brother's spirit became increasingly alive as the disease dragged his body toward death. She was amazed to see his faith in Christ grow stronger as his body grew weaker. She longed to have the faith and certainty her brother had. He approached death not with worry or fear but with a deep certainty of his eternal home.

Four months after the diagnosis, Victor died. Standing at his bedside as his earthly life ran out, Aida sensed that his desire was for her to know he was not saying, "Good-bye" but, "See you later."

Aida wanted that same confidence, that same certainty. Victor's life—as well as his death—had answered many of her questions. She discussed the rest of them with some of Victor's friends from the prayer house. Finally, her decision became clear: She would follow Christ in faith.

It was a decision that would prove very costly for the young woman, but one she would never regret.

AN EXCHANGE OF LITERATURE—AND THE WORD

"Do you wish to give the court an explanation concerning the charges against you?" the judge asked.

"Yes, I do," Aida replied, knowing the judge himself would do the initial questioning. For this trial he would serve as her accuser, judge, and jury. "I admit the facts about distributing literature as mentioned in the indictment and about the recipients as mentioned."

She admits the facts. This case is going to go even faster than I hoped. She should have kept her lawyer, the prosecutor must have thought to himself.

At the judge's urging, Aida recounted each of the people she had given materials to as outlined in the indictment. She quibbled over the indictment calling one item a journal when in fact it was no more than two or three pages in length, but she admitted to giving the items away, and even to giving them to foreigners.

"Everything else in the indictment is correct?" the judge asked when she had finished.

"Yes," she replied. "All the facts about my distributing the literature are correct. But this literature does not contain 'deliberately false statements slandering the Soviet state and social order'; that is, it does not constitute a crime under article 190/1, and the distribution of literature in itself is not a crime. Therefore, I plead not guilty."

Rather than tackle her assertion head-on, the judge asked about the Swede, Miss Jursmar, to whom Aida had given the materials, including transcripts of two Christians' trials in Soviet courts. Aida refused to say where she'd met Miss Jursmar, calling that "a private matter."

Listening to Aida present her case, the prosecutor perked up, wondering if perhaps the young Christian would put up more of a fight than he'd given her credit for.

Grudgingly, Aida provided details. She and Miss Jursmar had a mutual friend in Sweden, and the friend had arranged their meeting. Miss Jursmar had brought fifty New Testaments, which

Aida had planned to pass on to members of the underground church—until the police confiscated them. In exchange, Aida gave Miss Jursmar the literature, including some letters and the trial transcripts, for her to take back to her employer, the Slavic Mission. From there it would be printed and distributed around the world.

"Why did you give Jursmar copies of *Herald of Salvation* and *Fraternal Leaflet*,[1] as well as transcripts of trials in Moscow and Ryazan, and letters of Khorev and Makhovitsky?" the judge asked harshly.

"So that she could read them and learn about the life of our church," Aida responded matter-of-factly. "*Herald of Salvation* is my favorite journal, and *Fraternal Leaflet* speaks about the life of our church. Trials have become so much a part of our church life that to know about the churches in Russia, you must know about the trials."

Indeed, for those who chose to follow Christ completely, trials were an accepted part of life in the Soviet Union. Arrests, beatings, and imprisonment were part of the cost of following Christ here, and the underground church magazines accepted and publicized that fact.

The judge could not believe Aida would trust a woman she had only just met with such secret and important information.

"With believers, friendships develop more simply," Aida tried to explain. "I can go to a strange town, meet believers I didn't know before, and after a few minutes we can become close friends. Believers are one big family, and we are interested in everything about each other."

The prosecutor began to intersperse his questions with the judge's, asking Aida about all the foreign addresses in her address book. He wanted to know if she wrote to all of them.

"Some of them," Aida answered. Then, a little tartly, she

added, "I don't know of any law forbidding Soviet citizens from corresponding with friends abroad."

Some believers who had come to observe the trial hid their smiles as the prosecutor looked up sharply at Aida's remark. Then he began to read each name in her address book.

A Special Boldness for the Gospel

Aida hadn't started out to be a correspondent working on the front lines of the Soviet church. When she accepted Christ, she was a pretty young woman of twenty-one, full of excitement about her new best Friend and wanting to tell everyone she met about Him.

Her decision came as a revival was breaking forth in the Baptist Church in the Soviet Union. "For a while, faith was growing weak," she would later say, "and suddenly there came an awakening. What I saw was quite miraculous. I saw the dead—the spiritually dead—rising again, and the weak proved capable of great feats. I came to know the greatness of humility and patience, the greatness of the church's struggle. This revival quickened my spirit too, and from that time onward I have not been able to remain uninvolved."

Her new friends from Victor's prayer house encouraged her to witness. She had watched as they printed cards with gospel texts and messages urging readers to "Repent and believe the Good News." They placed the cards in mailboxes, which caused quite a stir in Leningrad, even meriting coverage in the local newspapers.

From the first days of her Christian walk, Aida possessed a special boldness and zeal for sharing her faith with others. Only months after becoming a Christian, Aida devised a special way to welcome in the first day of 1962. She purchased a supply of postcards showing a Claude Lorrain painting of the sunrise over a harbor. For days she worked during every spare moment, hand-lettering a simple message on each one:

HAPPY NEW YEAR 1962!
A New Year's Wish

Our years fly past
One after the other, unnoticed
Grief and sadness disappear;
They are carried away by life.
This world, the earth, is so transient,
Everything in it comes to an end.
Life is important. Don't be happy-go-lucky!
What answer will you give your Creator?
What awaits you, my friend, beyond the grave?
Answer this question while light remains.
Perhaps tomorrow, before God,
You will appear to give an answer for everything.
Think deeply about this,
For you are not on this earth to eternity.
Perhaps tomorrow, you will break
Forever your links with this world!
SEEK GOD WHILE HE IS TO BE FOUND!

The postcard poems concluded with a simple call, the same one she had seen earlier on the cards printed by her friends: "Repent and believe the Good News."

After she had filled out all the cards, Aida bundled up against the icy air and went outside. In the large square in front of the Museum of History of Religion and Atheism, the dark-haired young woman began to hand out the cards. She worked quickly through the stack, handing them to passersby as she shared New Year's greetings.

The cards were almost all gone when a strong hand grabbed her arm. "What is this?" an angry-looking man demanded, waving the card in her face.

"A New Year's card," she answered, trying to pull away. She seemed very small next to the glowering man, and she tensed as his grip grew tighter. He looked around then began calling for the police officer standing on the corner.

"We don't need this here," he told her through clenched teeth. He did not let go of her until the policeman grabbed her other arm and began leading her to his car.

A TASTE OF WHAT WAS TO COME

It was Aida's first forced visit to the local police station. She was held for several hours then released, but not until the police had opened a file on her and written down all the information about her "postcard evangelism." Aida sat calmly, answering their questions, silently amazed at the confidence she felt. God was with her, she knew; she need not fear the authorities. She wondered if anyone had told the officer of Christ's love for him.

The police reported the incident to both her employer and the dormitory where she lived. Her first brush with the legal system came that April, when a so-called "Comrades' Court" heard the evidence against her. Aida sat on a bench in front of the three "comrades" who would rule on her fate. "Accusers," local people from the community, were brought in to speak against her. One old man trembled with apparent rage as he screamed, "I don't want to breathe the same air. I don't want to walk the same earth as her."

Other witnesses claimed that Victor had died because the Baptists wouldn't allow him to seek medical care (a strange thing to say, thought Aida, since Victor had died in a hospital). Her accusers' statements surprised Aida in other ways, too. Weren't the charges against her for giving away a Christian card? What did that have to do with her brother? Aida tried to speak up and defend herself, and even Victor's widow tried to speak up, but the courtroom crowd angrily shouted them down. By the end of the trial, the onlookers were demanding that Aida's case be sent on to a court of higher jurisdiction where stronger punishment could be levied. "To the People's Court! To the People's Court!" they chanted.

Aida wondered how a few simple postcards had engendered such hatred among this throng.

The three Comrades' Court officials rescinded Aida's Leningrad residency permit and forced her out of her job. After the witnesses' testimony, the crowd of onlookers didn't think the sentence was nearly severe enough. They stood, stomping their feet and screaming at the petite girl standing in front of them, demanding a stiffer penalty. For her own safety, Aida had to be escorted by guards out the back door of the building.

The court's decision was not carried out for many months, giving police more time to watch and gather evidence against the young Christian—not evidence of criminal activity, but evidence of her Christian work. Aida continued to live in Leningrad, finding work where she could. Her life had become more difficult, but those early hardships were just a taste of what was to come.

"You *Refuse* to Reckon with Our Laws"

Now, in her current trial, the questioning continued, the judge and the prosecutor badgering Aida about every foreign contact, every piece of information that had ever changed hands.

Next, they delved into the Christian publications Aida had distributed. The judge took one of the magazines from among the evidence pile and slowly turned the pages, looking for the paragraphs he had previously marked. Finding what he thought were the most incriminating sections, he began to read aloud, line by line. At the end of each sentence, he glared at Aida, challenging her to explain or verify the statement.

The judge asked about different Christian denominations, pointing out that some denominations were meeting without facing persecution.

"I don't know about the persecution of believers of other denominations," Aida replied wearily. "We write only about the persecution of believers of the Evangelical Christian and Baptist Church."

The prosecutor claimed that anyone outside the country who read the literature would think that all Christians in the Soviet Union faced persecution. He picked up where the judge had left off, reading the magazines and badgering Aida over any sentence he found objectionable. He pointed out claims in one magazine that Christian children faced persecution in the Soviet school system. The schools, he suggested, are merely trying to undo the damage done by zealot parents who poison their children with stupid superstitions.

"The law forbids the imposition of belief on those under age," he said, looking up to make sure the judge was following closely.

"But the law does not forbid the imposition of atheism," Aida shot back.

"Atheism isn't a religion. A child grows up, and then he must himself decide his attitude toward belief. Atheism isn't imposed."

"Then what does one tell a child?" Aida asked, looking from the prosecutor to the judge. "That one is forbidden, by law, to say that God exists, but one is allowed to say that there is no God?"

No one spoke, and the judge changed the subject, knowing he had no answer. He demanded that "the defendant not digress from the main point."

The prosecutor continued, reading more comments from another magazine. "Do you know that a religious community must be registered?" he asked the defendant.

"Yes." Aida also knew that by registering, a church put itself under the control of the Communist government—a government that denied the very existence of the God the church served.

"Your community did not register; therefore you are prevented from holding meetings, but not because there is persecution of believers in our country," he said, like an impatient teacher lecturing a kindergarten child.

"Our community requested registration," Aida replied calmly. "We put in an application, but we were refused."

"You were refused because you refuse to observe the law."

"Which laws do we not observe?" she asked.

"You're demanding the creation of Sunday schools, and you want to organize religious activities for underage children."

"I don't remember that our community demanded a Sunday school," Aida countered. "And, by law, parents can bring up their children as they wish."

"*No they can't!*" the prosecutor snapped. "It is forbidden by law to involve children under age in religious societies. But you *refuse* to reckon with our laws."

"According to the constitution, we have freedom of religious belief. The term implies a confession of faith," Aida answered. "It means that it's possible to tell everyone about God—that is, to profess one's belief freely. Isn't that so?"

Here Aida was presenting the core of her case. The Soviet constitution said people are free to believe as they choose and to practice those beliefs. Yet Soviet leaders feared Christians' beliefs; they wanted all confidence and dependence to be placed in the Communist Party. Wiping out religious belief, they reasoned, would lead people to believe more passionately in the party.

Yet again, the judge had no answer for Aida's question. So once more he changed the subject, saying that, if the material in all the literature was true, why was Aida so secretive about handing it out?

"Because those who persecute don't like it when the fact that they're persecuting becomes known," Aida answered, sounding more and more like a trained lawyer and less and less like a simple factory worker. "I know that in the literature I gave Miss Jursmar there were no deliberately false statements. In the *Herald of Salvation* and in the *Fraternal Leaflets*, where the situation of believers is described, it's described as it really is. I agree with you that it's unattractive, but this is real life, and it *must* be talked about. When I was handing over the literature to Miss Jursmar, I knew that those materials could get me locked up. I understood that. But it doesn't change the truth of what the literature stated."

The prosecutor scanned his notes then sat down. Finally, Aida's direct questioning was over. But the trial was not. Now the witnesses came. First, it was her neighbors, Anatoli and Alla Lavrenteva. Both judge and prosecutor badgered them with questions: "Did she talk to you about her faith?" "Did she give you any literature?" "Did she have a TV or radio?" "Did she live according to her means?" "How did she dress?" "What did she cook?"

Neither Anatoli or Alla would say Aida was a criminal.

"Aida was on good terms with everyone," Anatoli said. "You could only speak good of her."

Another neighbor was called to testify and peppered with more questions about Aida's dress, demeanor, and employment.

Finally, a fellow believer, Marja Akimovna Skurlova, was called to the witness chair. She had known Aida five years. The two had worshiped and prayed together, and when Aida came out of prison after a one-year sentence, Marja gave her a place to stay.

Now Marja admitted to helping the defendant.

"You say that Aida was dismissed from her job because she was a believer," the judge asked. "Why aren't you dismissed from *your* job? Surely you work."

"My turn hasn't come yet," Marja replied simply.

Marja went on to admit that foreigners had come to the apartment she shared with Aida, but she did not know what, if anything, Aida had given them.

When Aida stood to question her friend, she asked Marja about the persecution of Christian believers. Marja recited the names of Christians who had been questioned or had had their houses searched by police, and others who had been arrested.

"I know that believers were fined," Marja testified. "Sukovitsyn was fined . . ."

"Why was he fined?" the prosecutor broke into Aida's questioning.

"Because he prayed."

"Where had he prayed?"

"He led the prayers at Lukas's flat. There was a meeting there."

"That's right!" the prosecutor said, almost shouting in triumph. "A meeting was held in an unauthorized place. You have a prayer house; go and pray there!"

Later, the prosecutor broke in again when Marja testified that she had been fined for attending a Christian meeting. "Where was the meeting held?" he demanded.

"In the woods."

"It's forbidden to hold a service in a public place. That's why you were fined." He nodded to the judge, a smug smile of satisfaction on his face.

"There was no one else in the woods; we were alone. We held our meeting and went away, but then some were picked up on the platform when we were already going home." Marja recited other instances where Christians were harassed and obstructed by police, then she was dismissed.

The final witness in the case was Yekaterina Andreyevna Boiko, Aida's friend and fellow believer. She identified Aida as her friend and testified that she was "good and kind."

Yekaterina told how police had come to her apartment, asking for Aida. The officers had strongly implied that Aida was a spy, and they urged Yekaterina and the other neighbors to let them know if Aida was seen in the building.

Yekaterina was clearly a witness hostile to the prosecution. At times, her answers were single syllables. At other times, she sat silently after being asked a question.

"What did you know about the visit of the Swedish tourist to Skripnikova?" the prosecutor demanded.

"I knew nothing about it. I found out about it the next day. The police called on Aida at the flat while I was there. A policeman said that literature had been taken from a foreigner and that Aida had given it to them."

The prosecutor asked about her education, which had ended after the tenth grade. "Why didn't you study any further?"

"I wanted to go to medical school," Yekaterina replied, "but in my character reference they wrote that I was a believer and a member of the schismatic Baptists. So I didn't enter medical school. I would have been expelled in any case."

"And you didn't even try?" A hint of mockery stained the lawyer's voice.

"I knew from the example of others that they wouldn't let me study anyway."

When Aida's turn came to question the witness, she looked at her friend. She began with general questions then honed in on the Soviet state's treatment of Christian believers. Aida asked about specific believers who had been fined by police, and Yekaterina listed them, giving details about some of the cases.

"Why do you hold prayer meetings in the woods?" the judge interrupted. "You have a prayer house at Poklonnaya Hill. Why don't you go there? Your community isn't registered. You hold prayer meetings in an unauthorized place, and you disrupt public order. That's why you're fined."

"We applied for registration. Our meeting in the forest disturbed no one in Lavriki."

The prosecutor asked if she believed herself to be a loyal citizen, obliged to observe the country's laws.

"I do observe the laws," Yekaterina insisted.

"You meet in the woods and in Lukas's home, and your community isn't registered," the prosecutor retorted. "So you do *not* observe the laws."

"The prayer meetings at Lukas's are not against the law." She daringly quoted Lenin, who had called laws against belief "shameful."

Not wishing to argue with one of communism's founders, the prosecutor abruptly dismissed the witness.

The Breaking Point

Aida had tried to practice her Christian faith within the bounds of Soviet law. During her first months as a Christian she went regularly to the prayer house that was registered and approved by the Soviet government. She was happy and pleased to worship with fellow believers—and not yet aware of the politics within the registered church.

As she continued to worship and minister, the restrictions began to chafe against her. She was involved in a Bible study with youth from the meeting, but she was warned not to let the church leaders know about it. Communist law prohibited the sharing of "religious superstitions" with anyone under eighteen years old, and the leaders of the registered church seemed to care more for Communist law than they did for lost souls.

Aida remembered the house church she had gone to with her mother. She remembered the sense of God's presence there, and the fact that children and young people were welcomed and trained. Keeping young people from hearing the gospel did not seem right to Aida, and it did not match the teaching of the Scriptures.

The breaking point came when Aida began to work on behalf of Christians who were in prison for their faith. Early on, her vision was to share their information and to develop a network of prayer and support for them. The leaders of the registered churches had lists of those who were in prison, but the lists were treated as state secrets, not as information other Christians needed to know.

To Aida, this was *exactly* the information that others *did* need to know. How could Christians—in the Soviet Union and around the world—possibly offer prayer and support for these imprisoned brothers and sisters in Christ if they didn't even know of their suffering?

Aida worked to get the word out, an effort that brought her into direct conflict with leaders of the registered churches.

"The thing is that, in a few words, the authorities tried to work in the church from the inside, through its ministers," Aida said later. "They wanted to introduce bans that would suppress the spiritual life of the church. And actually, by the 1960s they had quite a lot of success in that area."

The leaders' position was in direct opposition to Aida's efforts to get the word out about imprisoned believers. So she faced a choice: Remain within the registered church and work to protect herself, or join the underground church and work to protect her brothers and sisters in prison. The pull of the registered church was real. After all, it was the group her brother had belonged to before his death, and she had many friends there.

But Aida refused the easy, passive choice. She refused to follow leaders who were clearly more worried about government approval than about fellow Christians in prison. She threw the full weight of her personality and her hard work into the underground church, knowing she would pay a price for her decision.

On June 4, 1962, an article appeared in *Smena*, a newspaper that served as a mouthpiece for the Soviet government. The article, entitled "Don't Be a Corpse Among the Living," sought to discredit believers in general and the underground church in particular. Government policy said there was no God, and the article mocked and ridiculed those who chose to follow an imaginary messiah.

When Aida saw the article, she began to compose a reply, a defense of her faith and of those who followed it. She sent the response to *Smena*, but of course it was refused for publication. The issue might have ended there, but Aida showed the *Smena* article and her reply to fellow believers. Impressed, they asked for a copy. Then some believers came to visit from the Ukraine; they asked for copies as well and took them home. Soon hundreds of copies were being made and handed from believer to believer, all across the Soviet Union. Underground church members were alarmed to read an attack on their faith—and then encouraged to read the bold, well-reasoned reply of one of their fellow believers. Aida was at the forefront of *zamizdat*, a new practice of self-published communication. Government officials simply couldn't watch every mimeograph machine, photocopier, or printing press in the country.

Through her writing, Aida Skripnikova's name became known to thousands of believers she had never met. And it became well known in another sphere as well: the ranks of the secret police.

THE CORE ELEMENTS

Other witnesses had been scheduled to testify at Aida's trial, but they did not show up. The judge ruled that the trial would continue anyway.

Frustrated, Aida complained that the court had spent more time delving into her home, her dress, and even her cooking than it had in considering the essential matters of her case.

"I ask the court to pay a little more attention to the core elements of the case," she pleaded. "For example, I would like to explain why our community is not registered. To begin, tell me, please, which laws have we broken that would cause us to be refused registration?"

"Defendant," the judge replied testily, "the court asks *you* the questions, not you the court."

Seeing the judge's pique, the prosecutor chimed in, "I cannot even understand what the defendant is asking."

Aida took a deep breath, collecting herself. "I am asking the court to pay more attention to the essential questions of the indictment, and requesting that the side issues should not obscure the essential aspect of the case for the court's consideration. That is my first petition. My second is to ask you, the court, to find out the exact date when my residency permit was confiscated."

The judge asked why that piece of information was important.

Aida explained that the trial had revealed that the police had been collecting evidence against her long before her residency permit had expired. "If I am being tried for an expired residency permit, and not because of my Christian activities, then why was

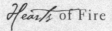

I under investigation *before the residency permit even expired?"* she asked.

"I can tell you why proceedings were started against me," she continued. "Twice in our prayer house I approached foreigners and asked them for a Bible. These two requests became known to the authorities."

"The question of a residency permit has nothing to do with the case," the judge said. "You're accused of distributing deliberately false statements slandering the Soviet state and social order."

"But the question of work and residency permit has received a lot of attention in the judicial proceedings," Aida shot back.

"These questions interested the court, not because you are being charged with this, but because the court must assess your personality. It may seem strange to you that the court even asks about your character. The court must know what sort of person you are. In passing sentence, the court takes into account the personality of the defendant."

Aida said that if the court truly wanted to know her character, it was all the more important to know the true facts of her story. Her last request to the judge was to call one final witness: Miss Jursmar, the Swede to whom she had given the literature. "This woman's notebook has been used as evidence against me," Aida reasoned, "but to understand it accurately we must have her here to explain her notes."

The judge made a show of considering her requests, asking the prosecutor for his opinions, and then he ruled: "After consultation, the court has resolved that the defendant's petitions be turned down."

There were a few final questions, then the trial adjourned for the day. All that was left was the final arguments. For the prosecutor, it would be a chance to defend the Soviet system, to explain that Christians did in fact have freedom of belief, *if* they were willing to abide by the law.

For Aida, it would be her last chance, her final opportunity to speak on her own behalf and on behalf of the brothers and sisters in the church. She felt burdened by the weight of the task, knowing the risk of being locked up again, but she was encouraged by the comfort of her heavenly Father.

AN ATTEMPT AT "RE-EDUCATION"

Getting locked up was not an idle threat to Aida. She'd been there before. After the Comrades' Court had rescinded her Leningrad residency permit in 1963, she had spent some time visiting her sister in the Ukraine, where Aida was impressed by the tenacity and the boldness of the believers. She returned to Leningrad with renewed determination. The police were watching for her, but Aida entered the city and managed to evade capture. Without the residency permit, she could be arrested at any time, yet she continued her Christian work.

Aida and her friends continued to gather in the forest outside the city to escape detection, and it was in the forest in 1965 that her first formal arrest came. Aida was twenty-five.

"The police arrived and began chasing us off," one witness would later testify. "They pushed us and grabbed us by the hair. They took away several people; some they fined, and some they imprisoned for two weeks."

Aida was one of those arrested, and the police arranged a trial for her. On paper, the charge had nothing to do with religion. Though she was arrested outside the city limits, Aida was charged with not having the proper residency permit for Leningrad.

At that trial, in a small hall at the Rayon court building, Aida was not even allowed to speak. The trial was an obvious facade, an attempt to exhibit justice where none really existed. When it was over, Aida's sentence was read: one year in prison.

She did not feel overwhelmed by the verdict. She fellow-shipped regularly with believers who had been in prison and many who were ready to go if that was where Christ led. Now it was her turn.

The goal of prison, to the Soviet leaders, was to re-educate the inmate. "These poor people had been misled," the officials explained, "and now they must be shown and convinced of the truth and power of the Soviet system: the glory of the motherland."

In addition to the monotonous re-education sessions, Aida was forced to spend many cold nights on a hard, cement floor. There was never enough food, and what there was of it was sometimes not fit even for animals. During her imprisonment, Aida was forced into a psychiatric facility. After thirty days of "evaluation," doctors said she was normal and returned her to her cell. The months in a cruel Communist prison system added years of pain and scarring to the outspoken young zealot.

Aida had not taken to the Soviet "re-education." Instead of weakening her faith, the experience made her faith in Christ stronger. Instead of stopping her from spreading the Word, she left prison even more passionate about sharing the truth of Jesus. Now she knew full well the price of doing so, yet she never wavered in her determination.

"The State Does *Not* Interfere"

Now it was time for the final arguments in Aida's second trial. The prosecutor's summation was first, and he chose to begin by recounting some of the history of the church in Russia.

"After the great October Socialist Revolution in our country, the church was separated from the state, and believers of all faiths received the right to freedom of belief," he proudly stated. But then the prosecutor went on to accuse the Evangelical Christians and Baptists and the Council of Churches of encouraging believers not to submit to the state's laws.

"The communities that support the Council of Churches are not registered," the prosecutor charged. "Their illegal meetings take place in private homes and in public places. Some believers were convicted for breaking the legislation on cults. The Council of Churches presents this as persecution for the faith. For seven years the Council of Churches has been carrying on this titanic struggle with the authorities."

From church history and the general situation among believers, the prosecutor finally moved into the specifics of Aida's case. "Skripnikova had links throughout the country, but her main task was to organize contacts abroad. It must be said that she measured up to the task well," he added snidely.

Then his tone became more patronizing. "Aida's life began unfortunately, in that she was born into a family of Baptists. Of course it's a pity that we let a person slip away, but we talked a lot to Aida and made the antisocial character of her actions clear."

His voice rose to a crescendo as he delivered his final comments, first quoting from some of the literature found in Aida's home. "One of the articles quotes a man named Kryuchokov saying, at his trial in Moscow, 'Those brothers who are in prisons and camps do not suffer because they have broken Soviet laws; they suffer because they have remained faithful to the Lord.'"

The prosecutor shook his head solemnly. "All this is a deliberately false statement that slanders the Soviet state and social order. In the Soviet Union there are various faiths, churches are open, and *no one* is persecuted for his faith. The state does *not* interfere in the activities of religious bodies if they do not break

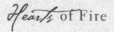

the legislation on cults. The defendant Skripnikova's guilt of systematically distributing false statements that slander the Soviet state and social order is *fully proved*. These actions are rightly covered by article 190/1 of the Criminal Code. Therefore I request that the court sentence the defendant, Aida Skripnikova, to two and a half years' imprisonment."

With that, he sat down, a smug look of confident satisfaction on his face.

"For the Christian There Is Only One Course"

The judge turned to Aida, motioning that it was her turn to present the final speech of her defense.

"I was intending to speak on the substance of the charges brought against me," she began, her voice clear and calm. "But other questions have been touched on here, so I must also deal with them, although, as has been said, they have no connection with this case."

She opened by refuting some of the minor issues the prosecution had raised, ranging from a letter she wrote to *Pravda* in 1958 to her work in a construction laboratory later. Then she began to deal with more substantive issues.

"When I say that I was dismissed from my work for my faith, I am told, 'That is a deliberately false statement.' But here is what happened: After my release from prison, I found work in a printing plant. A week after starting work, I was at a prayer meeting when the police arrived and took down my name, along with several others'. I knew they would report me to my place of work," Aida said.

"Everyone at the printing plant got alarmed when they found out I was a believer, and they began to tell me, right from the start, that if I did not change my views, I would be sacked.

They did not hide this fact from me. They told me straight out: 'The printing plant is a political institution. Not everybody can work here.' They said this even though that particular printing plant was under the management of the railways, and nothing secret was printed there—only railroad forms, boarding permits, and train timetables. I don't know what was there that I couldn't be trusted with," she continued.

"Things went on like this for three weeks. Then I was summoned to the manager's office and told that I'd been dismissed. Of course, they didn't say they were dismissing me because of my faith, because there is no such law that allows people to be dismissed for their faith. So they sacked me on the pretext of a staff reduction. When I went to the shop floor and said that I had been dismissed due to a staff reduction, the workers' eyes nearly popped out of their heads. One of the machines had been standing idle because there was no one to operate it.

"The manager told me, 'We can't employ you because your permit is valid only outside the city'—as if they hadn't previously seen that I had a non-city residency permit, and as if the manager hadn't previously looked at my papers."

Aida told the court that once the police began asking questions, she knew it wouldn't be long until she was arrested again. "Only six months had elapsed since my release, and I wanted to do something useful before going to prison again. I had work I had to finish."

She took a deep breath. Arguing her case was exhausting; it required a mental, emotional, and spiritual focus that was hard to sustain for long periods. She asked the judge for a ten-minute break, and he agreed.

When the trial resumed, Aida aimed her comments specifically at the case against her: "The distribution of any publication is not in itself a crime, and if the prosecution found no deliberately false statements in the magazines *Herald of Salvation* and *Fraternal Leaflet*, there would be no grounds on which to try me. Therefore, I must talk about the contents of this literature."

She then spoke about a forbidden meeting of Christians and Christian leaders that was discussed in the literature she had given out. "The law of 1929 says that believers have the right to organize congresses," Aida noted. "But instead of giving permission, the authorities began to persecute those who had asked for the congress.

"Next, the prosecutor's investigator noted seventeen 'seditious' phrases he had taken out of the literature. According to the investigator, these phrases contain deliberately false statements, slandering the Soviet state and social order."

Now Aida turned and addressed the judge directly. "During her testimony, Miss Boiko began to quote Lenin; I'll complete the quotation she began: 'Only in Russia and Turkey were shameful laws against religious people still in force. These laws either directly prohibited the open profession of faith or forbade its propagation. These laws are the most unjust, shameful, and oppressive.' Now, I should like to draw the court's attention to the word *propagation*. Lenin himself called the prohibition on the *propagation* of the faith unjust and shameful."

She drew in another breath and continued. "Now I will tell you how I was arrested. On April 11 I went to a prayer meeting. I noticed that I was being followed, but I didn't attach any importance to it. The next day, however, the police came to my flat and arrested me. Searches also have been carried out at other believers' homes. In connection with my case alone there were eleven searches: three in Leningrad, four in Perm, three in Kirovograd, and one at my sister's home in Magnitogorsk. One can more or less understand the search at my flat and at my sister's. But why make searches at the other believers' homes? They were only made because their addresses were found in my notebook. And in none of these places did they find anything connected with my case."

Next Aida turned to the question of "what we are being prosecuted *for*. We say we are prosecuted for our faith, but we are told, 'That's a deliberately false statement; you're being tried for infringing Soviet law.' I'm a member of an unregistered community, which requested registration—all our communities have sent in these applications, which include our statutes—and when we do, we are not told, 'You mustn't do this or that; it's against the law.' Instead, we're told, 'Sign a pledge that you won't break the law.' This isn't the correct procedure for registration."

Aida saw that the judge was getting restless, so she hurried to wrap up her argument. "Believers *cannot* promise to fulfill a law that forbids them to talk about God and forbids parents to bring up their children in the faith. For all their loyalty to the authorities, no Christian parents will accept a law that orders them to bring up their children as atheists. They would rather go through whatever sufferings you like—they would rather stand in the dock—than promise to abide by such a law.

"Christ said we are to preach the gospel to every creature," Aida continued, "and believers cannot submit to a law forbidding them to talk about God and about salvation. Not a single believer will do this. Even if he's not a missionary or a preacher, even if he's incapable of preaching a sermon, it makes no difference—he won't submit to such a law because even a person incapable of preaching a sermon will have an opportunity sometimes to tell someone about salvation. Therefore believers won't promise to carry out such a law. Despite all their respect for the authorities, they'll break this law.

"I'll repeat it once more: Believers can't keep a law that forces them to deny the gospel. So when we're tried for breaking such laws, we're quite justified in saying we're being tried for our faith.

"I know that the *Herald of Salvation* and the *Fraternal Leaflet* do not contain any deliberately false statements. But at the same time, I know what it means to send them abroad. I knew that act could bring me into the dock. I would never ask anyone else to send a *Herald of Salvation* abroad. I know it's dangerous; that's why I do it myself."

Aida paused, gathering her strength for the home stretch of her defense, the passionate final thoughts she wished to leave with those who would determine her sentence. "At one time people realized that it was unjust to forbid the propagation of a faith; now they don't understand this. Now they say, 'Believe yourself and pray, but don't dare talk about God to anyone.' To silence one's ideological opponent by force is no ideological victory. This has always been called barbarism."

The judge interrupted her, frustrated that this criminal was now preaching a sermon in his courtroom. "You are not to talk about the church; talk only about yourself," he said, punctuating his words by pointing at her.

Aida was undaunted. "For the Christian there is only one course," she said. "The Christian can't be anything but confrontational. Once you know the truth, this means following it, upholding it, and if necessary suffering for it. I can't be different. I can't act any differently. I love freedom and would very much like to be free with my family and friends. But I don't want to act against my conscience. What good is freedom to me if I can't call God my Father? The knowledge that my soul and thoughts are free encourages and strengthens me. That is all I wanted to say to you."

Aida sat down, her case presented and her heart clear.

EPILOGUE

Unmoved by her spirit and unconvinced by her argument, the judge sentenced Aida to three years in a Soviet prison, a sentence six months longer than the prosecution had asked for. Aida left the courtroom between two tall guards.

But locking her up couldn't stop her work. Appropriately, the transcripts of Aida's trial were copied painstakingly onto twenty pieces of cloth cut down from bedsheets and similar fabric, then they were smuggled out of the Soviet Union. Around the world, believers read the words of "Aida of Leningrad," and prayed for this faithful sister.

Aida left the prison labor camp on April 12, 1971. Upon her release, officials told her she had "learned nothing" from her punishment. In truth, she had learned much, but not what her Soviet captors wanted. She had earned a doctorate in God's faithfulness, and she had gained an even greater understanding of the deep joy and satisfaction that come from serving Him. She had become a full member in the fraternity that the apostle Paul called "the fellowship of His sufferings."[2]

Today, Aida Skripnikova lives in St. Petersburg. Her faith has outlived the regime that sought to destroy it. Today, it is legal for Christians like her to gather for worship and preaching. Her church recently gathered for a special time: to celebrate the fortieth anniversary of the church's ministry and to remember God's faithfulness to its members. A special display honored those who had been martyred for their faith.[3]

Sabina:
A Witness of Christ's Love

Romania
1945

The Russians had driven the Nazis out of Romania, and now they were taking steps to control all aspects of Romanian government and society. Their latest effort was to summon clergy of all religions to a meeting; the Russians called it the "Congress of the Cults." Their stated goal was to garnish support among the clergy. But to Sabina the tactic was nothing more than an attempt to gain control and turn Romania's religious leaders into puppets of the state.

Sabina was small in stature, nearly a foot and a half shorter than her husband, Richard, but she had a huge passion for Christ. Sitting beside Richard at the meeting and hearing yet another pastor publicly commit his loyalty to the Communists who had invaded their homeland, Sabina tugged on her husband's arm. "Will you not wash this shame from the face of Christ, Richard?" she pleaded. "You have to say something. They are spitting on the name of Christ!"

Richard looked around the assembled delegates within the

Parliament Building. It was quite a show. "Full religious freedom!" was the Communists' proclaimed motto. They advocated a peaceful coexistence between God and communism—or rather between God and the honorary president of the congress, Joseph Stalin. "How easily the world can be duped," Richard said softly.

Richard and Sabina were squeezed in among the four thousand other bishops, pastors, priests, rabbis, and mullahs who filled the galleries and the floor of the great hall. Moslem and Jew, Protestant and Orthodox, all faiths were represented.

There had even been a religious service in the patriarchy before the congress began. The Communist leaders had crossed themselves and kissed the icons and the patriarch's hand. Then the speeches had begun. Petru Groza, who was simply a puppet of Moscow, explained that the new Romanian government was in full support of religious faith, any faith, and they would continue to pay the clergy, as had been done before. In fact, they would even raise their stipends! Warm applause greeted this news.

After Groza's speech, the priests and pastors replied. One after another said how happy he was about this appreciation of religion. The state could count on the church if the church could count on the state. Simple as that. A bishop remarked that streams of all political colors had joined the church throughout its history. Now red would enter, and he was glad. Everyone was glad. And their gladness was broadcast to the world over the radio, direct from the hall.

"OK," Richard said, "I can go up and speak. But if I do, you will no longer have a husband."

Sabina knew he was right and that the other religious leaders were speaking out of fear for their families, for their jobs, for their salaries. But she also knew someone had to have the courage to expose the Communists instead of filling the air with flattery and lies. Looking straight up into Richard's eyes, she simply replied, "I don't need a coward for a husband."

Richard nodded silently. He filled out a card and sent it to the front, indicating he would like to speak. The Communists were delighted. Pastor Richard Wurmbrand, a Lutheran minister well known throughout the country, an official representative of the World Council of Churches, wished to address the assembly. Now they were making real progress!

A Time for Courage and Truth

A tense silence fell over the hall as Richard made his way to the platform. Sabina wondered what the crowds were thinking as she fervently prayed for her husband.

"Thank you for this privilege to join together and freely speak," Richard began. "When the children of God meet, angels also gather to hear the wisdom of God. So it is the duty of every believer, not to praise earthly men or leaders who come and go, but to praise God the Creator and Christ the Savior, who died for us on the cross."

The whole atmosphere in the hall began to change, and Sabina's heart was filled with joy. Finally, the focus was being diverted away from the propaganda of the Communists and onto Christ.

"Your right to speak has been terminated!" Burducca, the minister of cults, suddenly exclaimed as he jumped to his feet. Ignoring him, Richard went on to encourage his fellow leaders to place their trust and obedience in God, not in man. The audience began to applaud. They knew Richard was right, but he was the only one brave enough to say what needed to be said.

"Cut the microphone!" Burducca screamed to his subordinates. "Get this man off the stage. Now!"

As Richard's voice fell silent, the crowd began to chant rhythmically, *"Pastorul! Pastorul!"*[1]

The meeting dissolved into total chaos, a blessing for Richard as he snuck out the back before anyone could apprehend him.

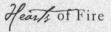

Sabina sat quietly watching the events. She was proud of her husband. Proud of his courage to stand up for Christ. But her pride was mixed with a sense of anxiety as she began to wonder about the price he would have to pay for speaking out against the Russians.

Sabina and Richard had always had a heart for the Russians. They often had discussed sending Romanian missionaries to Russia to preach the gospel. "Now God has brought the Russians to us," Richard and Sabina declared.

When the Russians first arrived in Romania in the summer of 1944, Richard and thirty-one-year-old Sabina went out to greet them with flowers and gospel tracts. As Romanian Jews, they both had suffered immeasurable loss from the Nazis. Sabina's entire family had been annihilated in the concentration camps, and Richard had already been arrested three times. When Sabina and Richard first became Christians, they had committed themselves to work among all who were lost, no matter their sins. In 1944 this conviction led them to reach out to the escaping Nazis as well as the newly arriving Communists.

During the Nazi occupation, Richard and Sabina had hidden many escaping Jews in their home. Then, when the Nazis had to flee, they had hidden them, too. One of the Nazi soldiers asked Sabina why she, a Jew, would hide her enemy, a Nazi. Sabina simply told him that she had no enemies and that God loved all sinners. He thanked her with a promise to imprison her if the Nazis regained power.

BUYING TIME

During the summer of '44, Sabina and Richard enjoyed a temporary window of religious freedom. The former Romanian dictator, Ion Antonescu, had been taken to Moscow then brought back and shot. Orthodox church prelates who had exercised tyranny over Jews and Protestants had lost their absolute domination.

Most Romanians thought that at last they had a democratic government, but Sabina knew better.

After the Congress of the Cults, no official move was made against Richard, but soon Communist hecklers arrived regularly to break up the church services he led. Week after week, rough-looking youths pushed their way into the back of the church to whistle, jeer, and interrupt.

"We ought to be glad," said Pastor Solheim, the church's senior pastor. "Better a rowdy audience that cares than a silent one that only pretends to listen!"

Then they received their first warning. Sabina was working in the church's mission alongside Richard one day when a plain-clothesman walked in and addressed her husband.

"Inspector Riosanu," he introduced himself. "You're Wurmbrand? Then you're the man I hate most in life." Richard and Sabina stared at him in disbelief. "But just to show you there are no hard feelings," he continued, "I've come to give you a tip. There is a big fat file on you at the secret police headquarters. I've seen it. Someone's been informing against you lately. Been talking to a lot of Russians, haven't you?"

Riosanu rasped his sandpapery hands together. "But I thought we might come to an agreement."

For a bribe, he said, he would destroy the report.

Sabina joined in the discussion, and they agreed on a sum. Stuffing the money into his pocket, Riosanu said, "You've got a bargain. The informer's name is—"

"No!" Sabina quickly broke in. "We don't want to know."

The inspector looked at the small woman curiously. But Sabina shook her head. She knew they didn't want to know who had informed against them. If they knew who it was, they might resent that person—and then the sin would be theirs.

Still, Richard and Sabina knew that the payment couldn't buy their safety. That was in God's hands. But perhaps they had bought themselves a little time—and a chance to further establish the underground church.

By late 1947, the arrests of Christians were occurring more frequently, and Sabina had lost many friends to prison. One cold winter afternoon Sabina was at home, sick with bronchitis, when she heard a knock at the door. She opened it and was surprised to find Vera Yakovlena, a Russian doctor she knew only slightly, waiting. The doctor had not come to treat Sabina's illness but to deliver a critical message. Her face was a mask of tragedy as she told Sabina her story:

Vera came from a town in the Ukraine where countless Christian leaders and lay people, including herself, had been deported to Siberian labor camps from which few returned.

"We worked to clear the woods, men and women together," Vera said. "We had equal rights: We could die of starvation or freeze to death."

The doctor leaned forward to clutch Sabina's arm with a hand that bore thick white scars and trembled with memory. "Every day people died, collapsing from overwork in the snow," she said.

One day Vera was caught speaking to another prisoner about Christ. As punishment, she was forced to stand barefoot on the ice for hours. Because the punishment made her unable to fulfill her work quota, the guards beat her.

Most of the other prisoners in the camp died under the inhuman conditions or the frequent torture sessions, but Vera had managed to survive. Now she had come to Sabina, not simply to tell of her tragedy, but to tell of God's faithfulness, even in the labor camp. In her sorrow and need, God had shown His might.

Sabina's head ached. Instead of pondering the miracle, she could think of nothing but her own likelihood of incurring similar suffering. *What does it mean? Why has she come to tell me such things?* she wondered.

As Vera stood up to leave, Sabina pleaded with her to stay the night. Or at least to wait until Richard returned so he could hear her testimony also and know what was happening to their brothers and sisters. But Vera was already at the door. Briefly she paused to say, "My husband was taken by the secret police. He's been in prison twelve years now. I wonder if we'll ever meet again on this earth." Then she was gone.

"Twelve years!" Sabina repeated the words with a shudder. How could anyone endure so long?

With the Communists' increased persecution of Christians, escape had to be considered. "It's not too late, Sabina," Richard began. "We can still leave. Many others are buying their way out."

Sabina didn't answer. She knew Richard wanted to leave no more than she did. But the dangers were real. And they had to think of Mihai, their precious eight-year-old son—their only child.

Richard continued, "When I was arrested before by the Nazis, I was released after only a few weeks. With the Communists, it could last for years. And they could take you, too, Sabina. And then what would happen to Mihai?"

Richard had touched on Sabina's soft spot. She knew if both she and Richard were arrested at the same time, Mihai would have noplace to go. He could end up living on the streets, begging for food. It was too much for a mother to comprehend. Still, Sabina would not answer.

Finally Richard reminded her of what another friend had told them: "'Escape for thy life,'" he said, quoting the angel's words to Lot. "'Look not behind thee.'"[2]

Then Sabina answered. "Escape for *what* life?" she asked.

Then she went into their bedroom and brought out her Bible to read aloud the words of Jesus: "Whosoever will save his life shall lose it: and whosoever will lose his life for my sake shall find it."[3] Closing the well-worn Book, she asked Richard, "If you leave now, will you ever be able to preach about this text again?"

For the time being, the question of leaving was settled. And a few months later it would be settled again . . .

Ceasing to Exist

On Sunday morning, February 29, 1948, Richard left for church, calling over his shoulder as he went out the door, "Sabina, I'll see you there."

But when Sabina arrived at church about thirty minutes later she found Pastor Solheim in the small office, looking upset.

"Richard hasn't shown up," he said. "But he has so much on his mind. He must have remembered some urgent appointment before church."

"But he promised he would see me here in half an hour," Sabina said, fear rising in her voice.

"Perhaps he met a friend who needed some help," said Solheim. "He'll come."

Pastor Solheim took the service while Sabina telephoned friends, only to find that Richard wasn't with any of them. Her fear intensified.

That afternoon Richard was supposed to marry a young couple in the church.

"Now, don't worry," Pastor Solheim encouraged Sabina. "You never know with your Richard. Remember the time we had that summer camp, and he went off to buy a newspaper in the morning and then telephoned at lunchtime to say he wouldn't be back for breakfast?"

Sabina smiled at the thought. Richard had remembered some urgent business and caught a ride back to Bucharest. "You're right. He must have done something like that again," she said, trying to reassure herself.

Sunday lunch at the Wurmbrands' small apartment was usually a happy, crowded occasion. There was never a lot of food, but Christians would gather there to talk and sing. For those who attended, it was the highlight of their week.

Now they all sat around the home, quietly waiting for Richard. But he never came. Pastor Solheim had to perform that afternoon's wedding. Sabina telephoned all the hospitals and even went around to the emergency rooms, thinking he might have been in an accident. She could not find him. Finally she admitted to herself what she must do: go to the Ministry of the Interior. Surely Richard had been arrested.

Then began the hours and weeks and years of searching . . . of trailing from office to office . . . of pushing at any door that might open.

Sabina thought of Vera, who had been separated from her husband for the past twelve years. She thought of the torture Vera had endured after sharing Christ with another prisoner, an offense Richard would surely be found guilty of as well. Sabina remembered how she and Richard had thanked God that they could be witnesses to the invading Russian soldiers . . . the same soldiers who now held her husband in captivity.

A rumor had spread that Richard had been taken to Moscow, as had happened to many others. But Sabina refused to believe he was gone. Night after night, she made a meal and sat by the window, thinking, *He'll come home tonight. Richard hasn't done anything wrong. He'll soon be set free. The Communists cannot be worse than the Nazis, who always let him go after a week or two.* She comforted Mihai when he cried for his father. She told her

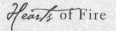

son God was looking out for Richard—and for all of them. Together they prayed that Richard was safe and that he would come home soon.

But he didn't come. And the conversation she and Richard had had a few months earlier began to haunt her dreams: *"When I was arrested before, I was released after only a few weeks. With the Communists, it can last for years . . ."*

Sabina's heart was in turmoil. She and Richard shared a love that had endured many challenges, but this time she didn't know how she and Mihai could go on without him. After a few weeks, Pastor Solheim took Sabina to the Swedish ambassador, their ally in the past, to ask for help. Ambassador Reuterswärd said he would speak at once to the foreign minister, Ana Pauker.

Mrs. Pauker's answer was obviously scripted: "Our information is that Pastor Wurmbrand has fled the country with a suitcase full of money entrusted to him for famine relief work. They say he is in Denmark."

The ambassador then brought up Richard's case with Prime Minister Groza. But he repeated the same words and added a jovial promise: "So Wurmbrand's supposed to be in one of our jails? If you can prove that, I'll release him!"

The Communists were so sure of themselves. Perhaps that was why it was said among the people, "Once in the clutches of the secret police in Romania, a man ceases to exist."

A Lifeline to Richard

After several months of wasted effort, Sabina was at church one night when she was summoned to meet a stranger waiting at the door. The man was unshaven and reeked of plum brandy. He had insisted on talking to Sabina alone.

"I've met your husband," he said simply. Sabina's heart turned over. It was the first she had heard of anything concerning her husband. "I'm a guard—don't ask what prison—just know that I'm the guard who takes him his food. He said you'd pay me well for a bit of news."

"How much?" Sabina asked, unsure that he really had information. There had been so many lies.

"I'm risking my neck, you know."

The sum he named was huge—and he would not bargain.

Pastor Solheim was as doubtful as Sabina. He told the guard, "Bring me a few words in Wurmbrand's writing." He gave him a chocolate bar from the famine relief stores. "Take this to Wurmbrand and bring back a message with his signature."

The guard left, and Solheim turned to Sabina. "It's all we can do," he said. "We have no idea if he is telling the truth, and he wants a considerable amount of money."

Sabina knew Pastor Solheim didn't want her to get her hopes up only to have them dashed again.

But two days later the man returned. He removed his cap, dug his fingers inside the lining, and handed Sabina the wrapper from the chocolate bar. Carefully unfolding it, she read, "My dearest wife, I thank you for your sweetness. I am well. Richard."

Sabina's heart skipped a beat. He was alive! It was his writing! Bold and clear, determined yet troubled. There was no possibility of mistaking the tempestuous hope within those lines.

"He's all right," said the guard. "Some can't take it in solitary. They don't like their own company." He again smelled of brandy. "He sends you his love."

Sabina agreed to give him money if he would continue to carry messages. Finally he said, "All right. But I'm taking quite a risk, you know. Some people have gotten a twelve-year sentence for doing this."

He agreed to risk his freedom out of a divided love: He loved the money and loved the drink it bought. But he also apparently admired Richard, and sometimes he slipped him extra bread.

Sabina was grateful for the man's sacrifice as he continued to bring her messages. A drunken guard had become her lifeline to Richard. For now, it would have to do.

PUNISHING THE PRISONER'S FAMILY

The Communists' laws were harsh. The wife of a political prisoner couldn't get a ration card. The cards were only for "workers." The wife of a political prisoner also could not work. Why? Because she had no ration card, and therefore she did not exist.

Sabina pleaded with the authorities. "How am I to live? How can I feed my son?"

"That's your problem, not ours."

Sabina worried about Mihai. Since Richard's arrest, she had watched him grow thinner from lack of good food. And she knew he still grieved for his lost "brothers and sisters," the six orphaned children Sabina and Richard had taken in after the Nazi massacres in eastern Romania.

But then, hearing that the Russians had decided to repopulate with refugees the two eastern provinces they had annexed, Bessarabia and Bucovina, Sabina and Richard knew sooner or later the children would be taken from them and sent east. Hundreds of other orphans faced the same plight. Sabina thought if they could get them to Palestine, where the new state of Israel was about to be born, everything would be fine. So, one fateful day, they sadly took the children to join a little army of refugees aboard the Turkish steamer *Bulbul*. It was hard to see them go, but sending them to Palestine seemed so much better than waiting for an unknown fate to catch them under the Russians.

Weeks passed, and there was no news of the ship's arrival.

Each day Sabina grew more worried. An international search began, spreading from the Black Sea to the eastern Mediterranean. But the ship had disappeared, and gradually, hope faded. It was thought that the *Bulbul* had hit a wartime mine and gone down with all aboard.

The pain they felt was terrible. Sabina and Richard had loved the children as their own, and Mihai had enjoyed them as siblings. When Sabina finally accepted the truth that the orphans were lost, she wouldn't see or speak to anyone outside their home. All her beliefs were put to a hard test. *How could God allow this to happen? How could God take my children?* she repeatedly asked herself.

Of course Sabina knew in her heart that she could not blame God for mankind's war and hatred, which had probably resulted in the accidental sinking of the ship. But she had loved the children, and she wondered how she could ever overcome the pain.

In her own grief, Sabina had reached out to comfort Mihai, who wept bitterly whenever he thought of the children who had swept into his life and brightened his days. She held him in her arms and repeated a story she'd often heard Richard tell:

It is said that during the absence of a famous rabbi from his house his two sons died, both of them uncommonly beautiful and enlightened in the Law. His distraught wife took them to her bedchamber and spread a white cover over their bodies. That evening the rabbi came home.

"Where are my sons?" he asked. "I looked repeatedly around the yard, and I did not see them there."

She brought him a cup of water to refresh him, but he continued to ask, "Where are my sons?"

"They will not be far off," she said, placing food before him that he might eat.

After the meal she addressed him: "With your permission, I wish to ask you a question."

"Please, ask it."

"Awhile back a friend entrusted to me two beautiful diamonds, and I have cared for these diamonds as if they were my own. Now she demands them back; should I return them?"

"What?" said the rabbi. "Would you hesitate to return to someone what is her own?"

"No," she replied. "Yet I thought it best not to give them back without first asking you."

She then led him to the room and lifted the white sheet from the boys' dead bodies. "My sons! My sons!" loudly lamented the father. "My sons, the light of my eyes!"

The mother turned away and wept bitterly.

After some time had passed she took her husband by the hand and said, "Did you not teach me that we must not be reluctant to restore that which was entrusted to our keeping? The Lord gave, and the Lord hath taken away; blessed be the name of the Lord."

The story was of little comfort to Mihai, but he understood what his mother was saying and drew strength from her courage. He was now ten and tall for his age, with sharp cheekbones and bright, questioning eyes. At school he was learning the hard lesson of how to be the son of a "social outcast." Mihai adored his father, and it was not easy for Sabina to explain that he had been taken away from them and locked in prison just for being a pastor.

And now, every day, more people vanished.

On one occasion a number of well-known prisoners were released. They came home in ambulances and showed their bruises and scars and told of the torture they had suffered. When word had sufficiently spread about the treatment they had received, they were all arrested again.

Sabina hated to think of the horrors her dear husband must be facing. She prayed he wouldn't break and betray his friends. He had promised that he would rather die than do so, but who can say how much a man can bear? Saint Peter had promised that he would not deny Christ, yet he had done so three times.

The Knock at the Door

Sabina took comfort in knowing that if Richard died they would meet again in the next life. They had agreed to wait for each other at one of the twelve gates of heaven, the Benjamin Gate. Jesus had made a similar appointment with the disciples, to meet them in Galilee after His death. And He had kept it.

But it wasn't the next life that concerned Sabina now. It was the pounding at her door at five in the morning . . .

Sabina had worked late the previous evening, volunteering at the church and doing home visitations. Mihai was staying with friends in the country, and one of Sabina's friends was staying with her in the small apartment. The harsh voice startled both women awake as it crackled through the early morning quiet: "Sabina Wurmbrand! Open up! We know you're in there."

Sabina made her way to the door, fearing the men outside would come crashing through at any moment.

"Sabina Wurmbrand?" shouted the bull-necked man in charge when she opened the door. "We know you are hiding weapons here. Show us where they are—now!"

Before she could argue, they were pulling out trunks, opening cupboards, and emptying drawers onto the floor. A shelf of books crashed down, and Sabina's friend rushed to retrieve them.

"Never mind that," one of the men barked. "Get your clothes on."

The two women had to dress in front of the six men, who trampled over everything as they trashed the apartment. From time to time they shouted out, as if to encourage each other to keep up the meaningless search.

"So you won't tell us where the arms are hidden? We'll tear this place apart!"

Sabina said quietly, "The only weapon in this house is here." She knelt down and carefully lifted her Bible from under one of the soldier's feet.

Officer Bull Neck roared, "You're coming with us to make a full statement!"

Sabina laid the Bible on the table and said, "Please allow us a few moments to pray. Then I'll go with you."

On the way out, Sabina snatched a package a friend had given her—a pair of socks and some underwear. They would be prized possessions where she was headed.

FREEDOM DAY

One of the guards placed blinders on Sabina so that she couldn't see, and she was rushed out of her apartment. After a short drive, she was dragged across a parking lot, and the blinders were removed as the men shoved their new captive into a long, bare room crowded with other women. Every now and then a name was called. Otherwise, the prisoners waited in silence. The "socially rotten" elements of Romania would wait for their name to be called so they could learn their fate.

It was August 23, Freedom Day. Or so the Communists called it.

Black bread and watery soup were served before nightfall and another day of waiting. Finally Sabina's name was called. The blinders returned along with another drive. This time Sabina ended up at what she later learned was the headquarters of the secret police. She was crammed into a small cell with several other women.

Questions at the End of the Maze

A few days passed, and Sabina was taken out of the common cell and placed in solitary confinement. Scanning the tiny room, she quickly realized what was missing. The bucket. In the short time she had been incarcerated, she had already learned that the bucket was critical. Now she didn't even have that.

Sabina could hear the heavy boots of the guards frequently stomping down the narrow hallway, and she wondered each time if they were coming for her. Finally her turn came. The cell door clanged open, and the guard shouted, "Turn your back!"

The blinders went back on.

"Move! Turn right. Now left. Another left. Move!"

A sudden fear came over Sabina as the guard quickly pushed her through what seemed like a maze. She began to wonder if the sharp turns would suddenly end at a firing squad and she would die without warning in the darkness. She tried to rein in her runaway emotions as the maze suddenly ended, and the blinders were removed.

She found herself standing before a tall, blond guard about Sabina's age. "You are aware of your offense against the state, are you not, Mrs. Wurmbrand?" Sabina was distracted by the officer's uncanny resemblance to a man she had once dated in Paris. "You will now write a detailed statement about it," the man commanded, motioning toward a pen and notepad.

"But what should I write?" Sabina questioned. "I do not know why you brought me here."

The orders continued. "Write your offense against the state!"

Sabina took the pen offered her and wrote a few words restating that she was not aware of any offense. The officer read what she had written and angrily sent her back to her cell. As the

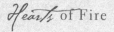

door slammed shut again, the guard told her, "Now you will sit until you are ready to write what the lieutenant told you. If you don't, you will get the treatment!"

Which treatment would it be? Sabina wondered. Bullying and mockery? Humiliation? Torture? So much had been said about what Christian prisoners faced in Communist prisons, she knew full well what they were capable of. Some former prisoners had even spoken of mental torture designed to soften up the prisoner for more "successful" interrogation. The Communists would play tape recordings of screaming voices and tell the prisoner it was the cries of his or her children as they were being tortured. How could any sane parent hold up to that?

The next session with the lieutenant outlined the issues surrounding Richard's arrest. "Mrs. Wurmbrand," he said, "your husband is accused of counterrevolutionary activities. He could be shot. His colleagues have spoken, and they support the charge against him."

Sabina's heart pounded wildly. The man was lying, of course, and watching for her reaction. She tried her best to look blank as the lieutenant continued: "They may just be trying to save themselves. Perhaps *they* are the real counterrevolutionaries. We can't judge, unless you tell us everything the people working with the mission have said. Everything. Speak out, denounce the real counterrevolutionaries, and your husband will be set free tomorrow."

Sabina was sorely tempted by the thought, but she did not trust the Communists. "I know nothing," she said, matching the lieutenant's gaze.

That night, nursing bruises from the guards' blows, she lay down on the small, narrow cot and felt her feet touching the end of it. *Poor Richard*, she thought. *He is so tall, his feet will be hanging over the end.*

What were they doing to him now? One moment she was ready to say anything to be safe with him again; the next moment she resolved not to give in to that temptation. Two apparently opposing wishes struggled madly within her heart: She wanted Richard to live, and she wanted him to resist.

A piece of chalky white plaster had fallen from the cell wall. Sabina picked it up and drew a large cross on her dark blanket. Then she gave thanks.

And in what seemed like a whispered response from the One who heard her prayer, a thought popped into her mind: *seven*. Sabina realized she was in cell number seven. A holy number. The number of days in the Creation.

It seemed like such a gift of encouragement, Sabina lay on the cot and sobbed. Her body remained in darkness, but her spirit rose up in imagined light that surpassed the bounds of prison. She rubbed her hands over the cross she had drawn on her blanket and as she fell asleep, she whispered, "We are crucified with Christ."

"Get up!" Mielu, the red-faced head guard, was in the doorway early the next morning. Sabina rose and faced the wall, as she had learned to do. The blinders were roughly slipped onto her head, and again she was directed down the black maze.

This time Mielu, a man much older than Sabina, grilled her for an hour. "Who did you sleep with? What did you do with them? I want to know with whom and how often—everything."

Emotionally and physically exhausted, the weary Sabina was dumbfounded at the turn the questioning had taken. She replied quietly, "I will not tell you what you want." "The worst sexual history will not prevent a person from becoming a great saint if God wills it," she told him. "Mary Magdalene was a harlot once. But she will be revered when we have long been forgotten."

Mielu grunted an obscenity and sent Sabina back to her cell.

"I'VE ALREADY BEEN BOUGHT!"

During the next session, Sabina was forced to look at pictures of different people. She recognized one of them, a Russian they had secretly baptized in their home. "Do you recognize any of them?" a bald interrogator asked. Sabina knew what would happen if she gave a single name. Then the interrogator sweetened the offer. "Tell us what we want to know, and we will let you and your husband go free." The temptation was real, but so was the willingness to lay down her life for her brother. "I do not recognize any of them."

The bald man suspected she was lying and finally asked her what her price would be. "Every woman has a price. What's yours? Freedom? A good pastoral position for your husband? Money? Name your price."

Sabina was fed up with his constant wielding of power and empty promises. His only interest was in more arrests, and Sabina would play no part in that. "I've already been bought!" she exclaimed. "Jesus was tortured and died for me. Can you offer a higher price?"

His face glowed red, and Sabina thought he was going to hit her. Instead he ordered her back to her cell.

Sabina was eventually placed back in a common cell. Months passed, and the cold of winter began settling in. She worried constantly about Mihai. Who was caring for him? Was he living on the streets? Was he cold? Sick? Maybe the Communists had taken him into custody too. A hundred doubts and anxieties pierced her heart every waking moment.

In November the prison director came to the cell where Sabina was being held. "We will read a list of names," the director explained. "Those whose names are read must be ready to leave in ten minutes."

There was no further information. The prisoners stirred as the guard accompanying the director started calling out the names, including Sabina's.

"What do you think?" Sabina whispered to a woman near her who was also gathering her things to leave.

"I think we're either going to be set free—or we're going to be shot," she said grimly.

"God Help You If You End Up in Jilava"

But they were not freed and they were not shot—at least not yet. Sabina and the others were taken to Jilava, the most feared prison in all of Romania. Sabina remembered hearing others talk about the infamous prison. And there seemed to be one particular cell that was a place of horror beyond description. "God help you if you ever end up in Jilava cell number four," the rumor warned.

A guard who had introduced himself as Sergeant Aspra led the prisoners down dark, arched passageways that led underground. Finally they stood in front of a large steel door with rusted bars running top to bottom. "Welcome to cell four!" Aspra proudly proclaimed.

It was the middle of the morning when they arrived, but the cell was almost completely dark. A single weak light bulb hung from the ceiling. Two tiers of wooden bunks lined the vaulted room. Up high, at the far end of the cell, was a barred window that had been painted over.

A hundred eyes stared at the new arrivals. Sabina, who was nearly suffocating from the lack of air, was assigned the end bunk directly over the bucket.

After a fitful night, Sabina was jarred from sleep by the wake-up call at five in the morning. Immediately, fifty women lined up to use the small bucket. Later Sabina learned that two hundred women were being held in four cells while three thousand men were crowded into the rest of the prison.

Jilava had been designed to hold a total of six hundred prisoners.

At eleven o'clock the women stood in line as a keg of soup was brought in. Sabina was surprised at how quiet her cellmates were as the soup was served along with a single slice of bread. But the instant the keg was removed, the quiet room dissolved into a wild brawl. Women began screaming curses at each other as they fought over the food. Within moments the guards returned and started beating the women with night sticks, knocking bowls right and left until the floor was covered with large pools of soup. Aspra angrily promised there would be no soup tomorrow.

Once more the cell was quiet as the women contemplated the next day with no food. Gradually, murmured conversations began. One of the prisoners asked Sabina why she was imprisoned. "You don't look dangerous," she said, causing all heads to turn Sabina's way and assess the new prisoner.

Sabina smiled. "I'm the wife of a pastor," she said.

Hearing her answer, a handful of prisoners spat out a few curses and turned away. But others were intrigued. "Then you must know some Bible stories," a prisoner named Elena said, settling next to Sabina on the floor.

"Yes, I do," Sabina answered, smiling again. "Would you like to hear one?"

Over the next few hours Sabina had a captive audience as she shared one story after another. In her church everyone had agreed: No one could tell a story like Sabina. Listening spellbound to the dynamic stories, the women forgot for a while that there would be no soup for another thirty-six hours.

Sabina was encouraged by her cellmates' interest in the Bible stories, but she soon began to see that the rumors about the Jilava prison were all too real. The female guards followed their orders with blind obedience. If they were ordered to beat a prisoner, they beat her mercilessly with sticks. Slowly. Severely. They showed no remorse, no pity. The prisoners might as well be carpets.

GIVE A LITTLE HOPE . . . THEN TAKE IT AWAY

"Come and get it! Carrot soup, my ladies!"

The guard's sarcastic invitation and the stench of the steaming pot preceded the meal's arrival. But many of the older women didn't stir. They were too weak even to stand in line for food. Although Sabina didn't know it then, the lethally spare diet was part of the preparation for the labor camps. And it had done its work, exposing the weaker women.

"It's slave labor, of course," a young teacher told her. "But at the canal you get a pound and a half of bread a day—and macaroni!"

The prison overflowed with rumors about the newest labor camp on the Danube Canal. Every newcomer had something to add about the huge project, which would cost billions even though much of the manpower came from prisoners performing forced labor. The canal was to run forty miles across the bare plains of southern Romania, linking the Danube River with the Black Sea.

"At the canal, you can get whatever you like from home!" one of the prison officials told the prisoners.

"Even chocolate?"

Sabina was amazed. Having given up on freedom, chocolate had now become a predominant dream.

Rumors also told of warm clothes that were freely available at the canal along with medical attention. But it was the last promise that caught Sabina's attention. Better than clothing or chocolate, it was said that canal prisoners were allowed daylong visits from family members!

Sabina grabbed on to the hope of seeing Mihai again and thought about little else.

"But not everyone will have the right to go to the canal and work," warned Viorica, a prison warden. "As the political officer told me just the other day, 'In a socialist society, work is a privilege, not a reward for bandits.'"

It was a typical part of prison culture: Give a little hope and then take it away. Later, offer it again with another agenda. On Mihai's twelfth birthday, January 6, 1951, Sabina discovered their new agenda.

"I'll make you an offer," announced Capt. Zaharia Ion one morning. "Instead of going to work on the canal, you can stay here as a special detainee in relative comfort. You will have all the privileges you would get at the canal but won't have to labor. It's really a very generous offer."

Sabina knew there were no privileges in prison without a price; she waited silently for the warden to drop the hammer. "All you need to do is report to me on the other prisoners from time to time—in complete confidence, of course. It's really quite simple, and no one has to know of our little arrangement."

Without a moment's hesitation, Sabina gave her answer. "Thank you," she respectfully replied, "but in the Bible you can read of two traitors, one who betrayed King David and one who betrayed Jesus. Both hanged themselves. I don't want such an end, so I won't become an informer."

In a flash, Ion's demeanor changed from charming to menacing. "Then you won't see freedom again!" he roared.

Sabina wondered if she had lost her chance of even going to the canal. She knew her name was on the list to go, and she knew the chosen prisoners were to leave any day. She dreaded the thought of forced labor, but she would do anything to see Mihai again—except become a traitor.

A few days later, Sabina was transferred to the Danube slave labor camp. Very quickly she and the other prisoners realized they had been duped.

The Canal

Sabina awoke the first morning in the camp to the acrid smell of rat dung. She heard a voice telling her neighbor, "You should leave some bread for them at night. It keeps them from biting."

Every day Sabina went out to work with the other prisoners— both men and women. They were building an embankment, and Sabina's job was to carry large rocks two hundred yards to the barge, drop them in, and then go back for more. She thought her back would break under the constant weight. It was difficult for her to even straighten up.

Each gang of laborers had a brigade chief whose helpers verified how much work the prisoners were doing. The normal requirement could be up to eight cubic yards a day. If the workers fulfilled their quota, it was raised the next day. If they failed to fill their quota, they were punished.

Sabina could never have imagined the conditions they endured at the camp. When she asked about the extra privileges they had been promised, she was laughed at.

More and more women began arriving to work on the canal. Like Sabina, each longed to be with her family, especially her children. Realizing the magnitude of the new canal project, most of the women began to lose all hope. But Sabina hung on to a hope that was greater than any canal project or prison system. Soon the other prisoners began taking notice. They wanted the same kind of hope she had.

"Please, Sabina, tell us some more stories from the Bible," they would beg after a long day of labor.

Sabina knew the dangers; she knew what could happen if they were caught. But she took every opportunity to share the gospel with her fellow inmates. More and more prisoners came to her, confessing their sins and asking if it was possible to be forgiven. Sabina assured them it was, and she told them something Richard had said: "Hell is to sit alone in darkness remembering evil you have done." Surely these women were experiencing that hell in this place.

While Sabina had refused the offer to be an informer, others had not. Sometimes the prisoners knew who the informers were, but they could never be too sure. It was a continual dilemma. Another prisoner might tell Sabina she wanted to know more about Christ as a trick to get Sabina to share her faith, a forbidden action that came with dire consequences. Or the woman might really want to know. There was really no way for Sabina to know which request was real and which was a trap. But more often than not, she chose to speak.

On more than one occasion after an informer had told on her, Sabina had been locked in the "carcer," a narrow cupboard big enough for only one standing person. She was sent into the carcer immediately after a day's labor, left there for the entire night, and let out in the morning just in time to return to the work assignment. The carcer became a common place for Sabina while she was at the canal.

A GLIMMER OF HOPE

She always asked new prisoners if they had heard any word of Richard. There was none until a prisoner told Sabina of a preacher she had met at Vacaresti. Actually she hadn't met him, she said. She had just heard him speak. His cell was close to the toilet, and while the prisoners were waiting in line, the "prison preacher" would encourage them to follow Christ and receive His love. Everyone in the prison had asked who he was, but no one knew. Now the prisoner told Sabina she was sure it was Richard.

Sabina's face lit up with joy. Her Richard was alive! The prison preacher had to be him. But then her hopes were crushed as her visitor finished her story. "One day we heard the preacher was very sick. After that, we heard him less often and eventually not at all. It was rumored that he had died. I'm sorry."

Tears streamed down Sabina's face, but she refused to speak. She would turn her troubles to God. She prayed for God to add years to the life of His faithful servant, her Richard, if he still lived. She also prayed for Mihai, fearing that he, too, might be arrested and sent to the canal. Her heart had stopped one day when she saw a boy Mihai's age laboring at the canal. Although she'd been relieved to see it wasn't Mihai, she still cried for the boy—and his mother, wherever she was—and she included them in her prayers.

A glimmer of hope finally came. There would be a visitors' day that Sunday! Sabina couldn't believe her ears. Oh, to see Mihai again—how glorious! When the day came, another prisoner lent Sabina a dress; hers was torn nearly to rags from carrying the large rocks. She was filled with eager anticipation, counting the minutes until she could hold her son in her arms again. But as the prisoners assembled for their visits, they were told they must stand across the room from their visitor and that they could speak for only fifteen minutes.

And then she saw him, and her mother's heart embraced him and her tear-filled eyes sent her love flowing across the room to warm him. How thin he was, how serious! The mother's and son's emotions wiped out time. Both could barely speak, and of course it was impossible to say anything intimate. When their time was up, Sabina called across the space that separated them: "Mihai! Oh, Mihai! Believe in Jesus with all of your heart!"

It was the best advice she could think to give.

Sabina's words were interrupted by a warden's rough shove. Then she was led out by the guards.

Back in her barracks-hut, the other inmates crowded around, asking what Mihai had said, how he looked. But she could only shake her head. For hours she could not speak; she was overcome with the emotions that filled her heart as she thought of her precious son.

Sadly, many prisoners had spent the day waiting for someone who never came. Sabina could only pray for them that night as they wept aloud on their straw mattresses.

Winter came, and Sabina and the other prisoners were even more miserable. She continued to work along the icy Danube, loading heavy rocks onto a barge. In winter, though, the harshness of the conditions was multiplied, because it was impossible to drop the rocks onto the barge without causing a big splash of frigid water to fly up into the air, drenching the workers. Within minutes of each workday's beginning, Sabina was soaked. Then the icy wind froze her clothes stiff, and she became encased in a layer of ice as stiff as a coat of armor. Her fingers, cracked and swollen from the work, were numb with cold until the pain of being crushed by one of the heavy stones awoke them.

In the evening, when she returned to the hut, she took her wet clothes to bed with her. There was nowhere to dry them, and any clothes that *were* hung up were sure to be stolen anyway. So she usually slept with her damp dress under her head as a pillow and put it on, still damp, in the morning. If she was lucky, it dried out a bit on the way to work, just in time to get soaked again. By now Sabina was as thin as a rail, and the cold wind seemed to blow right through her.

"Fit for Work!"

Sabina's next assignment was to load stones into wheelbarrows. Other women then wheeled the stones to the barges on the Danube. The work kept Sabina's knuckles raw, her nails broken and bloody. In a cruel irony, sheer exhaustion spared her from feeling some of the pain ravaging her body.

Finally, Sabina awoke one morning to the sound of water dripping from the hut's eaves. Spring had come. But with it came a new challenge: the formerly frozen, iron-hard earth had turned to mud.

The male guards who accompanied the workers to and from camp were the only men the women ever saw, and some of the women traded vulgar jokes about the men as they were transported.

Annie, a shrewish little prostitute, and her friend Zenaida usually led these sessions by trading off-color comments.

"That Peter has hands like a gorilla," Zenaida said one day, her voice low so the men couldn't overhear. "Look at all that hair on the backs of them! I'm sure he's covered in hair from head to toe, if one could see."

"Oh, there are women here who have!" Annie cracked, showing a mouthful of gold teeth. A laugh went up from some of the women.

"Ugh!" Zenaida groaned, pretending refined horror. "Though what they see in us to attract them, I can't imagine. Can you picture a more unappetizing and sexless band of creatures than ourselves?"

Annie's profane retort to Zenaida's comment brought screams of laughter from their friends. More filthy words went to and fro. Sabina stared straight ahead, trying to ignore them.

"Our little saint doesn't like our nasty talk," said Annie. "She thinks we're horrid!"

Sabina kept silent, a response that only made the others

madder. And this time Annie, whose loose chatter was raw but rarely maliciously directed, caused Sabina more cruelty than she intended.

At the end of the workday the women lined up as usual, worn and sore, to trudge the muddy path that ran along the Danube. Peter, one of the guards, nudged his companion, a dumb-looking youth with a flattened nose, then stuck a leg out to trip Sabina as she passed by. She fell full length into the slick mud.

The other guards roared with laughter.

Peter reached out and dragged Sabina to her feet. She was caked head to toe with mud.

"What you need now, my lady," he growled, "is a wash."

"Chuck her in the Danube!" screamed a woman's voice.

Sabina struggled against the man's grip on her, but another guard hurried to help him. While Peter held her wrists, the other guard grabbed her ankles to jerk her off her feet. They swung her once and then flung her through the air. She landed hard in the rocky shallows, the breath knocked out of her body. Sabina was stunned but still conscious as the icy water poured over her, the current dragging her small body over the rocks. There were shouts from the bank, but she couldn't understand them. Every time she tried to get up, the rushing water brought her down. It was no use. Sabina couldn't save herself.

Suddenly two strong hands seized her beneath the arms and dragged her up onto the bank. Someone else forced her to sit up and then slapped her back. She felt hollow and sick, gasping as a sharp pain pierced her side. Dizziness overwhelmed her, and a roaring sound filled her ears. Was it the water of life that flows through paradise? she wondered. But then she opened her eyes and saw the mud, the guards, and the thin, bedraggled women lining the riverbank, and she knew she was not in heaven yet.

"She's all right. Get up!" a woman said loudly, looking sternly down at Sabina. Then she said more softly, "Get moving or you'll freeze."

Rough hands pulled the pastor's wife to her feet. Sabina was shivering, but she was suffering more from shock than from the cold. She held her chest, in agony because of the pain in her side that was intensifying by the minute.

When they finally got back to the hut, Sabina inspected her wounds. Her side was badly bruised, and the skin on her hands and legs had been badly scraped. Trying to lift her arms caused pain so sharp it left her breathless. She managed to crawl up to her bunk and tried to sleep, shifting every few minutes during the night, trying to find a comfortable position. But there was none.

The next morning she saw the camp "doctor," an evil woman named Cretzeaunu. A huge purple-and-yellow bruise shaped like a map of Africa spread down one side of Sabina's body, and by now it was totally impossible to raise her arms above waist level.

"Fit for work!" Cretzeaunu pronounced.

Sabina started to protest but thought better of it. Arguing would only cause her more punishment, possibly the carcer. She moved toward the women waiting to be transported to the worksite but stood aside as the line moved forward.

"What's the matter with *you?*" the supervisor barked, glaring at her stooped form.

Sabina said, "I can't work today. I'm in great pain. I think my ribs are broken."

The supervisor might have considered a respite, but the menacing Peter quickly put an end to any such notion. He caught Sabina's wrist and jerked her out of the ranks, causing her to shriek in excruciating pain. "What's wrong with her is that she didn't fulfill her norm yesterday. Now, get on with it!" He spun her around and planted a large boot in her back. She wasn't kicked as much as heaved forward into the line of women.

Sabina went to work that day and every day following it, struggling to keep up even though, as doctors would later confirm, she had two broken ribs.

DIANA AND FLOREA

Summer finally came at the depressing compound, and Sabina felt increasingly hopeful. Two new girls had arrived at the camp and were assigned to Sabina's hut. They were known by some of the street women but spoke little to them. Shyly, they claimed beds in a far corner of the room.

Later, Sabina learned they were sisters, Diana and Florea. Dark complexioned and intense, both girls had good manners and quiet voices. But they were prostitutes, said the ones who knew them, and they had been swept up like the others to serve "administrative" sentences at the canal.

An aura of sadness and mystery surrounded the sisters. No one could learn much from them about their past, though many poked and pried. The sisters slaved and slept and might have remained a mystery if Diana had not heard Sabina's name called out one day by a guard.

Immediately Diana hurried to Sabina. "Do you know Richard Wurmbrand?" she asked.

"I am his wife," Sabina replied.

"Oh!" she said. "What can you think of me?"

"What do you mean?" Sabina asked.

"My father was a lay preacher," Diana said, her voice trembling. "He used to read to us from Richard's books; he called them his 'spiritual food.' Father was sent to prison for his faith, leaving a sick wife and six children. Florea and I are the eldest. We both lost our factory jobs when Father went to jail. Our family faced starvation."

Sabina lay a comforting hand on the girl's arm as she continued the heartbreaking story. "One day a young man asked me for a date. We went to the movies and then to dinner. He told me he could get me a work permit. And then . . ." Diana hung her head and wiped away tears that welled up in her eyes. "We drank wine, too much wine, and then, he . . . he seduced me."

Soon it happened again, she said, but this time nothing more was said about work permits. However, the man gave her money. Knowing how desperately her mother needed it to support the family, Diana accepted the cash. A week later, the man introduced her to a friend—and then left them together. When this man tried to make love to her, she was furious. But then he, too, produced badly needed money and said he had only acted on his friend's suggestion. Diana reluctantly gave in.

Soon Diana had a steady stream of "clients," and she ignored the shame and became accustomed to the life, even preferring it to the drudgery of factory work.

As terrible as Diana's story was, Sabina could sense that the girl was holding something back. Suddenly Diana stopped and searched Sabina's face. "I thought you'd be disgusted," she said. "Doesn't it upset you that I came from a Christian home to become . . . a prostitute?"

Sabina said gently, "You're not a prostitute; you're a prisoner. And anyway, nobody is a prostitute or a saint or even a cook or a carpenter all the time. The things you do are only attributes that make up part of your being. They can change at any time. And I believe you've changed already in telling me your story."

Diana wanted to believe Sabina's words, but she obviously was not comforted. She sat on her narrow cot in the bare hut, her hands clenched between her knees, her face taut with distress and guilt.

"If it were only me," she burst out at last, "it wouldn't be so

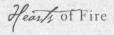

bad. But I made my sister join me. My boyfriend suggested it. He said it wasn't fair that I should carry all the responsibility for the family. So in the end I introduced him to Florea and let him take her out."

Soon Florea had been initiated into the life of prostitution. The sisters' main difficulty was keeping the secret from their brother, a fifteen-year-old boy who adored them both. Like his father, he was strongly religious with a keen, sensitive temperament but no knowledge of the world. "He wouldn't want a fly to suffer," Diana said, shaking her head. "We knew if he found out he would be beside himself with grief and anger. We tried to keep it from him."

But the sisters' new way of life—their late hours and the sudden indications that the family had money—made the neighbors suspicious. Soon one of them confirmed what was happening and told the boy.

"The shock drove him mad," Diana said sadly. "He ended up in a mental hospital."

And then their father was released. When he discovered the depths to which his daughters had sunk, he said, "I ask God for only one thing, that He will send me back to jail so I don't have to see what is happening to my family."

Now the tears were flowing unchecked down Diana's face.

"He had his way," she said. "He began teaching children's gospel lessons, and soon he was denounced to the police. The informer told me later he had done it to get my father out of the way so he wouldn't interfere with our 'business.' He was the same one who had first seduced me."

Sabina, stunned and saddened by the tragic story, reached out to hug Diana. "You feel shame over what you have done, and rightly so," she said. "In a world of suffering, where even God is nailed to a cross, you can't allow His name, which you bear as a

Christian, to be defiled. But this sense of pain and guilt will lead you to a shining righteousness. Remember, the soldiers on Calvary did not pierce Christ's side so much as they opened it, so that sinners like you and me might easily enter His heart and find forgiveness."

Diana thought about her words and replied slowly, "Shame and suffering—yes, I've known them. But there is still something else to confess. I didn't always hate the work I was doing. And now bad thoughts come into my head all the time. I can't keep them out."

Every day Sabina prayed for the tormented Diana, and eventually the poor girl was able to release her guilt. Sabina kept thinking of how Diana and her sister had sinned to get bread for their family. Perhaps the greater sin, she decided, belonged to Christians of the free world who had not taken the time to send food that would have saved them.

"In Your Eyes, I See Myself"

A few weeks later Sabina was brought before the deputy camp commandant, a red-faced woman with heavy forearms and large, splendid teeth. Her bulky uniform seemed to encumber her movements as though it were armor.

"You've been preaching about God to the prisoners. It must stop!" she warned.

"I'm sorry, but nothing can stop it," Sabina replied.

Furiously, the deputy commandant raised a fist to strike Sabina. Then she stopped and stared.

"What are you smiling about?" she demanded, her face blotchy with rage.

Sabina said, "If I am smiling, it is because of what I see in your eyes."

"And what is that?"

"Myself," Sabina answered. "When people come close to each other, they see themselves in each other's eyes. In your eyes, I see myself. I used to be impulsive too. I used to rage and strike out at others with sharp words and selfish thoughts—until I learned what it means to love. When you're able to love, you're able to sacrifice yourself for the truth. Since I learned that lesson, my hands do not clench into fists."

The officer seemed stunned by Sabina's boldness. In the silence, she continued, "If you look into my eyes, you'll see yourself as God could make you!"

It was as though the deputy commandant had turned to stone. Her angry demeanor did not change, but she quietly said, "Go away."

Sabina continued to witness for Christ among the prisoners.

Freedom

And then, unexpectedly, she was freed. Sabina tried to read the document ordering her release: "Certificate of Liberation" was the heading, but the sun had set, and it was too dark to read the rest as she was loaded into a truck and driven out of the camp. A short while later she was dropped off, well beyond the outskirts of Bucharest.

She walked for hours carrying her greasy, smelly bundle through the suburbs. For the first time in nearly three years, she saw people hurrying home after work, shopping with their families, going about the same everyday life she had lived before her imprisonment.

Sabina hurried, eager to get home—and then wondered if her home still existed.

She wondered how many changes she would have to deal with. She didn't know what had happened to her relatives and friends.

Mihai would be fourteen now. What had the years done to him? She was almost frightened to find out, yet she longed to see him.

Sabina passed near Victory Street, thinking sadly of the police station where she'd first been held. Nothing had changed. The gigantic portraits of the men the Communists called mankind's four geniuses — Marx, Engels, Lenin, and Stalin — still stared down on the crowds who tramped along the street.

Eventually she came to an apartment building she knew and climbed the stairs. She knocked on a door, hoping this, too, had not changed. She nearly collapsed with relief when the door was opened by a friend.

"Sabina!" her friend shouted, clasping her hands to her mouth and stepping back to look at her. "Is it possible?"

The two women embraced and began to cry. And then Mihai stepped into the room. Sabina felt as though her heart would explode when she saw him come through the door. He was pale, even taller than when he had come to the prison, and ever so thin. And now, she noticed, he was a young man.

As they embraced, the tears poured down her cheeks. Mihai leaned back and gently wiped them away with his fingertips.

"Don't cry too much, Mother," he said.

Sabina was so happy to hold her son in her arms again, she thought if she could just stop crying now she would never need to weep again.

ONLY ONE WORD IS NEEDED

In those first few days, Sabina was like a woman brought back from the dead. She was so excited to be free! But reality soon presented itself: While she was no longer imprisoned, she was still a social outcast because she was not only the wife of a prisoner, she was a former prisoner, herself.

Without a ration card, she couldn't even buy bread. And getting a card proved impossible. One morning she waited in line for four hours at the government office. When she reached the small window, the girl snapped, "Where's your work card? Without that, you can't get a ration card."

"But I'm an ex-prisoner. I've had no way to get a work card," Sabina explained.

"I can't help that. No work card and number, no ration book," the girl said, already looking toward the person behind Sabina in the line. "Next!"

Once again Sabina and Mihai were forced to survive on the charity of others.

The Wurmbrands' home and all their belongings had been confiscated. Fortunately, friends now lived in the house where their flat had been, and they invited Sabina and Mihai to live in the tiny two-room attic. The furniture was rickety, the old beds had broken springs, and there was no running water and no bathroom. But Sabina was thankful to have her son with her again and determined to make it a home.

One morning several months after Sabina's release an official from the Ministry of the Interior showed up at her attic door. He was a fat man with a booming voice and black hair parted in the middle. He carried a briefcase so full of papers it threatened to burst its hinges.

The man shouted that Sabina was a bad mother and that she was not caring for her son properly. Sabina sat silently looking at him. She knew what was coming.

What possible use, the man said at last, was it to remain tied to her husband, a counterrevolutionary whom she would never see again? It was only a matter of common sense that an intelligent young woman like herself should get a divorce from this enemy of the state. If she didn't do so now, she certainly would realize she should do so later. How long did she think she could stand up to the state in such blind, stupid disobedience?

The man alternately bullied and cajoled as he painted heart-breaking pictures of Sabina's ultimate fate. Love? he jeered, *love?* It was all rubbish. Love didn't exist. What Sabina needed was a new husband, a new father for her child, he said. There was to be no love for counterrevolutionaries.

Fuming inside, Sabina thought, *You dare say this to me in my home? I didn't marry my husband only for happy times. We were united forever, and whatever may come, I will not divorce him.*

The man argued and urged for another half-hour, and in that time Sabina said nothing. She remembered the old saying: Even God cannot contradict someone who remains silent.

Finally the man retreated, shaking his round head as he left. "Sooner or later you'll come to us," he said as the door closed behind him. "They all do, you know."

Despite the man's unpleasantness, the cloud had a silver lining. Sabina thought ruefully: If the Communists so wanted her to file for divorce, then Richard must still be alive!

Sabina heard him go noisily down the stairs. *Off to his next victim,* she thought solemnly, *where he'll probably have better luck.*

The authorities made every effort to force prisoners' wives to file for divorce—first, because a prisoner's will to resist, even to live, was often shattered when he heard he had been abandoned by the one who had promised to stand by him no matter what. Second, a divorce helped get the wives involved in the Communist way of life. Once the divorce was finalized, women were anxious to forget their husbands, perhaps out of guilt, and the easiest way to do that was to swallow the party line. Sabina knew scores of women who parroted the government slogans mocking the political prisoners, men they had once loved and whose children they had borne.

Third, fatherless children were at the mercy of the state, to be indoctrinated from the earliest age.

Only one word was needed to make it all happen. When a wife said yes to the divorce official, he took care of everything else. A few days later, the husband would be told, in front of his cell-mates, "Your wife is divorcing you." Then the man would think, *Who cares about me now? I'm a fool not to give in and sign whatever nonsense they want so I can go free.* But even if he did sign, he might not be released for several years. Meanwhile his wife remarried and had children by her new husband. Thus, homes and families—and lives—were destroyed.

Sabina encouraged women whose husbands were imprisoned to prepare for the officials' visits and to stand by their husbands, to love their men as they are, not for what they should be. She advised the women to think of the happy moments of their married life and use them to overcome temptations.

But all too often, she failed in her efforts. The pressures on prisoners' wives were too severe.

ANOTHER TEMPTATION

Then came the time when Sabina, by then forty-three, had another temptation to deal with. His name was Paul, and she knew he was falling in love with her. He entered her life when she had not heard any news about Richard for months, and she'd begun feeling the years slip by. Again she was questioning whether he was even alive. So many had come to her door saying they had been in prison with Pastor Richard Wurmbrand and that he had died. Was it true—or another trick of the Communists?

When she thought of Paul, Sabina found it difficult to listen to her own words of wisdom she had so often told others. Paul was kind and gentle, another Jewish Christian like herself. He lived in a single room with his elderly parents, and sometimes he would take Mihai to the movies or help him with his studies. Sabina often thought, *Here is someone with whom a woman could live in love and trust.*

Sometimes Paul caught hold of her hand when they talked, and Sabina found herself unwilling to withdraw it from his grasp. Their relationship never reached the point of what the church or the law would call adultery. Still, Sabina knew it was wrong.

One day Sabina's pastor came to her with a serious look on his face. "Sabina, you know how much I love and appreciate you," he said. "And that won't change, whatever happens. I've known both you and Richard for many years. And I hope you know that whether you sin or you don't, whether you lose faith or keep it, I will still care for you in the same way because I know what you are, not what you do." He spoke with rare emotion and sincerity; then he paused before he asked the question. "So forgive me if I ask," he said, looking directly into Sabina's eyes. "How is it between you and Paul?"

For a moment Sabina was silent.

He went on: "Don't imagine I haven't had such trials too. But please, Sabina, answer my question."

"He's in love with me," she said, her head dropping with the words.

"And are you in love with him?"

"I don't know," she answered honestly. "Perhaps."

The pastor continued, "I remember something Richard used to say: 'No passion resists before the bar of reason. If you delay, if you give yourself time to think, you see all the harm you could do to your husband or your wife, to your children, too.' Now I want you to make a hard decision, Sabina, the hardest decision there is. Don't see this man again."

The pastor was right. It was the "hardest decision." Sabina

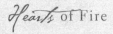

wanted to take control of her runaway emotions and deny her feelings for Paul, but she was also a mother and a woman. She knew Paul would be a good husband, a thoughtful companion who could take away the constant feeling of loneliness. And he would be a good father to Mihai. The temptation was almost more than Sabina could bear, especially when her own church friends told her, "Your husband is dead. You've lived a hard-enough life. Let this man take care of you. He is a good Christian and loves you."

Only her pastor had been bold enough and committed to her enough to say what needed to be said. And Sabina knew he was right. She knew Satan wanted to destroy her witness. So, with great difficulty, she told Paul they must never see each other again, and she rededicated herself to wait for her Richard.

Ten Lines on a Postcard

A few weeks later Sabina was in church, scrubbing the floor, when her friend Marietta rushed in, waving a postcard. Tears were running down her cheeks. "I think—Sabina, I think it's from . . ."

She could not continue but knelt, breathless, on the damp boards beside Sabina.

Sabina turned over the little card. It was signed "Vasile Georgescu." But Richard's handwriting, large and irregular and beautiful, was unmistakable. Sabina's eyes hazed over, and she clasped the card against her heart.

She knew political prisoners could write only ten censored lines—when they were allowed to write. What could Richard say, after so many years of not knowing if his wife and son lived? Sabina held her breath and read the words through tear-filled eyes. "Time and distance quench a small love but make a great love grow stronger," he had written. Then he asked her to come to see him on a certain date in Tirgul-Ocna, the prison hospital.

Richard's postcard was the best news Sabina could have had. And though it broke her heart, she knew she couldn't go. Every week she had to report to the police station in Bucharest, and they continually refused to revoke the ban on her leaving the city. So she would not be there on the appointed day to see her cherished husband's face. But she was happy to know Mihai would take her place.

Tirgul-Ocna is in northern Romania, on the other side of the Carpathian Mountains. The train from Bucharest travels several hundred miles around the mountains to reach the small town. Sabina arranged for a friend they called "Aunt Alice" to go with Mihai to the prison. But only Mihai would be permitted to see Richard.

Sabina waited anxiously behind. Mihai and Aunt Alice were gone for two days, and during that time a million thoughts and worries swirled through Sabina's head: Would Mihai really see his father? Would Richard be allowed to receive the few warm clothes and food she had sent? Since he was in a prison sanatorium, he must be very sick. Would he be able to stand? Could he even speak to Mihai? And what would Mihai's response be to seeing his father after all these years? Would he be devastated to see Richard in his undoubtedly weak health? .

They got home late on a December evening. Sabina heard them climbing the stairs, and then, even before she was through the door, Alice called out, "We saw him! We saw him! He's alive. He's up and about!"

They came in with snow on their shoulders.

"Mihai!" She clung to him, pressing her cheek against the cold, frosty wool of his coat.

"Mother! Father's well, and he said to tell you he knows he'll

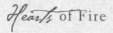

come back to us soon. If God can perform one miracle and let him see me, he said, then He can perform two and bring us all together again."

Soon they were all in tears. "We had to wait hours and hours in the snow," Alice said. "They let us in through the main gate, then we stood in a fenced-off compound away from the sanatorium buildings. The prisoners have to cross an open space to get to a big tin hut where they receive their visitors. It was terrible to see them. Frightening! They looked like gangs of dark, muffled shapes against the bright snow—like gray ghosts is how they looked! And among them, going along, I saw Richard! You couldn't miss him, he's so tall. I waved like a mad thing, but he couldn't pick me out. We were all in a huddle, and everyone was waving. I saw him— but only Mihai was allowed to speak with him."

In such conditions, they couldn't say much to each other, Mihai said. But his father's last words to him were, "Mihai, the only gift I can give you as a father is to tell you this: Always seek the highest of Christian virtues, which is to keep the right measure in all things."

Sabina had lovingly tucked Richard's postcard between the pages of her Bible. Now and then she would take it out and read it again. Later he told her that in prison and in the sanatorium he became a master at packing great meaning into the minuscule letters the prisoners were allowed to write—so much so that others came to him for help in making each of their allotted ten lines count. They also asked each other what Richard had suggested, so Richard's words went all around the facility. The result was that dozens of prisoners began their postcards with "Time and distance quench a small love but make a great love stronger." Thus, Richard's messages of love and hope were being read and cherished far and wide. The prison preacher was back in business.

One Lovely Morning

The year 1956 began with the whole Communist bloc in a rebellious mood. The Soviets' "five-year plans" had gone nowhere. Food was still in short supply, and wages were low. All the hopes raised after Stalin's death had faded.

Then, in February, during the twentieth congress of the Communist Party, Soviet premier Nikita Khrushchev made a secret speech denouncing Stalin and his works. The Russians never published it, but before long, in every country of Eastern Europe people felt the warm breeze of a political thaw trickling out of Moscow.

The signs of "de-Stalinization" came rapidly. The huge forces of militia and secret police were reduced in size. Million-dollar trade contracts were negotiated with Western countries to rescue the economy. Collectivization was relaxed. And most of all, hundreds of political prisoners were freed each day under an extended amnesty.

Sabina didn't dare hope that Richard would be among them. She had received no hint, no news, that he might be released early. After all, he still had several years to serve of his sentence. Then one lovely morning in June 1956 she went out to visit friends, and when she returned home, there he was. Head shaved and looking more like a skeleton than a living man, Richard was home at last. Sabina nearly fainted as he put his arms around her. It was an embrace she had feared she would never feel again. That evening, friends came from all over Bucharest to greet him, and together they shared laughter and tears—followed by more laughter and more tears.

Richard had suffered mightily in prison. He had been beaten with a variety of torture tools, and he had been doped with drugs. Eighteen torture scars stood out on his wasted body, and doctors later found that his lungs were covered with the healed scars of tuberculosis. They simply couldn't believe he had survived eight and a half years (almost three of them in solitary confinement in an underground cell) virtually untreated. He was now given the best bed in the hospital ward. Amazingly, released prisoners were treated with kindness and generosity by the people wherever they went. They were the most privileged group in Romania, a status that infuriated the Communists.

Soon after Richard got better, he and Sabina celebrated their twentieth wedding anniversary. Neither had a penny to buy each other a gift, but Richard managed to obtain a pretty, bound notebook in which he wrote verses every evening—love poems addressed to Sabina, the love of his life.

They had both survived temptation and torture. God had been their strength. Love had been their motivation. But while a tragic decade lay behind them, another nightmare waited on their doorstep.

"PUT YOUR ANGELS AROUND HIM!"

On the evening of January 13, 1959, a woman from Sabina's church arrived at the Wurmbrands' door in tears. The week before, she had borrowed some copies of Richard's sermons, and hundreds of photocopies were now circulating throughout Romania, a situation that was strictly against the law. Now the apologetic woman had come to warn Richard that the police had raided her apartment and taken all the remaining copies. It wouldn't be long, she feared, before they came for him.

They also learned through another friend that Richard had been denounced by a young pastor who claimed to be his friend. They knew the man might have been blackmailed, forced to sign the denunciation under threat of prison.

At one o'clock the next morning, angry police officers once

154

again battered on the Wurmbrands' door and burst into their tiny attic home.

"You're Richard Wurmbrand?" the captain in charge said loudly. "Get into the other room—all of you. And stay there."

Once again their tiny apartment was full of men opening cupboards, turning out drawers, throwing papers on the floor. On Richard's desk they found pages of notes, typewritten sermons, and well-worn Bibles. All were seized. Then they found Sabina's anniversary gift, the notebook in which Richard had written love poems to her.

"Please don't take that. It's a personal thing, a present. It's of no use to you," Sabina begged. They took it anyway.

The captain in charge put Richard in handcuffs and led him out of the back room.

Sabina spoke boldly, "Aren't you ashamed to treat innocent people like this?"

Richard moved toward her, but they caught his arms and pulled him back. He warned, "I won't leave this house without a struggle unless you allow me to embrace my wife."

"Let him go," said the captain. One of the policemen removed the handcuffs.

They knelt together in prayer, with the secret police standing around them. Then they softly sang a hymn, their voices melding in the words, "The church's one foundation is Jesus Christ, her Lord."

A large hand fell on Richard's shoulder. "We've got to get going. It's nearly five o'clock," the captain said quietly. He was obviously taken aback by Richard and Sabina's incredible love for each other. His eyes were watery.

The handcuffs were clicked onto Richard's wrists once more, and the policemen led Richard out the door. Sabina followed them down the staircase. At the bottom, Richard turned his head and said, "Give my love to Mihai." Then he paused for a

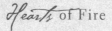

moment before adding, "and to the pastor who denounced me." Then he was gone. As the police vehicles drove away, Sabina ran after the van on the icy street, calling out and weeping as she slipped in the slushy tracks: "Richard! My dear Richard!"

Then the van vanished around a corner, and she stopped, breathless and heartbroken. Back at the attic apartment, the door stood open. Sabina fell to the floor, sobbing out her prayer. "Lord, I give my husband into Your hands," she cried. "I can do nothing, but You can pass him through locked doors. You can put Your angels around him. You can bring him back!"

She sat in the darkness, praying, until the sun came up. Aunt Alice came that morning and found her still on the floor. Through red, tear-filled eyes, Sabina looked at her and said, "Again, they have stolen my Richard."

EPILOGUE

Richard was gone another six years, and Sabina had only one opportunity to see him during that time. She diligently continued her work in the underground church and faithfully waited for her husband, never allowing herself to believe that God would not bring him home.

In December 1965 Richard was ransomed for ten thousand dollars by the Norwegian Mission to the Jews and the Hebrew Christian Alliance. The going rate for a political prisoner at that time was fifteen hundred dollars. Richard and Sabina did not want to leave their homeland of Romania, but believers in the underground church convinced them to go so they could be a voice for those who were being persecuted for their faith and a witness of God's incredible love in the harshest of times. The next year Richard, Sabina, and Mihai arrived in the United States.

Under death threats from the Communists, the Wurmbrand family immediately became a voice for their brothers and sisters whose faith was under fire.

In October 1967, with only one hundred dollars and an old typewriter that sat on their kitchen table, the Wurmbrands wrote the first issue of *The Voice of the Martyrs* newsletter. Since that first issue, the newsletter has continued to be published regularly, and nearly ten million copies have been distributed around the world in dozens of languages.

From the time Richard and Sabina arrived in the United States, they labored tirelessly to share a message of hope and love in the face of persecution and martyrdom. Their lives were enriched by the trials they endured.

Shortly before Sabina's death due to cancer in August 2000, she asked her beloved Richard (who was also very ill) to come to her bedside. In the presence of a small group of friends, Sabina told Richard again how much she loved him, and she asked him to forgive her for any shortcomings in her life. Sabina was in severe pain at the time, but she refused medication so she could be clearheaded and alert when she bade farewell to the temporal life that had inflicted so much pain upon her yet brought her so much joy.

Hers was a life sustained through Christ's love and the love she demonstrated to all who knew her.

Tara:
Life on the Run

Pakistan
June 1985

The postman walked up to the familiar mansion and peered through the window. The entryway alone was as large as many entire homes in the villages of Pakistan. "I have a package for Tara," the postman said when a servant finally answered the door. "I need her signature. May I come in?" He was carrying a medium-sized brown cardboard box under his arm. His pen was already out.

"No, you cannot come in," the servant answered sternly. "Give the package to me, and I will take it to Tara. Her father will not permit her to come to the door."

"OK," the postman reluctantly agreed. "But I must get a signature from Tara or someone in authority. Otherwise I cannot leave the package; do you understand?"

"Yes, yes," the servant said impatiently, his hands extended. "Now please give me the package."

Tara was watching from around the corner, wondering what

the fuss was about and who would be sending her a package. "What is this?" she asked the servant. "Who's it from?" The servant shrugged and handed Tara the paper to sign. She scribbled her name then reached for the package. It was heavier than she expected. She wrapped both arms around it and shuffled to her room, shutting the door behind her. Although Tara's family was quite large, she had her own well-furnished room. Opposite her large windows were built-in dressers, and on each side of the bed were attractive nightstands, each topped with an elegant crystal lamp. Tara's father had a soft spot for his young daughter, and her room was filled with the lavish gifts he showered upon her.

Now she was as excited as any child of twelve would be to receive an unexpected package in the mail. She placed the box on the floor, knelt down in front of it, and ripped back the tape that secured the cardboard flaps. Peering inside the box, Tara gasped. Her joyful curiosity quickly turned to trepidation. She jumped to her feet and ran back to her door, opened it just enough to poke her head out, and peered up and down the hall to make sure no one was near. Again she closed the door, but this time she locked it before returning to the open box in the middle of her bedroom floor.

An inner voice said she should just turn the box over to her father. *That would be the safe thing to do*, she told herself. She could simply tell her father she had no idea why it had arrived with her name on it. But the truth was, Tara *did* know why the box had arrived. It contained something she had sent for. A few weeks earlier she had filled out a small coupon in the local newspaper and mailed it. Now the ordered item had come, and she feared what would happen to her if she was caught with it. Her young mind began to race. She had to decide whether to keep it, in hiding of course, or tell her father.

Her curiosity overruled her fear, and she lifted one of the

small books out of the box. The book had a single-word title on its soft ivory cover: *Genesis*. Sitting on her bed, she opened the cover and began to read.

From the first day the Bible curriculum arrived, Tara pored over the material, completing two or more courses nearly every week. She sealed her completed tests in the envelopes that came with the curriculum and asked a house servant to mail them. A short while later, a new certificate would arrive in the mail, congratulating Tara on her success.

Tara, who came from a very prominent and strict Muslim family known throughout Pakistan, had no intention of changing her faith. She was simply caught up in the study of the Bible and especially enjoyed receiving the fancy certificates. It was easy and fun, and it also offered an exciting element of peril as she carefully tucked the box and its contents under her bed each day. The servants who helped her send and receive the mail were sworn to secrecy. Everyone knew her father would be furious if he found out. But everyone also knew Tara was her father's favorite girl. He would be mad, yes, but more than likely he would simply scold her and take away the curriculum. She was just having fun. *What harm could come from studying?* she asked herself.

Two and a half years later, Tara mailed in the last test. She had completed the entire course, studying every book of the Bible. She felt a sense of satisfaction in completing such a large curriculum and still marveled that it had all been provided for free and her secret had gone undetected. A few weeks later she was even more surprised when another box arrived. It was much smaller than the one the course came in but was still relatively heavy for its size. Tara knew it was from the same people who had sent the course and the completion certificates, but she had no idea what was in the small box. To her amazement it was a beautiful blue Bible with page edges that were gilded in gold. It was the most beautiful book Tara had ever seen. Opening the front cover, she noticed her name written in fancy script in an acknowledgment of her successful completion of the entire Bible course. Tara carefully flipped through the onionskin pages before hiding her new gift under her bed with the other books. The curriculum was dangerous enough. If she was caught with a Bible, she knew there would be hell to pay.

Actually, she didn't know the half of it.

THE CHRISTIAN

The following year, after completing her tenth year in school with high honors, Tara was invited to do a comparative religion study in Iran. Her family made pilgrimages to Iran quite often, and Tara was eager to take on the challenge of studying there. She also believed her secret study of the Bible would give her a nice start in her study of Christianity.

Her family accompanied her on the study trip, and it was while they were in Iran that Tara met a Christian for the first time. It happened when she left the hotel one afternoon, planning to take pictures of the courtyard outside the local mosque for a presentation she had been assigned for her class. It was dangerous for a young foreign girl to be moving about alone, but Tara promised her eldest brother, who was looking out for her that day, that she would stay close to the hotel, and he had reluctantly agreed that she could go.

As she walked through the courtyard snapping photos, she came upon a curious sight. A man was sitting on the ground next to a girl a few years younger than Tara. His hands were folded tightly, and he was looking into the sky, apparently speaking with someone.

"What are you doing?" Tara asked, feeling a strange draw to this man.

"I'm talking to God," he answered simply.

"You can't talk to God," Tara argued, punctuating her remark with innocent laughter. "He will not come down to speak with you, and you cannot go up to Him unless you die. So how can you say such a thing, that you are *talking* to God?"

The man patiently looked at Tara, and with a smile he added, "I not only spoke with God, I got an answer."

Now Tara was sure the man was crazy. "You got an *answer*? You are not a prophet or an angel. How could you possibly get an answer from God?"

"Do you want to know how you can talk with God?"

"Yes, of course I would like to know," Tara answered. She didn't believe him for a minute, but she wanted to hear his explanation, futile as it probably was.

"Then meet me tomorrow at four o'clock. Here, I'll write down the location for you." Pulling out a blank piece of paper, the man wrote down the address and directions to his church. "You come here, and you will not only know that you can talk with God, but you'll know He loves you too."

When Tara got back to the hotel and shared her experience, her brother was furious. "What are you thinking?! You cannot go to that place. It is a Christian church! This is Iran, and you are a Muslim. You could be hanged for being caught in such a place!"

"I have been assigned to do a study on different religions. How can I complete my studies if I do not do my research?" Tara protested.

The argument ended with Tara's brother agreeing to make an official request at the local police station to visit the church. From there he was then sent to the courthouse, where permission was granted. But the officials required her to be accompanied by twelve security officers and her older brother when she visited the church.

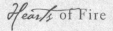

"You will not have to be afraid," her brother said. "I will be right outside the door with the police should anything happen." Tara wondered what went on in a church that would require such high security.

The following afternoon at four, Tara entered the church. She walked in slowly, her body slightly trembling, as the security guards and her brother waited outside. Except for the man in the courtyard, Tara had never met anyone who was not a Muslim. She wondered what Christians looked like, how they acted. Were they dangerous?

She found a seat near the back of the church. She chose a spot that was close to the main entrance so she could make a quick exit if she needed to. Most of the wooden benches were already full, and the singing had already begun. The church members sang different choruses, and Tara thought she recognized in the lyrics some of the verses she'd studied in the Bible curriculum. After the singing, a man stepped up to the podium and began to speak about prayer. He said that anyone who had a prayer request should come forward.

As a few people began to make their way to the front, Tara saw the man she had met in the courtyard the previous day. He was carrying a small girl of about eight; Tara assumed it was another one of his daughters. This one seemed to be completely crippled. Her arm flopped loosely against her father's back as he carried her. Her eyes were empty, and she barely looked alive.

The man walked to the front and began to pray aloud, asking God to heal his child. Others in the church joined in and began pleading with God to heal the girl. Tara again thought a person would have to be crazy to try to speak with God this way. Why would God come down to help this child? To Tara, it made absolutely no sense. But despite her skepticism she was mesmerized by the activity and wanted to remember all that was happening so she could write about it in her thesis.

Then Tara noticed that the crippled girl was beginning to move. Her legs slowly straightened, and her father gently lowered her to the floor, helping her stand. *My God!* Tara thought, *I can't believe this is happening.*

Those in the church were again singing praise songs to God as the little girl, now healed of the affliction that had left her crippled, walked down the center aisle of the church and looked right into the eyes of Tara. When she got to the bench where Tara was seated, she simply said, "Emmanuel," and then turned and walked back up the aisle to her father.

Tara was terrified by what had happened—and by all the thoughts swirling through her head. Why would this young girl come up to her, of all the people in the church? How had her legs been restored? And what did *Emmanuel* mean? The religions study Tara had set out to do was producing more questions than answers. She was determined to understand what was going on.

She didn't dare tell a soul what she had witnessed in the church. But she certainly couldn't forget it. Later, when she arrived back home in Pakistan, she went to the only place she could think of to find some answers. She went to the blue Bible. This time Tara wasn't reading to pass a test; she was diligently searching for the truth. Each day she pored over the Scriptures, trying to understand the difference between the Bible and the Koran, and trying to find out why Muslims were so against Christians.

The Christians' God must be real, she thought. *How else would He hear them when they pray?*

Betrayed

Finally Tara knew she had gone as far as she could on her own. She had to talk to someone. Instead of enlightening her, the religion course—and what she had witnessed in the church and

165

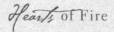

read in the Bible—had created additional questions, and she desperately wanted to understand what was going on.

"Daddy, I'm going out with some friends," Tara told her father as she prepared to leave. It was the first time in her sixteen years she had ever lied to her father, and guilt swept through her body as she hurried out of the family's large, luxurious home. But she had to find out what the Christian faith was all about. And going back to a church was the only way she knew to do that.

She made her way across the city to a church and again slipped into a pew at the back of the sanctuary as the service was beginning. Afterward, she introduced herself to the man who had conducted the service and told him she hoped to ask him a few questions. The pastor agreed. Tara had assumed a church was a church, a Christian was a Christian, and any of them should be able to help her. Unfortunately, in this case, she was wrong.

The pastor grew a little uncomfortable with Tara's many questions as she came week after week to talk with him. He was worried for his own safety and told her on more than one occasion that it might be better if she no longer came. "But where else can I go to find these answers?" Tara replied.

Her persistence won him over for a while, but finally the pastor felt the risk was too great. Thinking he would free himself from any future trouble, he met with Tara's father and reported that she had been coming to his church and asking many questions about the Bible. Within a few minutes, he had betrayed a teenage Muslim girl who was seeking to know who God really was.

"What the hell did you think you were doing?!" Tara's father screamed at his daughter when she arrived home that afternoon. "Do you have any idea what embarrassment you have brought upon me and this family? How could you possibly meet with that man? He is not a Muslim. He is a Christian! How stupid could you be? Are you now one of them?"

Tara was shocked at her father's rage; she had never seen that side of him. She tried to explain that she was just asking questions and didn't have any intention of converting to Christianity, but he wouldn't listen to her. He angrily ordered her away from his presence, and Tara ran from the room in tears. She had no idea what she had gotten herself into or how she would appease her father's wrath.

She also still had unanswered questions. Back in her room, despite the scene she had just endured, Tara found herself drawn back to the little blue leather-bound Book. Wiping away her tears, she opened the Bible and struggled to read as her father's furious tirade continued to echo loudly through her mind.

Gradually the ancient words drew her in, soothing her anxiety and encouraging her with God's love. She became so absorbed in her Scripture reading that she lost track of time and failed to notice that her father had stepped into her room. At first his countenance revealed a man who was sorry for yelling so viciously at his youngest daughter. But when he saw what she was reading, his repentant face turned to fury.

"You *are* a Christian! Now I know you are!" he screamed.

"Daddy, I promise, I'm not a Christian. I'm just curious. You have to believe me!"

"Don't lie to me! Why else would you be reading a Bible?"

"Please, Daddy! It's just a book I'm reading. You know I've been doing a lot of studying lately." Tara was trying desperately to convince him of her innocence when his hand came flying hard against her face.

"How could you do this to our family? We are Muslims!" She had retreated from him in shock and pain, her eyes wide in disbelief that he had struck her. Now he came after her and slapped her again. "We were born Muslim, and we will die Muslim. And you—you are no longer my daughter!"

Tara's wailing sobs brought her oldest brother running to her room to find out what was going on. "Your sister has become a Christian! She has been visiting with a pastor, and now I find her reading a Bible!"

Hearing the accusation, Tara's brother changed instantly from concern to fury, and he swung at Tara, joining his father in beating her. His eye fell on the blue Bible, and he viciously began tearing its gold-edged pages. Tara's father found a cloth belt, folded it in two, and swung it wildly across Tara's face and back as she cowered on the floor, sobbing hysterically.

"Father, you need to find her a husband. And do it quickly before this goes any further," her brother said, his face red from anger and exertion. As the two men finally left the room, her father was nodding his head.

"EMMANUEL, EMMANUEL"

As Tara lay crying in the middle of the floor, she uttered her first prayer: "God, I do not know what my father and brother are talking about. I am not a Christian; I am a Muslim. But now I do not know which way I should go. Please. Just show me, and I will follow."

Tara felt strangely peaceful after she prayed and, lying there on the floor, she fell into a deep sleep. After a while she felt someone lifting her head and softly caressing her cheek. She could hear a voice; it sounded like someone in the background was moving toward her. The voice was saying, "Emmanuel, Emmanuel." Tara sat up quickly and looked around her room, only to find it empty. As she recalled the strange dream—it *was* a dream, wasn't it?—she tried repeating the bizarre word she had just now heard for the second time: "Emmanuel."

Tara lay on her bed, thinking again about the incident in Iran.

"What does it mean?" she wondered aloud. "And why do I keep hearing this word?"

She touched her face tenderly, wincing from the pain. In all her life, her father had never hit her, and Tara was devastated by his anger and his willingness to beat her. She and her father had always been so close. But now she knew they would never be close again. She knew the rage in her father would not be easily restrained.

And neither would her own stubborn search for the truth.

A few days later, Tara's father sat down with his daughter, her face still bruised from the beating. Again he approached her with a sorrowful look in his eyes. "Tara, I am very sorry for what I did to you," he said. "It is shameful for a father to beat his daughter. You must understand that I did not mean to hurt you. This impression that you gave me was simply more than I could bear. Please forgive me."

Tara sat quietly, not allowing herself to fully trust her father's newfound tenderness. "I know now is the time," he continued, "that you should be married."

Tara remembered what her brother had said after the beating. But she was only sixteen and had no intention of getting married. "Daddy, I am too young to get married. I want to finish my studies." She tried to sound calm.

Her father stood up, his voice a little firmer. "I said it would be best if you got married. It is not a suggestion."

Tara shivered at the growing coldness in his voice, but she wasn't willing to give in that easily. "No, Daddy, I don't want to. I am so young, and I want to finish my education first. I don't want an arranged marriage, Daddy! Who is he? What is his name? What is his religion?"

The words slipped out before she realized what she was saying. It was a stupid thing for a Muslim girl to say. For their family, there was only one religion: Islam. Her father, infuriated again, screamed, "What do you mean, what is his religion? We are only one religion here! We are Muslim!" He grabbed her arm and jerked her closer so he was glaring straight into her eyes. "You are a Christian! You are! Now I know it for sure!"

Before Tara could offer a word in her defense, she again felt her father's swift, hard hand against her face. He was firmly convinced that his daughter had converted to Christianity, and in response, he did what he thought was his duty.

Coming into the room just as another blow fell on Tara's face, one of her sisters screamed out in shock and fear.

Unmoved by the pleas of family members or servants who happened to be nearby, Tara's father and brother dragged her into her room and locked the door behind them. Shrinking back into a corner and trembling in terror, Tara had good reason to fear for her life.

Her father and brother beat her with whatever weapons they found quickest: the electric cord from one of the crystal lamps and the rod from Tara's closet. Then they grabbed, pushed, and carried all her belongings—her rugs, bed, clothes, electronics, everything—and dumped them in the hallway. When the terrible scene ended, Tara lay in a bloody heap in the middle of her now-barren room. Her father's last words to her before he slammed the door shut were, "Either you marry, or you die. Your choice. If you are a Christian, then there is no place for you in this city. But if you marry, then you can be my daughter. Otherwise you will die here alone."

RUNNING AWAY

Tara lay on the cold tile floor, drifting in and out of consciousness. No one was allowed to help her. Her family thought she would surely come to her senses if left alone with no food or medical aid. On the third day, Tara started to sit up, but a pool of dried blood caused her hair to stick to the floor. Dazed but trying to grasp all that had happened, she felt a wave of nausea and sadness wash over her as she inspected her wounds. She never could have imagined that her search for God would bring her to such a terrible place. But now she had only one thought, to escape for her life. Having never before spent even one day away from her family, she had no idea what to do, but it didn't matter. She knew she had to go.

She struggled to her closet to see if anything was left and found the one thing they had missed, a small travel bag from her last trip to Iran. In it were a few clothes, a little money, plus some jewelry and her passport. Tara quietly changed her bloody clothes, grimacing with pain at every movement. When she was ready, she stood in the middle of her room and looked around one last time. She knew if she left she could never come home again. In her culture running away was almost as bad as being a Christian, and she knew her family would never be able to accept the humiliation. If they caught her, they would kill her now, for sure.

With a heavy heart, she snuck out her bedroom window and discreetly made her way to the bus station. Tara was sore, stiff, and heartbroken, and the only thing that kept her going was the fear of what her father or brother would do if they found her—and the hunger in her heart to know more about the Christian God. When she reached the bus terminal, she bought a one-way ticket to a city several hours away, a place she was vaguely familiar with. She had been there a few times with her family, and she planned to seek refuge in a church she had seen there. Surely any Christian person there would help her, she thought.

The bus ride was long, and people stared at and whispered about the bloodied teenager. As an attractive girl from a prominent

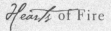

family, Tara cringed with humiliation, knowing what her fellow passengers must be thinking. It was a new experience for her, and she only hoped her quest for God was worth all she had given up. As she tried to avoid the glaring eyes around her, she also hoped these strangers wouldn't turn her in to the police. Women in her country have few rights and are seldom seen out in public without a male family member.

When the bus finally arrived at the intended destination, Tara quickly got off and tried to blend in with the crowd, not an easy thing to do in her bruised and bloody state, but she thought that as soon as she got to the church, she could clean up.

When she arrived at the church, she was met by a Salvation Army officer standing outside the door. Surprisingly, the man tried to dissuade Tara from seeking help there. "If I were you, I wouldn't want to be alone with the leader of this church. There have been rumors," he said.

Tara was on the verge of tears. "What is this?" she asked. "I thought a Christian was a Christian, and now you're telling me this church isn't good for me? Is this what I left home for?"

"Come home with me," the man said kindly. "I can help you and protect you."

Although Tara had great misgivings about going to the man's home, she seemed to have no other choice. Reluctantly, she went with him. It turned out he had a wife and two sons, and everyone in the family treated her kindly—for about two weeks. Then family rumors started flying; the wife suspected maybe her husband wanted to have an affair with their pretty young guest. Finally, Tara couldn't take the tension any longer; she asked the man to take her somewhere else. "You must know someone in another city who could help me," she begged. "Just take me there, please, and I'll find a job. I appreciate your help, but I don't want to cause any more trouble for your family."

"I do know of a man who might help you. He is actually from your hometown," the Salvation Army man said.

Tara was overcome by fear when she heard his words. "I don't think that's a good idea," she said. "Please, my father doesn't know where I am—and I don't *want* him to know. Please don't do this to me."

"Don't worry," the man assured her. "I know this man. He will help you."

THE DISOWNED UNCLE

With her options quickly expiring, Tara agreed to meet with the man. But the first time she saw him, waiting at the prearranged spot, she almost fainted. "That's my father! You tricked me!" she screamed.

"No, it is not your father. I promise," the man said. "Go in and meet him."

To Tara's utter amazement, she discovered the man was actually an uncle she had never met, a man who had an uncanny resemblance to her father. "Why didn't my father ever tell us about you?" Tara asked him.

"I became a Christian in 1952, before Sharia law came into effect," explained her uncle, referring to the country's adoption of the Islamic code. "Back then it was legal to convert, but it wasn't socially acceptable. Your father disowned me. Since then I have been working here as a pastor. Now I see that God has sent you here. Don't worry. I'll take care of you; you can be my daughter."

Relief flooded over Tara; she began to feel a tendril of hope growing within her; maybe she could settle down, get a job, and continue her schooling.

She soon learned that her uncle was a kind, generous man, and she quickly grew to love and admire him. He spent long hours talking to Tara about Christianity, and he answered all her questions. He even explained what *Emmanuel* meant. After a couple of months living in her uncle's home and studying with him, Tara felt she had a solid understanding of who Jesus was, and she finally prayed, asking God to forgive all her sins, and she gave her heart completely to Him.

Tara's search for God was paying off, but her trials were just beginning . . .

Trouble started again when Tara's uncle received a visit one day from a cousin who thought he recognized Tara. "Oh no," her uncle assured him. "She's just a friend who's visiting awhile."

But the cousin was not convinced, and when he returned home he called Tara's father and told him he thought the girl staying with his cousin was Tara.

Just a few days later, Tara was working in her uncle's kitchen when she heard hurried footsteps coming from the front room. Tara headed that direction and nearly collided with her uncle as he burst into the kitchen, waving his arms frantically, "It's your father! He's coming. You must go—right now! Leave! Go to my friends' farm outside of town, the one I told you about. Here's some money; now *run*! And don't worry. I won't tell your father anything. I'll check on you in a few days."

Tara's father and brother were literally on the front doorstep when she flew out the back door. She didn't have time to think, only to run. Pure adrenaline kept her going as she ran as fast as she could. She fumbled in her pocket for the address her uncle had made her carry with her constantly, just in case something like this ever happened. Out of breath and in pain, Tara finally reached the main street and slowed to a brisk walk. In this busy part of town, she didn't want to arouse suspicion. After hailing a taxi, she slouched in the seat and closed her eyes. She couldn't believe she was on the run again after only two short months with her newfound uncle. But even though the adrenaline rush of having to run so quickly had caused her heart to pound wildly in her chest, Tara felt a strange sense of calm creeping through her. She prayed silently for her dad and brother, and she prayed they wouldn't give her uncle too much grief.

Tara ended up staying at the farm ten days while things settled down back in the city. Finally her uncle came to see her, and Tara was eager to go back home with him. But when she saw the look on her uncle's face, her heart fell. "What's wrong, Uncle?" she asked.

"Tara, you know how much I have enjoyed having you these past two months," he began, his eyes never leaving her face. "It felt like God gave me the daughter I always longed for—in both blood and in spirit. But you can't come back with me. It's just too dangerous. I'm sorry to be the one to have to tell you this, but your father said you have to die. He said it was a matter of honor for him and his family."

Tara knew her uncle was telling her the truth. She knew her father and brothers would never stop looking for her—and she had no doubt about what would happen if they ever caught her. She felt pangs of self-pity trying to cloud her mind, but the sadness in her uncle's eyes tugged at her heart, helping her move her focus away from herself and onto him and his misery.

"Uncle, please don't be sorry," she said, clutching his hand. "I am the one who should be sorry for causing you so much trouble. I am so thankful God led me to you. You gave me the answers I was looking for, and now I have peace like I have never experienced before. I can never repay you for that."

It was a tearful good-bye as Tara prepared to once again be shuttled off to a new home. Her uncle had made arrangements for her to live with a family he knew in a distant city. She tried to hide her worries from her uncle as they parted. But inside, she wondered if she would ever be able to stop running . . .

A Prisoner of Refuge

Tara was welcomed into her new home with open arms. The family was composed of a local pastor, his wife, and their three sons. The boys immediately adopted Tara as their new sister. The oldest son, Rubin, especially admired Tara for her courage.

To protect her from her father and brothers, who continued their relentless pursuit of her, Tara's new family asked her to remain in her room most of the time. She was there throughout the day and in the evenings whenever anyone was visiting (which, with the husband and father being a pastor, was nearly all the time).

Tara's room was divided into two parts: one for sleeping, the other for sitting and studying. The two sections combined were less than half the size of the bedroom she had grown up in. Tara was relieved to be staying with a family she could trust, but the confinement was getting to her. She knew she couldn't take it much longer.

"Please, let me come out of my room," Tara pleaded one morning. "I know you are trying to keep me safe, but I feel like a prisoner. This is no way to live."

The pastor wanted to let Tara roam free, but he knew her father and brother were still looking for her. In fact, they had come through town asking questions and revealing their intentions to kill her.

"Tara, just a little while longer, then we can let you out," he told her. "Please bear with us. It's for your own good."

Tara knew she had no choice. If she was seen in public, she would endanger not only herself but her adopted family as well. She tried to make good use of her time studying, but there were many days when all she could do was cry. Her small room would remain her home for an entire year.

Finally one evening Tara overheard the pastor speaking about the church needing a new secretary. When he came into Tara's room the next day, she pleaded for the job. "Please, Pastor," she begged, "please let me have this job! I have been typing your sermons for you all this time; I know I can do the job. It has been a year since I came. Surely my father and brother have moved on."

The pastor was uneasy about the decision, but he knew he couldn't keep Tara in her room forever. He agreed to ask the church's senior pastor if he was willing to give the job to Tara.

The following week, Tara was the church secretary. "Tara, listen very closely," the pastor instructed. "You are my niece visiting from another town. Please stop referring to me as 'Pastor.' From now on, you must call me 'Uncle,' and we will call you 'Rebecca.' Do not tell your story to anyone. Do you understand?"

Tara not only understood, she was delighted.

She excelled at her new job. She had studied English, and the senior pastor, who was British, took an immediate liking to her. She was given oversight over the church finances and even began to teach a Sunday school class.

The senior pastor, knowing of Tara's prior situation, also allowed her to minister one on one with secret Muslim converts. Tara began to feel that this work would be the heart of her ministry, and she thanked God for allowing her to experience similar trials as these converts, who couldn't help but be encouraged by her incredible testimony.

Six months after starting her new job, Tara was secretly baptized in a small cistern in the church basement. Only her adopted family, the senior pastor, and her uncle were allowed to attend.

The Passion to Evangelize

After spending two years with her new family, Tara was eighteen years old and longing to get out and do more ministry. She was happy with her job as church secretary, but she had a longing to evangelize. Most of the mission workers had been born into a Christian home, but Tara could speak to Muslims as a former Muslim herself. Tara had survived the brutality of her father and brothers, and she had been ostracized from her family. She had a testimony to share, and she knew others would listen to her.

"Please, Rubin! Please let me go with you," she begged one day as the pastor's oldest son prepared to leave on an evangelizing trip.

"No, Tara," he said, hating to refuse her because he knew how passionately she wanted to evangelize. "It's just too dangerous. Someone will get offended by your testimony and report you to the authorities. I may be arrested, but if you're caught you will surely be killed."

Rubin had grown to love Tara like a sister, and he couldn't bear to endanger her. But he knew she would insist on coming with him—and he was right. She had her argument ready. "Rubin, what is more important," she demanded, "my safety or the lost souls you are trying to reach?"

Rubin admitted defeat, and Tara began traveling with him as he taught her the art of evangelism.

Another two and a half years rolled by without any trouble. Tara had settled into her new life as the pastor's niece, and she had completed part of her college studies. She had also found a new role in arranging secret baptisms for former Muslims and Hindus. Most were the result of her and Rubin's evangelical outreach work. She also helped start a literacy program and a children's ministry.

Tara always remained on guard, but after all this time she was finally feeling that she had settled into a life far away from the threats of her father and brothers. Her only troubles came from a few church members who refused to believe Tara was the pastor's niece and who were jealous of her growing ministry alongside the church leadership. It was a problem she could handle. The problem she couldn't handle was waiting outside the church one bright Sunday afternoon as Tara walked out the door.

RUNNING AGAIN

Tara recognized him immediately; he was her cousin. Every muscle in her body tensed as the young man tried to stare directly into her eyes, but Tara was determined to walk past him without giving any indication she knew who he was.

"Wait! I want to speak with you," he called after her.

Tara knew by the tone in his voice that he wasn't positive of her identity. She had been gone more than four years and had changed considerably. She simply ignored his request as though she hadn't heard him and continued on by him. Then she heard the word she had dreaded most . . .

"Tara!"

Tara turned and answered with false courtesy, "Oh, hello. Are you talking to me? My name is Rebecca. I don't believe I know you. I hope you'll excuse me; I'm in a bit of a hurry."

If Tara's face didn't give her away, her voice did. She knew her cousin had found what he was looking for. Now it would only be a matter of hours before her father and brother showed up. She felt panic welling up inside her heart as she quickly continued on her way and tried to get lost in the small crowd of people bustling about. Her heart was pounding so hard she thought it would burst through her chest.

Out on the busy street Tara grabbed a taxi. "To the airport, please," she said. She had money in her purse but no idea where she would go. Once again she was running out of options; she only wanted to get away before her brother or father found her. At the airport she scanned the outbound flight board, desperately trying to decide where to go. She ended up flying to a city in the eastern part of the country; she thought she would be out of danger there, at least for the moment. She had no idea where to go once she landed, and she ended up spending a long, difficult night at the airport. She had phoned Rubin so her adopted family wouldn't worry. But other than that, she could only sit alone with her thoughts and memories and try to calm herself with silent prayer. She resisted the urge to ask God, "Why me?" But she was tired of living as a fugitive, and she wondered if she would ever in her life feel safe and securely settled.

The next day, exhausted and emotionally drained, Tara returned to her adopted family. She felt bad for them. They had given her so much love and support, and by helping her they had put themselves and the whole church community at risk. Now Rubin told her he was trying to get her a visa so she could leave the country. Tara was apprehensive but also a little relieved as she thought about leaving. At least in another country she wouldn't have to carry the burden of getting her dear friends in trouble. And not only her friends. She knew if she was caught the government could use the whole incident to create a huge scandal for the entire Christian community in Pakistan. Yes, it would be best if she left.

Tara assumed that if she lay low for a while she would be safe. But two church members who were jealous of the attention Tara received from the pastor's family decided to take matters into their own hands. They called the CID, Pakistan's intelligence service, and reported that a young woman in the church was actively evangelizing.

The Apostate Daughter

Tara was summoned to the CID office, where she was told the agency would be opening a file on her and gathering information to see if the allegations were true. The agents also wanted to contact her family. Tara couldn't believe she had escaped so many times only to be turned in by one of the church members. She knew most of the congregation members were kindhearted, and she understood that it was necessary for her to keep silent about her past. But it only took one or two to turn the tide. Now she felt like she was caught in an undercurrent pulling her down so deep she would never recover.

Tara cried out to God to save her one more time. The word *Emmanuel* came into her mind. She now knew it meant that God was with her, and that thought was enough. She believed if God could make a fish spit Jonah onto the shore, He could get Tara out of the mouth of the CID!

But it wasn't going to be easy. The CID confiscated Tara's passport and continued asking questions and filling out forms. Rubin was usually with her and tried to convince the CID that she was his sister, but they weren't buying it. The names on the passports didn't match. Tara's passport also identified her as a Muslim. So what was she doing with a Christian family?

After spending a full day in CID custody, Tara was allowed to return home—but not before a warning not to leave town. The agency would be contacting her soon. Tara needed a sign from God, needed something to hang on to. She was now without a passport, and it was only a matter of time before the CID connected her with her true family—a turn of events that would be the end of her. Sometimes she wondered what method her father would use to kill her . . .

On the way out the door of the CID office, one of the officers whispered to Tara. He knew her family but hadn't spoken up, knowing the danger she was in. "Tara, listen to me," he said. "I am a friend of one of your cousins. I know who you are. You must leave the country as quickly as possible. It is not only you who is in danger."

Tara was surprised but also relived. It was a miracle the CID officer hadn't turned her in. But not only had he kept her secret, he also had confirmed what she must now do. She must leave Pakistan. But how? She had no passport. And even if she had one, where would she go?

Rubin immediately went from one foreign embassy to another trying to get her a visa. He was repeatedly turned down. The embassies said she had to have a connection in their country, someone who could sponsor her. Finally a country in the Middle East offered a three-month visa for one thousand American dollars. Tara wasn't excited about traveling to another Muslim nation, but once again she lacked any other options. The same day she paid the money, she learned that the CID was preparing a warrant for her arrest. Its agents had discovered that she was arranging baptisms for former Muslims and that she herself had converted to Christianity from Islam. She had been labeled an apostate. Tara also learned that her parents had filed charges against her as well. They confirmed her conversion, and in accordance with Islamic law, they had personally recommended that she be hanged.

Falling deeper into despair, Tara began locking herself in her room for days on end. She expected that any day her family would catch her and kill her. Worse, they might kill her new family, too. And it would be because of her. Her prayers became shorter but always contained a passionate cry to God not to leave her, to be her Emmanuel, even if it was while she stood before a noose.

"God Must Have Quite a Job for You"

While Tara was losing hope, Rubin was busy trying to secure a new passport and identification papers to go with the visa they had obtained. He made Tara cut her hair short and wear sunglasses for the picture, and he had a document forged to say she was extremely sick and could not travel to the government office to get her documents. On Easter Sunday 1996, Rubin walked into Tara's room with the good news: "Tara, I have all your travel documents. Happy Easter!"

"I can't believe it!" Tara exclaimed. "How did you do it? And how much did it cost you?"

"Never mind that," he answered, smiling widely. "I told you God would come through. He hasn't brought you this far to be handed over to the CID. He must have quite a job for you to do, Tara, especially considering all the trouble you've been." His brilliant smile told her he was glad to have been part of that "trouble."

Tara was humbled by his faith and perseverance. He had been more than a brother; he had been a friend in a time of need, and he had never let her down. With those thoughts, a new sadness came over Tara, the sorrow in parting from her Christian family and all the church projects she had been able to serve in.

"I have one more request before I leave," she said. "I want to take part in the baptism we have been planning for the new converts."

Rubin was about to say no, but the truth was, he was too worn out to argue with Tara. And he knew who would win anyway. "Sure," he said, shrugging and smiling, "but you must leave immediately after."

The following night, Tara attended the secret baptism. She knew each of the six converts, and each knew Tara's incredible story. Tara knew she could trust them. They were all in the same boat.

Some of the converts were from Pakistan, but most were from other countries. One was from China, another was from Afghanistan, and two others were from Iran and Iraq. It wasn't uncommon for converts to be traveling through Pakistan from foreign lands.

Tara marveled at how God had used her. She would be leaving the country the following day because of her faith while others had come to her country and found faith. And most of the Christians in her community, including those in her own church, never even knew what was happening. It was hard to trust those who clung so tightly to their own safety.

BETRAYED AGAIN

Tara left the challenges of Pakistan only to be thrust into a new set of trials. She was free, for the time being, from her family's pursuit, but she had to be careful not to give away her identity. Even in another country there was the constant risk of being arrested by the Islamic police and exported back to Pakistan. And if she was ever returned to Pakistan, she would be handed directly into the hands of her father. Her fate would be sealed.

Tara also faced another challenge. In the Muslim world, a woman is expected to marry before the age of twenty-five. If she doesn't, she is assumed to be a prostitute and is usually detained, re-educated, and designated for an arranged marriage. Tara had no desire to get married, at least not with her life in such disarray, and she certainly had no desire for a marriage arranged by Islamic officials. And on top of all this, she was now without the support of her adoptive family and had only a three-month visa.

She quickly realized that focusing on the reality of her situation would only serve to destroy the hope she carried. *I have lost everything*, she kept telling herself, *but I have found God—a minor loss for such a great discovery. Emmanuel—God is with me. Who can ultimately be against me? I have gained more than I can ever lose. Emmanuel. God be with me.* It became her prayer, one that carried her, one more time, to hell and back . . .

Rubin had arranged for her to get a part-time job as a church secretary in her new country, but it provided barely enough money to pay for food, let alone rent. She was also working part-time cooking for the pastor's wife, who spoke more of jewelry and fashion than of Christ. Tara began to wonder if this was the faith she was risking her life for, and she again grew restless. She now found herself battling depression while hopelessness tugged at her soul.

She eventually got another job working for a clothing designer and became eligible to apply for a three-year residency permit. One problem solved, but a greater one was coming.

With her residency permit secured in her new country, Tara began volunteering in some of the church's outreaches. Making new friends was easy for Tara; knowing which ones to trust proved a little more difficult.

Although Tara didn't realize it at the time, one of her new friends was a man who worked for a Pakistani Christian magazine. He knew, from contacts he had in Pakistan, that Tara was not who she claimed to be. Wanting to "get the story," he approached Tara one day after church. "Tara, I know it must be very difficult for you here in a foreign country, with a new language and no family," he said. "Why don't you come to our house for fellowship and a warm meal? Let us help you."

Tara agreed. *It will be nice to make new friends*, she told herself.

For their first few visits, the reporter was true to his word. He invited Tara and a few other Christians her age to his house to share an afternoon of food and fellowship. However, with each visit, the reporter began asking Tara more questions—specific questions—about her past.

"Please, I'd rather not talk about myself," she answered politely, not wanting to offend her new friend. When the next invitation came, Tara declined.

Not ready to give up so easily, the reporter called Tara the next day. "Tara, I know you're having financial difficulties here, and my friends and I really want to help," he told her. "Please come over and share your testimony with us, and we will raise some money for you. We're your friends. You can trust us."

Tara reluctantly agreed. At that point, the only Christians who really knew her complete story were her adoptive family in Pakistan. She had been very careful not to let anyone know who she was. Keeping her identity secret was a matter of life and death.

A month went by, and Tara had conducted a number of interviews with other reporters. Each time, those who interviewed her showed compassion and promised to do what they could to help. Another month went by with more interviews, more tears, but still no money. Tara began to wonder what was going on. Finally a lady called one day and asked Tara how much money she was getting from the bank each month.

"What are you talking about? I don't have a bank account. And the bank certainly hasn't sent me any money. Why would a bank do that?" Tara asked the woman.

"Oh, there must be some mistake," the woman said. "People have been sending money to this account, believing it was for you. From what I understand, it has grown into a fairly large amount."

Tara had been used; she confirmed the awful truth. A business had been set up, and others were profiting from her testimony. Soon afterward she saw the magazine. The cover story featured a teenage Muslim girl who had miraculously found Christ and was on the run from her own family, who wanted her dead. The story contained her name! Tara couldn't believe her eyes.

"How could this happen?" she gasped. And more importantly, she worried, "How will I keep my family from finding out about me?"

Tara was reaching her limit. She was wondering how much more of this deception and subterfuge she could take, when another man from the church caught up to her as she was leaving the Sunday morning service. It was the same story: "Share your testimony with us," he said, "and we can raise money to help you." But this man presented an appeal with a twist. He said he thought Tara was very beautiful, and he suspected she must be lonely.

That was it. Tara drew back her hand and slapped the man across the face. "You have a wife and a daughter!" she scolded him. "You are a Christian! How can you go on like that?"

The man was completely taken aback by Tara's aggression. He put his hand on the side of his now-reddening face and growled, "You will pay for this." He didn't dare make a bigger scene because there were people on the street not too far away.

"Fine," Tara replied, still fuming at the man's suggestion. "You tell me how much I have to pay, and I will pay. Just stay away from me!"

The only problem was, it wasn't money he had in mind.

Three nights later, a brick came crashing through the window of Tara's small apartment. Tara could hear men shouting on the street below, but she couldn't tell what they were saying because they were speaking a broken Arabic she couldn't understand. She peeked from behind the curtains as the men picked up more stones from the street. They hurled them at her windows again, finishing off any glass still attached to the frame. Now she could make out a few words they were saying: "Muslim . . . now a Christian! . . . an apostate! Police! Call the police . . ."

She peeked around the curtain again just in time to see the men jump into taxis and speed away. She had recognized two of them. They were friends of the man she slapped.

Tara prayed their threats to call the police were just bluffs, an attempt to scare her. Well, if it was a bluff, it was working. She was scared. But it wasn't a bluff. A few hours later, the police were at her door asking what had happened. They took Tara to the police station.

GIVING IT ALL TO GOD

"We have reports that you are a Muslim and that you have converted to Christianity—and you are also single," the questions began. Tara knew the police could easily trace her back to her father in Pakistan and access the file on her there. She gave short, elusive answers, repeating a single word to herself between each question: *Emmanuel.*

After a few hours, the police let her go but promised to keep an eye on her. They kept asking why she wasn't married, and they strongly suggested she find a husband. They even offered a particular man who they knew would take her.

Amazingly, Tara had quickly gone from being a victim whose apartment had been attacked to becoming an accused person. Such are the "rights" of a Christian in a Muslim land.

A HUSBAND FOR TARA

The next four months went by without any major incidents. Tara excelled as a clothing designer and become more active in church programs. She was also able to help other Muslim converts who were on the run, fitting work for Tara, who now had more than ten years of practical experience in the field. Still, she knew the man she'd slapped was not satisfied with the way the initial problems he had instigated had been resolved. He wanted more. Tara could tell by the way he looked at her. He wanted either to have Tara or to destroy her.

For Tara, neither was an option.

Tara was sitting in her apartment when the phone rang. It was that same man, and he had news. He was proud to announce that he had written an article and posted it on the church bulletin board. The article claimed that Tara was a prostitute. That's why she wore such nice clothes and was still single. He invited her to come view his handiwork.

Furious, Tara slammed down the phone. This man was not going to give up. She wasn't really worried what the church members thought. Those who knew her would know the truth. She couldn't marry because of the continual danger she was in; the nice clothes were samples of her own designs. The real problem would be with the police; it was only a matter of time before the report made it to them. They had basically told her to marry, and this article would only fuel their position. When they found out, she would be brought in.

A week later, Tara's fears were realized. She was placed in an Islamic detention center where she was to be re-educated in the teachings of Islam and ultimately married off to a Muslim man. Confined to a small room, Tara quietly prayed. She had no idea how she would manage to leave the detention center without agreeing to marry. Now it seemed that everything had come full circle. Her father had wanted her to marry and was willing to kill her if she refused. It wouldn't be much different with the detention center. If Tara couldn't be "rehabilitated," she would be returned to her parents in Pakistan. But Tara had refused her father's plan for her, and she wasn't about to give in to the center officials. Without any further options, she prayed, giving it all to God.

Nearly three months went by. Tara was subjected to daily lessons on the Koran. When not in class, she was a prisoner to her own room. Finally one day an official broke the monotony with an announcement: "Tara, you have a visitor."

"How can I have a visitor? No one even knows I'm here."

"He says he wants to speak with you. We think it would be a good idea if you go with him."

"Go with him?" Tara questioned. "I don't even know this man, and you are sending me out with him?" Tara was obviously upset, believing it was another trick to marry her off. However, the man promised he would have her back after lunch. Tara wasn't happy with the idea, although it would be nice to get out of her room. She decided she would go, but she would ignore the man during lunch.

The man was Tara's age, handsome, and he spoke with a quiet, gentle voice. "Tara, I know who you are," he told her. "I learned about you from a Muslim friend." Tara tried to ignore him. But the more he talked, the more he got her attention.

"I am also a Christian," he said, his voice continuing its low, mellow tone. "But no one knows. I fled from Pakistan just like you did. Actually, I came from the same city. I also know that the center has arranged for you to marry a Muslim man who already has three wives."

Tara cringed. She had already been told of the plan. She tried to act completely disinterested in what the man was saying, and she almost succeeded, until he told her, "If you refuse, you will be deported back to Pakistan—back to your father."

Tara didn't know what to believe. How could the center have arranged for a single Christian man from her hometown to have a meeting with her?

"So what do you want?" Tara finally asked.

"I want to marry you," he said.

A MIRACLE IN THE FLESH

When Tara returned to the detention center, three officials were waiting for her. "We've made a decision, Tara," one of them said. "You are to marry Zahid. He already has three wives, and he is willing to take you, too. He is a good man. We will make all the arrangements. You don't have to worry about anything. But if you refuse, you will be deported back to Pakistan."

That was it: the moment of decision. She hadn't answered her lunch date when he had proposed to her. It was all too much to comprehend. Everything was happening too fast, and she needed time to think. Time to pray. She longed to speak with her adoptive family—with anyone who knew the whole story, anyone who could give her advice.

"I will not marry Zahid," Tara answered to the surprise of the officials.

"Then you can pack your bags. You are going back to Pakistan."

"I will pack my bags, but for another reason. I am getting married. Just not to Zahid. I'm marrying the man who took me to lunch," Tara answered.

The officials were surprised but agreeable. Anything to bring this young woman under control.

Tara contacted the man she had shared lunch with and told him the news. She would marry him. She was still unsure if his motives were true, so it was a risk. Not as big a risk as marrying Zahid would be, however. She knew where he stood.

The decision made, Tara cried out again to Emmanuel, the God who had brought her this far. She was nearly twenty-seven years old, and she had been on the run for more than ten years. If her husband-to-be had deceived her, she knew the problems she would face. But if he was sincere, he was a miracle in the flesh. He would allow her to escape the detention center and the continued rumors of her prostitution. She would even have a helper in her work of ministry to others who had secretly converted from Islam. But was she just setting herself up for another fall? There were just too many questions.

Finally Tara remembered the prayer she had prayed when she entered the detention center. She had given it all to God. And she did so again. It was out of her hands now. "Emmanuel, God with us," she prayed, "be with both of us."

EPILOGUE

The man Tara married turned out to be that miracle in the flesh. A committed Christian, he has served alongside Tara in her continued ministry to others who have converted to Christianity from Islam.

He and Tara now have a baby boy, James, and they are still on the run. She and her husband are continually watched by the detention center officials. She is frequently brought in and questioned about her activities. "Who comes over for lunch?" the officials might ask. "Why did that woman stay at your house last night?" "Why were you gone for four hours today?"

For Tara, life is a constant game of cat and mouse.

Her biggest challenges may still be ahead. In a few years, when her son is old enough to speak, he undoubtedly will also be questioned by the Islamic officials. Another challenge is much closer at hand. Just a few months before being interviewed for *Hearts of Fire*, Tara was spotted by another one of her cousins who has been employed to find her so that she can be returned to her father and "justice" can be done.

For Tara's protection, nothing more can be said of where she lives, nor can details be given of her Christian activities. But one thing is sure: She lives a world apart from most Christians. For the most part even those in her own church remain ignorant of her life as a converted Muslim, of the risks she faces each day. Perhaps it is not possible for them to comprehend. Perhaps that's why God needs those like Tara who can light the way for other apostate sons and daughters to follow.

Ling:
In the School of Suffering

China
1973

Nine-year-old Ling had been out in the village all morning with her older sister, begging for food. They were taking a rest under the large ginkgo tree that overshadowed their hut when her mother called her. "Ling, come quickly," she said. "Your father wants to see you."

She and her sisters spent most of their time outside the tiny, overcrowded bamboo-and-grass hut their family called home. Most of the time they were either begging for food or scavenging for coal from the iron factory nearby; they gave the coal to their parents to sell or use for cooking. As far as Ling knew, her family had always been extremely poor, but lately things had gotten even worse. Her father's poor health was deteriorating dramatically, and Ling was worried about what the future would bring—and about her mother.

"Ling, please, let's not keep your father waiting," her mother's weary voice pleaded. Ling reluctantly left her peaceful spot under the old tree and joined her mother, sisters, and little brother around the family bed—a bed all six of them shared. It was the main piece of furniture in the one-room hut.

"Ling, come nearer," her father said. "Let me see your beautiful face." Ling sat on the edge of the bed and tried to smile. She hated seeing her father like this. Ever since he came back from the hospital the last time, he had been so weak, nearly helpless. Her mom didn't say so, but she knew her father was dying. The cancer was ravaging his body, and he hadn't been able to work for months.

Now her father lifted his hand and waved it gently along the bedside where his wife and children stood, most of them weeping. "Children, please promise me that you will take care of your mother. And take care of each other, too. I will not be here much longer, but always remember that I love you." Ling's mother was sobbing quietly now as her father reached up to caress her face in his hands. "Promise me that after I'm gone . . ." He continued speaking directly to his soon-to-be-widowed wife, ". . . you'll marry a stronger man. Someone more dependable, who will take care of you better than I have. And please remember to keep praying to God."

The love between the two was obvious to all who knew them. Ling had never heard them shout or even speak a harsh word to each other. She couldn't bear to watch her father die, and she hated seeing her mother so distraught. And the way they always talked about God and prayed, she never understood it. Ling had frequently seen her parents kneeling by the bed. She had asked them once what they were doing, and they had said they were "talking to God."

So where is God now? Ling wondered doubtfully. *If there really is a God, why is my father dying?* She choked back a wail and ran out of the room.

Later that afternoon Ling's mother told the children that her in-laws—their grandparents—would be coming to visit. Ling was surprised; she knew her grandparents didn't particularly care for their son and his family. Actually that was an understatement. Her grandmother had cursed the family for not being able to produce more boys!

The grandparents did come a few days later, but they had barely stepped into the tiny home when their son passed away. They refused to help with his burial.

With no money to buy a coffin and no help from her in-laws, Ling's mother carefully wrapped her deceased husband in the nicest blue cloth she could find. It would be a "soft burial," the type reserved for the poorest of the poor.

Ling and her grieving mother and siblings thought surely things couldn't get any worse, but they were wrong. As they were preparing to leave, the grandparents announced they would be taking Ling's little brother back with them. Ling's mother and the rest of the children vehemently protested, but it was no use. The little boy was taken away from them.

The three girls were left behind with their mother in the hut, all of them wondering how long they could survive.

"Please, Ling, kneel down and pray with me," her mother invited one morning. Reluctantly, Ling joined her mother beside the bed. Winter was setting in, and the floor was cold on her tender knees. Ling resented her mother's request, thinking they had been through enough suffering.

Beside her, Ling's mother was softly weeping. At first, Ling thought she was crying in grief; then she realized her mother was pouring out her heart as she talked to God again. Ling herself had nothing to say. She would suffer on her knees in support, but that's as far as she would go. After all, what was the point in talking to the air? And even if God *did* exist, she wouldn't want to talk with Him. Not after all He had put them through.

For a few months after her father died, Ling's family managed to scrape by with the help of some neighbors who took pity on them, but life grew increasingly difficult for them. Finally Ling's mother announced they would be going to live with her parents in Henan Province. In the Chinese culture, women were reared to believe they had to depend on a man. It was not proper for them to be out on their own, and the government refused to help them in any way.

When Ling arrived at her grandparents' home, she was amazed by the size of their house. Her mother's parents were not rich by any means, but they had a mansion compared to the hut where Ling had grown up. Ling's grandmother led the girls through the narrow kitchen into a back room. It was a small, shabby room previously used for storage. "You can all stay here," Ling's grandmother said gruffly. Ling looked around the cramped, unappealing space and chuckled sardonically to herself. She felt at home already.

Their new life brought on a constant battle between Ling's mother and grandmother. And conflict arose because Ling's mother wanted to apply to the production team (the local labor bureau) so she could secure her own home, but Ling's grandmother wanted her daughter to remarry instead.

THE STEPFATHER

One day when Ling came home from school, she heard the usual arguments erupting before she even reached the door. "But, Mother, I don't want to marry again!" her mother was saying, her voice breaking with emotion. "I could never love anyone like I loved Jun. You knew I planned to stay single when I agreed to move in with you. If you would just speak to the production team about letting me work and help me get my own house, I know I can take care of the children. Please, Mother! Please don't do this."

"You've been here two years," Ling's grandmother shouted in response. "I cannot bear it any longer! It's not the way things are done. Shu-Tan is a decent man and can provide for your children. Besides, your father has already arranged it: You're getting married next week."

The following week, Ling had a new stepfather.

Ling bristled at the sharp edge of her new stepfather's voice and longed for the gentle tone her father had always used. Shu-Tan treated Ling and her siblings like animals, and Ling secretly despised him. Being poor was one thing, but it was even worse to be poor and have to live with a stepfather who regarded her as no more than a servant.

Still, Ling persevered and kept her thoughts to herself. Now that Ling's mother had remarried, they were allowed to work, and when Ling was not in school, she worked in the fields with the shepherds in the production teams. Local officials had a point system to determine the workers' pay and benefits. A hardworking man could earn up to ten points in a day. Young Ling earned nine.

Ling also helped design a simple machine to make tofu. When turned by an ox, the machine could be used to pulverize soybeans between two large stones. Shu-Tan loved the idea, but he couldn't afford an ox. Instead he put Ling and her older sister to the task. And for the next four years, the "ox work" became part of their daily routine.

As a result of all the hard work, by age fifteen, Ling was strong and healthy and longing for the day when she could strike out on her own. Her contempt for her stepfather grew each day as he profited from the tofu Ling and her sister's work produced. Yet he refused to buy a single ox. Why should he? He had his stepdaughters to do the drudgery.

Her mother, who had cried relentlessly the first few weeks of her marriage to Shu-Tan, prayed less frequently now. There were only a few secret believers in the village of Ru Tain and only one Bible, which, because she was illiterate, Ling's mother could not have read anyway. A single prayer remained on her lips. Ling would hear it sometimes in the quiet of the night: "Please, God, protect my children, especially Ling and her sister. They are being forced to labor so hard. Please watch over them. It is all I ask."

Ling wondered why her mother talked to God about the slave labor she and her sister were enduring when she should be speaking with the slave master himself! God obviously wasn't helping matters, Ling thought bitterly each time her stepfather forced more work upon them. Probably suspecting Ling's growing animosity toward him, one day he suggested that she find herself a husband. He even offered to help pick one out for her. "It would be best for everyone," he told her.

Ling knew he just wanted to be rid of her. It would mean one less mouth to feed.

An Invisible God

Ling was caught between her own determination and her obedience to her family. If she refused to marry, she would dishonor the whole family and shame her mother, a pain that would be difficult to endure. If she married, she feared her husband would be like Shu-Tan. Only one choice remained for her: She would kill herself. Death seemed to be the only way she could escape enslavement as the pressures in her mind slowly became the pain in her heart.

Ling's mother knew her daughter was falling into a deep depression, and she feared for Ling's well-being. "Ling, you are a natural-born leader," she told her daughter, trying to boost her spirits. "Surely God has something special planned for you."

Ling refused to listen to her mother talk about her invisible

God. It all seemed so futile. Having to deal with her mother's vain superstition and her stepfather's harsh workload only fueled Ling's feeling of hopelessness.

Knowing how low her daughter's mood had fallen, Ling's mother did not dare let Ling out of her sight, worried that she might kill herself. One day she finally succeeded in bringing her distressed daughter to one of the small house-church meetings that had formed in the village. Ling agreed it was better than grinding soybeans to make tofu, and she was actually amused by the gathering. Only four people were there: Ling, her mother, and two others.

As Ling sat there listening to the other three sing a hymn, she thought about her mother's faith. *How can she believe so blindly in a God she cannot see?* Ling wondered. Despite her skepticism, Ling couldn't ignore the rapture that shone from her mother's face. She looked as though she was singing to unseen angels.

Becoming Something God Can Use

A few days later, Ling heard her mother praying for her again, but this time her words definitely caught Ling's attention. "Oh, God," her mother prayed softly, "please save my children, especially Ling. You know how strong willed and naughty she can be. Please turn that headstrong drive of hers into something You can use." That part of her mother's prayer was familiar, and hearing the words again, Ling couldn't help but smile. It was the next part of her mother's prayer that caught her off guard: "I have heard the story of Abraham, who offered his son, Isaac, to You as a sacrifice," her mother continued. "Now I, too, would like to offer one of my children to You. I would like to offer Ling."

Ling shuddered. *Sacrifice me? Has my mother gone mad?*

Her mother's prayer stayed in her mind for several days,

tormenting her with confusion. Finally, as Ling overheard her mother praying again one morning, she stormed into the room to confront her. "Are you sacrificing me to your God again, Mother? Will you have Him kill me with hard work or just strike me down with lightning? And just where is this Lord Jesus you keep talking about? Make Him stand before me so I can touch Him, then I will believe! And what kind of people go to heaven anyway? Hopeless old ladies like you? And how do you get there? Do you think you can climb a tree or a ladder and get to heaven?" Ling could see in her mother's face the pain she was inflicting on her. She hated to hurt her, but she'd simply had enough.

Ling heard the harsh, commanding voice coming out of her mouth and realized it was the same tone she used with her sisters. She had established herself as the self-appointed leader among her siblings with her boldly persuasive tactics. The sisters usually acquiesced to Ling's demands; they knew she could make trouble for them if they didn't. Now Ling heard herself scolding her mother with that same callous voice, and she regretted the hurt she was causing. But she couldn't stop herself. She'd had all she could take of her mother's ridiculous prayers to her nonexistent God.

Time passed, and Ling continued to work hard. She managed to successfully avoid her stepfather's suggestion that she should marry, and he finally gave up and went back to simply ignoring her. Ling felt certain the change in her stepfather was due to her mother's influence. While she was relieved, she also felt guilty about how she had confronted her mother so brazenly. Hoping to make up for her outburst, she continued to accompany her mother to the weekly church meetings.

By the time spring came, Ling had put aside her thoughts of suicide.

She was laboring at the tofu grinder one day when her mother rushed up to her, shouting, "Ling, he's here!"

"Who's here?" Ling asked.

"The evangelist we've heard so much about!" her mother answered. "Don't you remember my telling you? He will be preaching here tonight, and I told the others we would be there. Go get cleaned up. Hurry!"

Before Ling could even think of objecting, her mother had hurried away.

Oh, great, Ling thought, *a self-appointed authority on God.*

She went to the church meeting that evening, partly to please her mother. The old preacher spoke eloquently and effortlessly, not so much preaching as simply telling them about Adam and Eve, explaining how sin entered the world, and assuring them that God loved them so much He sent His own Son to die on the cross so their sin could be forgiven. Ling felt her heart soften as his words penetrated deep into her soul. She had never known such love and sacrifice. She had heard the story before, but it had never made much sense—until now.

Later that evening, the stirrings in her soul escalated as she stared at a picture of a cross hanging on the wall of her aunt's home. She moved toward it, reaching out her hand to touch the print while recalling the story the preacher had so vividly told. *If Jesus died for me, what have I done for Him?* she asked herself as a flood of repentance filled her soul. Ling fell to the floor and wept, crying out to the invisible God she had so adamantly denied. Soon she felt her mother's hand on her shoulder.

"Oh, Mother! I'm so sorry," Ling sobbed. "I'm so sorry for all those bad things I said about your God and for the way I mocked you and didn't believe the things you told me. I am such a bad person. How could God ever forgive *me*?"

Ling's mother's eyes glistened with tears of joy as she hugged her daughter—and her new sister in the Lord. "Ling, my dear, it is forgiven," she said. "God's grace has drawn you here tonight, and now you will be His child forever. Nothing could make me happier. I believe He has a very special plan for you; I've believed that for a long time."

Ling hadn't cried so much since her father died.

LAMBS AMONG WOLVES

For the next year she continued to go with her mother to the weekly Bible meetings, no longer as just a spectator but as a member of their growing fellowship. Her depression had been replaced with an inner joy, and she believed her troubles were behind her. Then she had a dream: *The narrow path cut straight through the field. On the left side the wheat was slender and green, blowing easily in the wind. But on the right side, the wheat was ripe, and some of the stalks were falling over from the weight of the large, tan heads of grain. Ling looked from side to side as the wheat disappeared into the distance. She wondered how queer the weather and soil must have been to produce such a crop.*

Ling related the unusual dream to her mother the following morning. To Ling's surprise, her mother reported a similar dream. She had seen the heavy, ripe stalks of wheat, but she also saw a small bean shoot growing in the midst of the field and heard a voice instructing her to "water this tender shoot, or it will dry up."

Neither of them knew what the dreams meant, but both knew there had to be a reason why they had shared the same vision. Their answer came the following week at the prayer meeting, when the text for the evening came from the Gospel of Luke, chapter 10: "The harvest truly is great, but the laborers are few; therefore pray the Lord of the harvest to send out laborers into His harvest. Go your way; behold, I send you out as lambs among wolves."[1]

Wondering if this was the meaning of their dreams, Ling was both scared and excited about what God had in store for her. She was also curious what the second half of the passage referred to. "But how could I be a preacher?" she asked her mother as they discussed the passage. "I'm too young, and I know next to nothing. I don't even own a Bible."

Her mother just looked at Ling and smiled. She knew exactly what the dreams had meant: Her daughter would bring the gospel to the lost souls of China. This she knew for certain.

Shortly after her seventeenth birthday, with very little money or food, no Bible, and no destination, Ling set out alone to preach the gospel in China. She wanted to wait until she had studied more, but her mother was insistent. "You don't have to know much. Just share the story of Jesus. Tell people what you know. If it's of God, He will bless your ministry." And with her mother's encouragement, Ling was off.

Ling simply walked from village to village, sharing her faith. Whenever she came across a village that possessed a Bible, she would study to memorize verses for her next message. She also learned hymns. She had never realized how beautifully she could sing until she saw that people were drawn in by her voice, then they stayed to hear what the young preacher had to say. Just the fact that she was a young, single woman traveling alone through China was enough to get most people's attention.

God blessed Ling's ministry. The more she traveled and preached, the larger the audiences became. She was amazed to see groups of seven in the early villages grow to crowds of seventy in the villages she visited the next week. The scripture was right: The fields *were* ripe. People were so hungry to hear the gospel, and God had called her to be one of His messengers. It was an overwhelming thought, and Ling continually prayed that she would be found worthy of the call. Most of all, she wanted to be an example. She wanted to preach what she knew and experienced.

She also longed for a Bible and began asking God to provide one. "How can a preacher of God's Word not have a Bible?" she asked Him.

Young people were especially drawn to Ling's charismatic personality and fervor for the Lord. Some of them offered to accompany her, and the young evangelist gladly accepted.

As the crowds grew and her passion for the gospel increased, Ling felt she couldn't go much longer without a Bible. She had visited one village where believers possessed only portions of the Gospel of Matthew, and they had read in chapter 25 the parable of the ten virgins. Five of the virgins were prudent and took along extra oil for their lamps, and five were foolish and did not take extra oil to keep their lamps burning. Taking the passage literally, every church member in the village carried extra oil with them at all times to make sure they would not be without when the Lord returns.[2]

Ling longed to have a complete Bible of her own so she could study it and help other believers understand it. So when she overheard that a woman only four miles away had Bibles available, she couldn't get there fast enough. It turned out the woman had a few Bibles that had washed ashore after members of a Christian mission group had been forced to throw them overboard while attempting to smuggle them into China at night. Some believers along the shoreline had recovered the Bibles, and this woman had carefully dried the pages one by one in the sunlight.

When Ling asked her for one of the Bibles, explaining how God had called her to preach the gospel, the woman became alarmed. "No, no, no!" she answered. "These Bibles are very valuable. Do you know how hard it is to get a Bible? And how do I know you are even a believer?"

Ling persisted in her pleadings, but she was unsuccessful. The woman would not part with a single one of her Bibles. Poor Ling looked so crestfallen the woman told her that if she could recite the Lord's Prayer without a single mistake, she would reconsider.

Ling left, encouraged that there still might be hope. She traveled back to a village where she knew there was a Bible in the home of an elderly believer. The brother cherished the Bible with a holy reverence, and when Ling saw it, she understood why. The old man's Bible was completely handwritten. In fact, the brother's hands were now permanently twisted from the thousands and thousands of hours he had spent carefully copying each verse character by character.

A Dream Planted, a Mission Begun

When Ling made her request, the old man carefully presented his Bible to her and allowed her to copy the Lord's Prayer so she could put it to memory. Ling was awestruck by the neatly penned characters and wondered how many years he had spent copying the thousands of verses. She would see many more Bibles like this one as she continued her journey. These laborious works of love gave her a new appreciation for the importance of God's Word, and she committed to memorizing as many passages as possible. She also vowed to distribute Bibles all around China to other believers . . . if God should make that dream possible.

On her way back to the woman's house, Ling began to wonder if she had memorized the Lord's Prayer correctly. What if the man had made a mistake? What if she had copied it wrong?

But she needn't have worried. She passed the test and recited the Lord's Prayer perfectly. Afterward, though, the woman had Ling pray aloud so she could make sure Ling was sincere. Then she asked question upon question about Ling's ministry and how she had come to Christ. Finally the interrogation ended, and the woman knelt down with Ling, hugged the Bible, and presented it

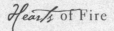

to her. She apologized for being so meticulous, but then she explained, "After our brothers collected these Bibles from the shore, they began to distribute them about China. It was very dangerous, and some paid with their lives. Remembering their sacrifice, I treasure these Books even more."

Ling left with her Bible. Part of it was still wet because the woman hadn't finished drying all the pages. Ling turned to Luke 10, carefully lifting the damp pages, and read the familiar words with tears in her eyes: "The harvest truly is great, but the laborers are few; therefore pray the Lord of the harvest to send out laborers into His harvest. Go your way; behold, I send you out as lambs among wolves."

Ling had fully realized the first part of Jesus' directive. She had gone out, alone, as the Lord's laborer, and the harvest had indeed been great. Now, wondering how the second part of this passage would be fulfilled, she prayed for strength.

WANTED

The poster looked ominous: "Wanted for Crimes Against the State," the heading proclaimed. "Anyone seeing the persons listed below are to immediately report them to the local authorities. A reward will be given." Ling read the words and shuddered as her eyes scanned down the list, her lips moving as she read names she knew. Many were her friends and co-workers. And then, there on the list, was *her* name.

She wasn't surprised, but still, the discovery was sobering. Things had gone smoothly for quite a while. Ling had become quite effective in her itinerant ministry. Remembering how the old evangelist had changed her life when he'd come to her village and spoken simply about Adam and Eve, about sin, and about the great sacrifice of Jesus Christ, Ling followed his example. Soon she learned that one of the most powerful ways she could reach people was simply to read selected passages of Scripture aloud. Many Chinese people knew how rare a Bible was, and they eagerly listened to the story, quickly absorbing the message.

Surprisingly, the troubles started with her own relatives. As Ling traveled around the villages, the news of her ministry quickly spread, and her relatives accused Ling of bringing a great embarrassment upon the family. "She is getting old," they quarreled among themselves. "She should be getting married, not tromping around the countryside like a lunatic!"

Ling had considered going home but for a different reason. Her stepfather was furious that his tofu maker had departed. At first he believed she would be back as soon as she was hungry. But as the months passed, he realized Ling was gone for good. Sure, she returned occasionally, but never for more than an afternoon visit.

Refusing to hire help or buy an ox, Shu-Tan put Ling's mother to work at the grinder. When Ling heard about her stepfather's heartlessness, she slipped home and told her mother, "This is too much for you. I will stay home."

"No! Absolutely not," her mother responded. "You must promise me you will be faithful to God's call. I can handle this. It is a small price to pay to have you preach the gospel. Do you understand? You *must* continue your work in the Lord's harvest."

Ling did as her mother told her. But soon she had other problems. In some of the villages the local police had begun cracking down on "unauthorized meetings" and "cult activities." Many believers were afraid to let Ling stay in their village; in some places she was refused even a single meal. Ling found herself traveling farther and farther by foot, moving deeper into the countryside. She could have traveled much of the distance by bus for only fifty cents, but it was more money than she had.

Fortunately, when her supporters heard of her travels, they donated shoes to keep her going. Ling happily accepted.

Despite the mounting pressures, Ling was experiencing increasing results in her ministry. The crowds often numbered more than a hundred, and her voice remained strong as she addressed the building throngs in the open-air meetings. House churches sprang up in many of the villages, and they caught the eye of the government. At first the Christians denied that they had rejected the official government-sponsored church, called the Three Self Patriotic Movement (TSPM). And even if the Christians *were* willing to join the TSPM, there wasn't a single congregation within a hundred-mile radius!

Soon the police stepped up their persecution of Christians. In response, believers moved their meetings into the wilderness, and the singing and preaching became quieter. Ling had to be careful about whom she confided in, and she refused to stay in any one area very long. She had become known to many of the foreign missionaries in the area, and they often asked to meet with her. Ling knew these meetings brought added dangers and unwanted attention from the police, but she was eager to meet with her Christian brothers and sisters from abroad and let them know what God was doing in China. The missionaries brought Bibles, which Ling gladly distributed among the new house churches. They were still quite rare wherever she went, and she could often give just one Bible per congregation. The hand copying continued.

MUDDY KNEES, FULL HEARTS

By the winter of 1983, the persecutions and arrests of Christians were rampant. Ling was now constantly on the run, knowing that she and many of her co-workers were on the government's wanted list. Going home to see her mother was out of the question now. The police would surely be watching. During a visit to a village called Towkil, Ling had to lead the villagers deep into the fields to safely share the gospel with them. It was pouring rain, and there was no cover. But everyone stayed, transfixed by the message and absorbing every word.

When Ling led them in a prayer of repentance, the listeners knelt down in the thick mud. Ling's knees were completely buried—as were everyone else's. More than a hundred people accepted Christ that day, and Ling rejoiced with them while she also dreaded what was ahead. But she also knew the fire of persecution would cause the wind of the Holy Spirit to blow stronger and further. She committed herself yet again to be faithful to her call, no matter what lay ahead.

Twenty miles away, in the village of Datwin, Ling met some other preachers who had been traveling through the countryside sharing the gospel while attempting to avoid persecution. One of them was known as Uncle Qiang, and he and the others shared Ling's vision and passion; they had been serving the Lord for many years. Uncle Qiang was the eldest member of the group. He had already served a five-year term in a forced-labor camp.

Ling and the others joined together—ten evangelists: nine men and Ling—and committed themselves to continue preaching the simple message of Christ until the house churches were set up with local leadership. They also agreed among themselves that those of the group who were still single, like Ling, should remain so until their work was firmly established.

The biggest challenge the evangelists faced was not persecution but the overwhelming need for Bibles. They agreed that Ling would be responsible for bringing in more Bibles since she already had developed contacts with the foreign missionaries who had smuggled in Bibles. When she was not in the countryside planting churches, Ling, with help from Uncle Qiang, pursued any rumor of where Bibles might be available.

HARD WORK, INCREASING DANGER

Between evangelizing and distributing Bibles, Ling was traveling thirty or more miles every day—now mostly by bicycle. The journeys were increasingly dangerous; Ling knew the police were watching her. She expected it was only a matter of time before they arrested her. In preparation, she took to reading more and more passages about persecution to the village churches. She wanted them to be prepared, and if it happened to her, she wanted to be a good example.

The work grew steadily harder. She often had to go more than a day without food, and some church members criticized her. She was only twenty years old, single, and a woman, they said. What business did she have taking on such work? Some of the sneers were due to the critics' cultural upbringing; others were simply jealous. Either way, the comments were hard for Ling to take.

Throughout the 1980s, as Ling and her co-workers continued with their travels, they heard more and more reports about Christians being harassed, arrested, and even tortured by the authorities. China's central government was becoming increasingly concerned about the rapid growth of the house churches all across the land while the official TSPM churches lost members. To Ling and the other evangelists, it was clear that believers were seeking out the fresh new outpouring of God's Spirit that resulted in the burgeoning house-church movement. In response, government leaders led a nationwide campaign to squelch the growth of these churches. Persecution intensified as local police were given broad authority to deal with the Christians, especially Christian leaders, however they chose. This often meant torture and imprisonment without trial.

By the early 1990s, Ling was known by thousands of believers as a wise and compassionate leader. Somehow she had escaped the grasp of the authorities—at least for now.

KEEPING A COMMITMENT

In April 1994, Ling was physically exhausted. "You should rest a little," Uncle Qiang told her. "And maybe it's God's timing for you to marry."

But Ling resisted his suggestion. "You know I made a commitment to the others in the leadership group. We said we would not rest or marry until the church was built up on a solid foundation. The believers need leadership to keep them strong so they stand against the terrible persecution that's been going on. Besides, another shipment of Bibles has arrived in Guangzhou. I'm taking Teoh and Jan with me to pick some up. We'll be back in a few days."

The elder Qiang felt a slight unease, but he suppressed the urge to argue with her. Ling could be stubborn, but that was the reason he had brought her into the group at the beginning. He knew God could use her fiery commitment to help the budding house churches grow and flourish. Besides, Uncle Qiang and his wife had come to love her like a daughter.

He knew Ling's struggles, how she sometimes had to deal with jealousy from church members because of her position, and how she put up with the constant misunderstanding of those who just couldn't figure out why she had never married. Thinking of all the challenges she faced, Uncle Qiang breathed a silent prayer as he watched her go.

FINALLY CAUGHT

It was early evening after Ling and her co-workers had picked up their supply of Bibles and arrived at their friends' house on the way home. They enjoyed some warm fellowship and soothing rest after their long journey, and it was quite late when Ling excused herself to make a telephone call before bed. As she

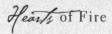

stepped outside the apartment on the now-quiet street, she heard a man calling her name. He was hurrying toward her, and as he came nearer, under the streetlight, she could see it was a police officer. Ling's first instinct was to escape, but as she turned, she was confronted by another officer.

Well, Ling thought, *they've finally caught me.* Ever since seeing her own name on that wanted poster years earlier, she had been expecting this moment. But she had firmly believed she would not be caught until God allowed it in His timing; now she took solace in that thought.

"You must come with us," one of the officers said as they showed their badges. Apparently they had been waiting for her, and although she had a pretty good idea of what was to come, she breathed a sigh of relief, thinking they were going to take only her, without bothering the other believers or searching the tiny apartment.

But instead of leading her to a waiting car, the officers led her back toward the apartment.

"Where are you taking me?" Ling asked.

"Inside," replied the first officer. He was tall, like Ling, and he spoke with a calm voice that unnerved her. As they escorted her back into the building, Ling's mind raced: *Teoh and Jan are both married; surely the police won't send them to prison. How many Bibles are they going to find? Did I destroy those directions to the pastor's house after I picked up the Bibles there?*

Stepping into the apartment ahead of the officers, Ling quickly whispered to Teoh and Jan, "Just tell them I hired you and that you don't know anything. Let me take the responsibility."

The police quickly separated Ling from the others, shoving her into a chair and spreading an official-looking document on the table in front of her. She saw her name written over one of the lines in the first paragraph. "Sign this," barked Mr. Tall-and-Mean. He shoved a pen into her hand, and Ling quickly scanned the document. It was a warrant saying they could search and remove all "evidence" from her room. She signed the paper and suddenly felt overcome with fatigue. She knew it was going to be a long night . . .

The officers set to work tearing through the apartment. She watched them rifle through her clothes. And then they found the boxes of Bibles . . .

Ling was taken to Prison 91, one of four famous prisons in China. The officers who interrogated her only wanted three things: names, names, and more names. "Who is supporting you? Who are the other leaders? Who gave you these Bibles?" Knowing the consequence of identifying anyone in the group, she refused to answer.

The questioning occurred repeatedly during the next two months.

Along with being frequently questioned, Ling had to work alongside the other prisoners. The inmates' current job was to make cigarette lighters, and the quality control was strictly maintained because the lighters were to be exported to the West. Ling fell ill; she ran a high fever and became quite sick. But if she didn't fulfill her daily quota, she was beaten.

"We Know How to Open Mouths"

In July Ling was moved. Police in her hometown had found out she had been arrested, and they had her extradited. After pursuing her for nearly ten years, they were thrilled to discover she was in custody. The hometown police were much more experienced at interrogating prisoners. As one of them told her, "We know how to open mouths."

Already weak from the fever and the forced labor at Prison 91, Ling suffered mightily as the interrogations proceeded. Her lips were cold, and she felt close to passing out. The interrogation sessions had been harsh, but she hadn't given them anything. They used techniques different from those of the first police questioners, but they wanted the same information: names. "Who are the others you work with?" they asked again and again. "Who are the people you have connections with overseas? Tell us about your illegal meetings. Who gives you your books and Bibles?" The questions were dizzying, but time and time again Ling held on and didn't reveal the others' identity, although the temptation to do so was strong. Sometimes the interrogators showed Ling pictures of herself with her co-workers. *If they already know who I was working with; why do they want me to provide their names?* Ling wondered. *And what further harm could it do now?*

One terrifying day, ten men came into the interrogation room. One was holding a small clamp that was open on both ends. Two of the guards roughly forced Ling onto her stomach on the floor. They pulled one of her arms around her side to her back and jerked her other arm over her shoulder so that her hands were a few inches apart above her spine. Then another guard rested the heel of his boot on her back so he had enough leverage to pull her hands together while the two arm-holders hurriedly attached a clamp to her two thumbs. They screwed the clamp tight, forcing her thumbs together.

Ling heard her bones cracking as her shoulder joints were strained into the unnatural positions. Then the men released her arms, and the full force of her torturously twisted position sent a lightning bolt of pain through Ling's body.

The "thumb clamp" was so cruel, the government had outlawed its use on women. In her misery, Ling moaned, noting the irony: Many in the villages had discouraged her from her ministry because she was a woman doing what was considered a man's job. Now she was being tortured like a man.

Ling knew what was coming. In that moment she thought she

had a choice: face death or betray her brothers. She decided death would be less painful.

"Get up!" an officer screamed as he kicked at Ling's feet. She was struggling to get up onto her knees when she was knocked back down by the vicious blow of a cane across her back. The pain seared her body like a bolt of lightning. She could not breathe; she could barely move. Her wrists were swollen, and her arms cramped from being locked behind her.

"Please! I can't . . ." Ling's voice quivered as she fought to stay conscious. Beads of cold sweat ran down her forehead and burned her eyes as she cried out to God in her agony. She wondered if this was how Jesus felt as He prayed in Gethsemane, knowing He was to suffer and die. She wondered if she was going to die . . .

For three hours they continued the interrogations with Ling's thumbs clamped together behind her back, her body agonizingly contorted. Finally she passed out from the pain.

When Ling woke up she was facedown on the floor of her filthy cell. She could hear voices nearby, and eventually someone came into the cell and lifted her onto her wooden bed. She couldn't move; the pain was too great. She couldn't even get up to eat or use the bucket. For fifteen days she remained on the bed while the officers decided what to do with her.

Gradually, she recovered from the torturous treatment, and she survived the appalling conditions in the prison for five more months. Then, because the authorities had no real evidence against her and couldn't get her to reveal the names of other believers in her vast network, they reluctantly released her.

SUFFERING IS A SCHOOL

It was a cold, blustery day in January 1995 when Ling knocked at the door of a co-worker. "Ling!" her friend Ruth exclaimed when

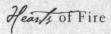

she saw the frail form standing in front of her. She quickly pulled
Ling into the house, threw her arms around her, and peppered
her with questions: "Ling, we were all so worried about you. Why
didn't you contact us? You are so thin! Are you all right? The
police wouldn't tell us anything about you. How did you survive?
How did you get out?"

An impromptu celebration quickly ensued as the news of
Ling's return circulated among the believers. Ling was exhausted
but elated to be with her Christian brothers and sisters again. As
they gathered around to give thanks and pray, Ling said, "Thank
you so much for your earnest prayers for me during these past
months. I know I couldn't have made it without God's help and
your prayer support. Believe me, there were many days when I
didn't think I could go on, but God was faithful to always remind
me of His love during those times. I think suffering is a school. If
you successfully graduate from this school, you have done your
job. But if you fail, you are destroyed. For me, prison was that
school. While I was there, I couldn't dwell on anything but my
complete dependence on God, and that dependence forced me
closer to Him. I have always taught you to be strong for God and
to face any trial. Now I can tell you with even greater certainty that
Jesus will be with you, no matter what you have to go through."

Prior to her arrest, Ling had been studying and teaching on
the life of Paul and the other New Testament apostles who
suffered for Christ. Now she joked with her co-workers that when
she got to heaven, she wanted to greet Jesus then shake hands
with Paul and ask him, "When you were alive on earth, was your
life as hard as mine?"

Barely thirty years old, Ling had been through so much
physical abuse it was hard for her to function normally. Yet,
wanting to set a good example, she resumed her work among the
house churches right away, teaching and leading Bible studies,

meeting with overseas contacts to coordinate help and information, and making sure the flow of Bibles continued to the inland areas of China. Because of the severe persecution by the government during the 1980s, believers had scattered all across China, and the network of house churches had grown to several million people. With even more urgency now, Ling worked to make sure every church had at least one Bible.

One evening in September 1996, Ling had said good-bye to a missionary couple from Europe and returned home when she and her friends heard a knock on the door about 10:00 p.m.

A man's voice called out, "Hello! We just need to check your residency card."

Ling looked at Qiang and Teoh and shook her head. She knew it had to be the police. Ling opened the door, and five officers pushed their way in. "You're under arrest!" an officer proclaimed as the other policemen handcuffed Ling and her friends. Ling watched in dismay as once again the officers tore wildly through her things. It was going to be another long night . . .

OLD FRIENDS

When they arrived at the police station, Ling was presented to the commissioner, a smooth-voiced man who had dealt with her during her last arrest. "Sir, this is Miss Ling . . . ," the subordinate began.

"Yes, I know her," replied the man in charge as he flashed a smug smile. "We are old friends. Well, Ling, this time I don't think you'll be going anywhere for a while. The file on you and your group has grown quite impressive. And we picked up two more of your leaders tonight. All in all, I'd say it's been a good day's work." He jerked his chin dismissively. "Put her in cell block twelve," he said over his shoulder as he walked out the door. "I'm going home."

After a week, Ling's anxiety increased as she considered the officer's lax attitude. Why weren't they interrogating her? Why was the officer so relaxed? How did they find out about the others who had been arrested? Ling fought wave after wave of panic as she realized how much they must know. She thought the police surely understood even more clearly than before how influential she had become. They probably had been following her ever since she'd been released from her first arrest, so they undoubtedly knew how often she had met with her overseas contacts. And they surely knew about all the people who had visited her province and asked to meet with her in regard to the house-church movement.

Well, thought Ling, it all made sense. The church had grown exponentially, so the police were bound to learn the details of her activities sooner or later. She resigned herself to prison life, shuddering to think that Jesus' words—"behold, I send you out as lambs among wolves"—were becoming real for her again.

The next four months were agonizing for Ling. "Please," she sometimes begged her captors, "if you want to kill me, then kill me. If you want to sentence me, then sentence me. If you want to release me, just release me! But don't keep me here with no excuse or reason, like you did the last time."

She brazenly said such things, but little attention was paid to her except when a guard occasionally spat at her or mocked her.

Sometimes Ling thought she would go crazy. Every day she sat on the hard wooden bench that served as her bed. The tiny cell, intended only as a temporary holding chamber, was constantly wet due to a water leak. At times it was crowded with as many as twenty women who had to spend much of their time scooping water off the floor.

Although other prisoners frequently moved in and out of the holding cell before being transferred to another prison or before being released, Ling was virtually ignored there by the authorities and rarely left the tiny, cramped space. She was not allowed to lie down during the long days or even to lean against the wall but was forced to either stand or sit upright on the wooden board that served as her bed. Swarms of flies and mosquitoes made the filthy cell an even more miserable place.

Finally, the police commander appeared at her cell door one day with a form in his hand. "Sign this," he ordered.

Ling reached through the bars for the form. "What is it?" she asked.

"Just sign it," the commander snarled, thrusting the paper at her. "You're being relocated."

Ling's heart sank as she quickly scanned the document and saw that it was a notice saying she was being sent to a "labor reformation camp" for a sentence of three years. China granted prisoners fifteen days to sue or to try to defend themselves after receiving such a notice, but for Ling, there would be no such rights. "You will be leaving today," the commander told her.

Before Ling could protest, he had strutted away, the heels of his shiny dress shoes clicking importantly against the concrete as he disappeared down the long prison corridor.

Three years.

Oh, God, please watch over the churches, Ling prayed silently as a prison car took her to the area known as Eighteen-Mile River, where the labor camp was located. She was thankful for all that she and her co-workers had accomplished, but at the same time, she was anxious about what was happening to them now. Out of the ten top leaders in their network of house churches, at least four, she knew, were now in prison. Besides herself, Uncle Qiang had been detained in the local jail, and two other leaders had been sent to another labor camp.

When they arrived, Ling was given a bowl of rice and a small box of personal items, then she was led to her cell.

Prayer in Prison: As Essential As Breathing

"Welcome, Ling! We were told you were coming!" a voice greeted her as the cell door clanged shut. It turned out that some believers from one of Ling's groups would be her cellmates at the camp. She had to smile, hearing their cheery hello. They actually seemed happy that she was imprisoned, but she knew they were just happy she had been assigned to their cell. As they hugged each other and whispered a quiet prayer, Ling wondered how many more believers would be joining them.

She had been assigned a top bunk. That first night, Ling climbed up to her bed and began to pray out loud. "Hey!" one of her cellmates shouted. "You can't do that here. If they catch you, you'll be punished."

"But there is no such thing as not allowing Christians to pray. It would be like not allowing them to breathe," Ling replied.

"Well, that's how it is," the other woman said. "And not only that, but you're not allowed to have long hair, either."

Ling ran her fingers through her long, silky black hair. She was not vain about her appearance, but she couldn't imagine having her hair cut off. She had always kept her hair long, like her mother's. She wondered how ugly she would look with it short. She felt the first tears welling up in her eyes as she silently asked God to spare her hair. She knew it was silly even before she finished asking. She looked around her cell, noticing that all the other women had short hair—and that they all were ugly.

Life in the camp was different from life in prison. After the long weeks of confinement, Ling was happy to get outside during the day. The food was a little better here, but for the three-month probationary period, she had to work fifteen to sixteen hours a day making wigs. Again she thought of the irony as she rubbed the stubble now protruding from her head. The wigmaking work was tedious and difficult, and it was not uncommon for the laborers to

vomit under the pressures of the daily quotas. Ling found it difficult to think about anything else.

Life became a monotonous routine of waking, eating, working,
and sleeping—and then waking, eating, and working again. At
times the inmates even worked through the night if the load was
heavy or if the day's quotas weren't met. For Ling, the greatest
challenge was finding time to focus on God and prayer the way she
was accustomed to doing. And after so many years of traveling
freely throughout central China, preaching, teaching, and caring
for people, this new life with all of its rules and limitations was a
blow.

"God Has a Purpose for Us Here"

Each morning the inmates jumped out of bed at five o'clock
when the whistle blew, then they had ten minutes to make their
bed and line up in the courtyard, fifteen minutes to eat, and all
day to work at the factory. They followed this schedule without
respite seven days a week. For most of them, including Ling, life
became a perpetual state of exhaustion and monotony. Ling
labored beside prostitutes, drug dealers, thieves, kidnappers, and
others who had been labeled "the garbage of society."
Completely drained by the long hours of work, she found it more
and more difficult to pray at night because she craved sleep so
desperately.

After a few weeks, however, Ling felt her old self re-emerging
as she surrendered her situation to God. She once more felt
compelled to share her faith with the other believers. "God's
ultimate aim in every situation is for us to learn obedience,
right?" she told them. "So I know God has a purpose for us here.
We are surrounded by criminals with foul mouths who act out in
all kinds of ways, and I know God wants us to learn to love these

221

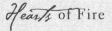

people and to show them His love. It's easy to love those on the outside—our friends and co-workers. But God wants us to learn how to love these people, too."

Ling was thankful for the handful of other believers in the large labor camp population. When one believer felt discouraged, another was there to pick her up. And although Ling found it frustrating that they could not meet openly to pray and share, she found other times and places where she could pray for and encourage the women— when they were allowed toilet breaks during the workday or when they were standing in the lunch line, for example.

Before long, Ling's leadership abilities were obvious to the camp officials, and they put her in charge of her division as a team leader. This promotion gave Ling more opportunities to witness as she took charge of the fifty women in her dormitory and also worked as a production supervisor overseeing two hundred women in the wigmaking factory. While the work was challenging and the fighting among the prisoners sometimes infuriated her, Ling nevertheless performed her duties with excellence, and eventually she won the hearts of several under her supervision.

"Why are you here?" some of the women would ask her. "You are so kind and such a good leader. You could have a good career on the outside."

Ling took every opportunity to share the reason for her imprisonment, and as a result of her testimony, many became secret believers. Though they had no Bibles, Ling taught them Scripture verses and songs she had memorized, and she taught them how to pray. She remembered the old brother's carefully hand-copied Bible and her own commitment to memorize large portions of Scripture. And now she was glad she had done it.

"CAN A PERSON LIKE ME BELIEVE?"

Prison officials continued to notice Ling's excellent work record and the fact that her team came out best in production and seemed to have fewer fights and accidents than the other teams. One day Ling's supervisor, Ms. Tao, stopped her in the factory hallway.

"Ling, I saw your file," she said. "I know about your activities and the fact that you were an influential Christian leader. And now that you've been here for eleven months, I've also seen your work and your behavior with the other prisoners, especially those coarse and perpetually angry ones who so easily cause trouble. You seem to have great affection for these prisoners, yet you don't act like them. Why?"

Ling felt a nervous excitement as she told her boss, "I don't act like them because I'm a Christian, and I've surrendered my whole life to Jesus Christ. He's the reason I live. He's the reason I can love all these unlovely people." Ling held her breath, waiting for Ms. Tao's reaction. The mere mention of religion could add more time to her sentence or get her locked in "the box," a solitary confinement cell. She never knew if an inquirer might be trying to trap her. But to Ling's surprise, her boss blurted out, "Can a person like me believe in Jesus?"

"Of course!" Ling replied. "But aren't you afraid of losing your position? Aren't you afraid the government will drive you out of the army?"

"Aren't *you* afraid I might punish you by adding time to your sentence for talking such nonsense?" Ms. Tao shot back, not missing a beat.

"As long as I know that my time here has purpose—as long as I know you have come to believe in Jesus—I can stay here forever."

"You *enjoy* staying here?"

223

"No, not at all," answered Ling. "But it is because Jesus loves you that I am here. My life and your life were given by God."

Ms. Tao argued a little more, but Ling answered every question as she continued to tell her boss about the loving goodness of God.

Ms. Tao was interested, but she wasn't easily convinced, and they continued their clandestine conversations over many months. Finally, one day she told Ling, "Even if I believe, I will have to believe secretly. You know, there are some Christians in my neighborhood, but I have never talked to them. It's difficult because of my position. You're the first Christian I've ever really known."

Ling could only smile in response and pray in her heart for Ms. Tao.

She continued to work and serve God in the labor camp as best she could over the next two years, but her health deteriorated from the long hours of labor and the lack of nutrition. Some days she wondered how much longer she could hold up. Then one December day Ms. Tao called Ling into her office. She was sitting behind her desk with a stern look on her face, holding a piece of paper.

"What is it?" asked Ling.

"I have been given a sentencing recommendation for you, and I need to sign it," Ms. Tao answered.

Ling was dumbfounded. She searched her memory for any recent incidents that would cause her sentence to be increased. Certainly there was nothing she could remember, although someone could have set her up by lying to the officials. Ms Tao and Ling had become friends, and Ling continued to speak with her about Christ. Perhaps someone had overheard them talking and reported her.

Her mind had wandered. She reconnected with the present

situation just as she heard Ms. Tao, reading from the paper, say, ". . . your sentence by one year."

Ling's heart sank. Then Ms. Tao looked up at her, surprised at the downcast look on Ling's face. "Ling! Did you hear me?" Ms. Tao said sharply. "They have classified you as completely rehabilitated and *reduced* your sentence by one year!"

Ling was speechless.

"Well, I must say, this is the first time I have ever seen you short on words." Ms. Tao was smiling now. "Congratulations, Ling; you will be released in less than three weeks."

A WORLD APART

Three weeks later, the morning cold cut through Ling's thin body as she waited anxiously outside the camp in the ankle-deep snow for Uncle Qiang. *Rehabilitated,* she mused. That just meant she hadn't gotten caught teaching and evangelizing the other prisoners. It also meant, she hoped, that they would leave her alone for a while.

Ling was excited to get back to her work of evangelizing and encouraging the church members, but she also knew her physical state was not what it used to be. There were many components of prison life that would be hard to shake. *Oh, Lord, please help me readjust to life outside the prison. And please continue to be with the sisters who are still there.*

Ling enjoyed a joyously enthusiastic reunion when Qiang and Teoh pulled up in the small car. Because it would have created great difficulties for any of the believers to see her in prison, she had had very few visitors over the previous two years. Now she was about to learn that some of the leaders had married, other church members now had babies, and several new fellowship groups had begun.

As soon as the car pulled into traffic, Ling felt a wave of nausea sweep over her. *Here's another thing I haven't done in a while*, she thought, *ride in a car*. The four-hour trip was miserable for Ling, curled up in the backseat and suffering car sickness while trying to focus on the thrill of being free.

As she expected, Ling did have difficulty adjusting back to normal life. Prison was a world apart. When she was in the labor camp, the officials had never allowed the lights to be turned off. The production tables were nearly always occupied, and even the cells were well lit. The leadership in the church had now become well established without her, making it even more difficult for Ling to resume her leadership role, especially since she was a woman. She felt sad that there seemed to be no place for her now among the church's leaders, but she also knew she had to rest and keep her responsibilities light while her body healed. So maybe it was for the best.

ARRESTED—EVERY ONE OF THEM

Ling moved in with the family of one of the Christian leaders. They lived in a large house in central China, and Ling was given a room on the second floor. The leaders were scheduled to meet secretly at this house from the nineteenth of August through the twenty-third. Ling had intended to attend, but instead she was given an important assignment in western China during the week of the meeting. She suspected the leaders were trying to keep her out of harm's way, but she couldn't know for sure. Over thirty key church leaders were expected at the meeting, and it would be a great opportunity to resume old ties—and to renew her commitment to a leadership role. But it wasn't to be.

She had completed her assignment in western China on the evening of August 23, when she received an urgent message. "Ling!

Come back quickly," she was told. "All the leaders have been arrested—every one of them. You are the only one left!"

Ling arrived home the next day and found the believers in a panic. Some of the church leaders' spouses took out their frustrations on Ling, somehow thinking she was responsible. She had only been out of prison a little over six months, and friends told her the police were looking for her also.

Ling immediately took charge of the situation. First she called together all the local believers and assigned each group the task of keeping track of one or two of the arrested leaders. They were to collect clothing, food, and money and deliver them to the police station for "their" leaders.

The arrest had a huge impact on the church throughout China because the pastors were the main Christian leaders in their respective areas. News of their arrest quickly traveled to the outside world via e-mail, and it spread quickly throughout China through The Voice of America radio broadcasts. Ling sought to coordinate the flow of information as people from all over China and the world began calling to find out the latest details. Soon the pastors' families began to arrive, and Ling hosted each one, answering their questions as best she could.

After five weeks, all but six of the leaders had been released, but not before paying steep fines (up to ten thousand yen each), which Ling was also responsible for securing. The believers were so poor, it was extremely difficult to raise the money for so many leaders. But Ling wouldn't take no for an answer. Her imprisoned brothers were worth more than any amount of money, and she kept on begging and collecting the funds until she finally had enough.

Ling was exhausted and felt as though she would crumble from the pressure, but she couldn't rest until she had done everything she could to help secure the release of the remaining six pastors, the most influential leaders in their organization—and thus the biggest prizes for the police. She now feared the leaders might be executed.

There was only one thing left to do. Ling called the police station.

"I wish to speak with the commissioner, please."

"Who is this?" the station clerk asked.

"My name is Ling. The commissioner will know who I am; he is looking for me."

"Ling, my old friend! I'm surprised to hear from you," the commissioner's familiar smooth voice came on the line. "Where are you calling from?"

"Never mind. I need to speak with you about my friends you are holding in prison."

"Sure, just come down to the station, and we can talk."

"No. I will only agree to meet with you at the Bright Moon Hotel. And you must come alone. I will be watching, and if anyone comes with you, I will not show up."

Ling knew he would agree. If nothing else, his curiosity would get him there. Why would the evangelist who had eluded him for the past several months be inviting *him* to a meeting?

"OK. When would you like to meet?"

"Tonight at seven," she said.

After hanging up, Ling met with one of the brothers she knew she could trust. She explained the situation to him and asked if he would accompany her to the hotel and wait outside. "If I do not come out, then you will know I have been arrested."

At 6:50 p.m. Ling and the brother stood near the hotel, watching and waiting but hidden from view. They saw the commissioner; he was accompanied by a group of officers. Ling's heart skipped a beat; she was ready to walk away when she noticed that only the commissioner went inside the hotel while the other officers waited out front. Entering from the back of the hotel, Ling joined the commissioner in the restaurant.

"Ling. So good to see you," he said warmly, as though they were, indeed, old friends. "But aren't you afraid I will arrest you?"

"If I was afraid, I wouldn't be here. But here I am."

They both ordered, and Ling instructed the waiter that she would be paying. Then she got down to business. "What are you doing with my friends? You've released the others with fines. If you want money, I will give you money. How much do you want?"

"Slow down, Ling!" said the commissioner. "We haven't even eaten yet. Besides, there is nothing I can do for them, and that is *your* fault. You are the one who made this a public spectacle."

Ling knew he was trying to intimidate her, and she refused to back down. But she was willing to try other tactics. They spoke over dinner for another two hours, and Ling slipped in statements about her beliefs; she explained why she and the imprisoned pastors were so passionate about sharing the message of Jesus Christ. The commissioner listened respectfully, seeing the concern in Ling's eyes for her friends, but it was futile. He refused to offer her any hope that they might be released.

Ling ran her fingers through her black hair. It was finally growing back. She remembered her mother's prayer about being a sacrifice, and she recited from memory the Scripture passage that had brought her this far: *"The harvest is truly great . . . the laborers are few . . . lambs among wolves."*

Ling wondered if it was time to go back to the school of suffering.

BACK TO SCHOOL

As the commissioner finished his meal, Ling knew her time was running out. She was aware of the officers waiting outside the

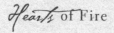

door of the hotel. She made a final offer. "Well, you have been looking for me, and here I am. Take me, and let my friends go."

The commissioner cocked his head and smiled ever so slightly. "Ling," he said sincerely, "you're surely one of the most unique women I have ever met."

Then, without another word, he stood up and left the restaurant.

Ling sat quietly for a few minutes, feeling that she had failed. Her heart was heavy, and she returned to her home with a sense of despair. She knew it would not go well for her co-workers—her friends—who remained in custody.

As time went by, Ling learned that two more Christian workers had been arrested, and the leaders who were still incarcerated had been turned over to the authorities from their local districts, where they were severely tortured. Their sentences ranged from twelve to twenty-four months of hard labor.

Ling continued her work, feeling a deep sense of loneliness. She was still quite ill from the last prison term, and seeing her declining health, many of the other leaders encouraged her to back away from her responsibilities. But she refused, remembering how much her mother had encouraged her and how hard her mother had worked on the soybean grinder so Ling could go about her ministry. She missed her mother. It had been years since she had seen her. But it was just too dangerous to visit her now.

Ling remained the sole woman among the group of leaders, and she often found herself crying alone in her room, asking God to give her the strength to finish her course.

On April 16, 2002, Ling's phone rang again. Thirty Christians from her group had been kidnapped by a fanatical Chinese cult. Ling called her "friend" at the police station. Back to work . . .

EPILOGUE

Ling continues to live a difficult life, but the rewards of her work are readily apparent. Through her "arranged" meeting with the commissioner, God opened a door for her to speak out on behalf of the injustices inflicted on Chinese house-church Christians. But, at the same time, her contact with the authorities has also brought about more controversy, and many Christians have strongly opposed what she is doing. In response to their criticism, Ling replies, "We may be Christians, but we are still Chinese, and this is still our country."

Ling has never compromised her views or shrunk back from her evangelical activities. Neither has she let fear or risk of imprisonment prevent her from taking every opportunity to boldly stand for her brothers and sisters. She remains on a government watch list, but she's also on God's watch list, and He has miraculously protected her and kept her from going back to prison.

But Ling is ready to go back if that becomes necessary. "I'm ready to go back to school," she says. "I know if God counts the hairs of my head, he will have His way with me, and I will remain in His will."

Another challenge for Ling has come from her commitment to remain single until the church leadership is firmly in place. The group estimated it would be a ten-year commitment, and Ling assumed she would have plenty of time to marry after that. (She was only a teenager at that time.) However, in China it is very difficult for a single woman after age thirty—an age group Ling now belonged to.

She has been told repeatedly (even by pastors of house churches she has helped establish) that a woman's position is in the home, cleaning, cooking, and taking care of the children. Ling doesn't deny this vital role, but she also knows God sometimes has different plans from those that are expected. She reminds her critics that, during the initial growth of the house-church movement, it was women who took on the dangerous work of evangelism. She also points out that, as many Chinese leaders are aware, two-thirds of the evangelistic teams that were sent into the remote areas of China were women.

Ling now has a vision for the International Olympics, which is coming to Beijing in 2008. She believes this will be an incredible opportunity for the house churches to grow and flourish.

Back to work . . .

Gladys:
A Lifeline of Forgiveness

India
November 1981

It was a warm, humid day when thirty-year-old Gladys Weatherhead arrived in the district of Mayurbhanj, about 110 miles southwest of Calcutta in the state of Orissa, which borders the Bay of Bengal. *I can't believe I'm really here*, she thought as her senses took in every sight and sound. The pungent aroma of chilies drifting through the open windows of homes and shops mixed with the putrid smells arising from piles of trash, open sewers, and the sacred cows that freely roamed the streets. The heat accentuated the smells, but Gladys was glad to be back in a warmer climate after the chilly air in the north.

Driving down from the Pakistani border had been an experience in faith for Gladys as her driver zigzagged in and out of traffic, dodging trucks, rickshaws, taxis, cows, bicycles, and a never-ending throng of people, all crowding the streets in an disorderly mass of chaos. Having grown up in a quiet rural town in Australia, Gladys was completely amazed that such chaos seemed to be accepted as an everyday part of life in India.

She had watched the swirling scene below her hotel window with nervous apprehension, holding her breath each time a mother with children in tow stepped out into the unrelenting traffic, and she said a silent prayer whenever she saw ladies riding "sidewinder" on the backs of motor scooters, clutching their packages instead of holding on to the driver. They often came within inches of swaying buses or trucks in the jam-packed streets.

India's total population was nearing one billion, and Gladys was astounded at the sheer numbers of people that seemed to be absolutely everywhere. She marveled at the variety of people now surrounding her on the street: barefoot children with dirty faces, mothers dressed in brightly colored saris with the traditional Hindu marking on their foreheads, old men with skin resembling parched leather, every single one God's creation.

Gladys loved what she was experiencing. After twelve years of frequent discouragement, she was finally realizing her dream and heeding God's call upon her life: to serve the poor in a foreign land. She had often wondered if this day would ever come . . .

Drawn to a Life of Service

Gladys was only eighteen when she had attended a Christian missions conference in her native Australia and answered God's call to mission work. Growing up on a farm in Queensland, Gladys had heard a lot of sermons in church, and she had even met several missionaries her parents had invited into their home. Every Saturday afternoon Gladys's mother gathered all the children around her and read missionary stories to them. Africa, India, China . . . Gladys was fascinated by the exciting stories of life in far-off places, and she had admired the missionaries' commitment.

With this strong emphasis on mission work in her background, Gladys shouldn't have been surprised that the missions conference affected her so dramatically, but she was. There was no doubt in her mind that God was drawing her to a life of service on a foreign field; she knew the moment when something in her heart felt different. She was beginning to understand the reason missionaries had such passion for their work.

Throughout her twenties, Gladys filtered every decision through her commitment to being a missionary someday. She completed nurses' training, an obvious choice for a foreign aid worker, and she did her best to keep any potential boyfriends at bay if they didn't feel the same call to foreign work. That part was harder, but Gladys knew God wouldn't want her to get involved with a man if it meant losing her focus. She excelled in her career and eventually earned a leadership position in a small clinic. She also taught Sunday school and helped out in the church wherever she could.

Gladys was especially energized each time a Christian humanitarian worker visited their small congregation; she hung on to every word of the presentation while envisioning what it would be like for her someday. She wondered if she would ever have to do any public speaking; that part of being a missionary wasn't so exciting—it was frightening. Not because Gladys was all that shy, but because she simply didn't believe God had gifted her in that fashion. *I will be content demonstrating God's love in a practical fashion, with my nursing abilities,* she told herself.

By 1980, Gladys was twenty-nine and beginning to wonder if she would ever realize her dream. Deep in her heart, she had confidence that God was in control and that all things happened according to His time. But her mind was full of questions, and she fought the internal struggle to go in a different direction and marry. She wasn't getting any younger, and in their testimonies, many of the foreign workers revealed how God had placed them in the field in their early twenties or even their late teens. Meanwhile many of Gladys's colleagues were getting married and having children; watching them delight in their growing families made it increasingly difficult for Gladys to hold on to her dream of ministering to the poor in a foreign country.

Later that year Gladys met Mike Hey, a worker in Operation Mobilization. He had been active in India for a couple of years, and she was immediately struck by his enthusiasm. In her restlessness she pelted him with questions about OM's work in India: "What are the people like? Are you able to preach to them openly? How receptive are they? How does OM operate? Where do you get support?"

Mike smiled, sensing her rising excitement as he patiently tried to answer all her questions.

Maybe this is it, Gladys thought. *Maybe this is the answer to all my years of waiting!* Over the next few weeks, Gladys pored over every piece of literature about Operation Mobilization. She learned that a two-year commitment was required and that each person was to seek God's guidance on which country to serve in. As she continued to understand the character of OM and the deep level of commitment of its workers and leadership, she knew this was the organization for her. She felt an inner peace and set about arranging a term with OM.

By May 1981, Gladys was ready to leave Australia for the first time in her life. She still had no idea where she would work her two-year stint, but she was off to spend the summer in Europe for orientation and training. Her heart was full of eager expectation as she said her good-byes to family and friends. The idea of working in India stuck with her as she replayed her encounter with the enthusiastic missionary Mike Hey, but she wanted to remain completely open to whatever God had in mind. On the eve of her departure, her family gathered around her and sang one of their favorite hymns, "Because He Lives."

"I *can* face tomorrow," Gladys told them when the song was finished, "because I know He holds my future."

That summer in Europe was a real learning experience for Gladys, and she absorbed it all with the same spirit of commitment that had led her there. Sleeping on cold floors, bathing once a week, cleaning the toilets in the dorms, ministering to the Asian population in England, and seeking God's direction about where she was to go after the summer term were all part of training for the foreign field. Gladys met every challenge with a tenacious sense of purpose as she continued to dream of India. She didn't know much about the country or its people, but the curiosity and drive that grew within her wouldn't let up.

Near the end of the summer session, Gladys was sharing a meal with a couple who had coordinated the ministry teams in England. They asked her where she was going on her long-term program.

Gladys explained that she had applied to OM's ships ministry and also to its India teams. "I'm really not completely sure which direction to go at this point," she said. "I just want to go where God can use me most."

"Gladys, you're an older person," the wife said gently. Gladys perked up at being labeled "older." She might have started her foreign work later than most, but she was still only thirty. Seeing her puzzled look, the woman smiled and hurried to explain. "No, no. You're not an *old* person. You're just *older* and more mature than most of the new OM workers. You've had more Bible and leadership training and a lot of experience in life. India *needs* people like you."

Gladys smiled and thanked God for the woman's words of wisdom and encouragement. It was basically the same advice Mike Hey had given her, and now she felt the overwhelming reassurance and confirmation she had been praying for. The words to the song that had become her life's theme flooded through her mind: "I know He holds my future, and life is worth the living just because He lives."

THE LEPROSY HOME

She was en route to her first OM station in Cuttack, India, when her driver asked to make a side trip. Distracted by the endless crowds of men, women, and children flocking the busy road, she hadn't really been listening to the driver until she heard him say, ". . . at the Mayurbhanj Leprosy Home. You don't mind, do you, Gladys? We won't be there long."

At the leprosy facility, her driver met with a tall, handsome Australian aid worker named Graham Staines. Gladys had heard there were other Australians working in the area but didn't recognize any of their names. Graham escorted Gladys into the mission house, where she waited alone while the two men conducted their business.

Looking around her and then browsing through a little booklet about the home's first worker, Kate Allenby, Gladys was completely taken in by the home's intriguing history. The seventy-year-old bungalow had a peaceful feel to it, Gladys noted. Every part of the single-story structure defied its age, from the cool, concrete floors to the eighteen-inch-thick walls covered by layers upon layers of whitewash, to the sweeping veranda that helped shade the interior from the unyielding heat.

While she waited, Gladys wondered why Graham's wife hadn't come out to offer her some tea, as she had quickly learned was the

Indian tradition. But no wife appeared, and soon Gladys and the driver were off again, headed south to Cuttack.

Life with the OM teams the first few months was hectic and wonderful as Gladys attempted to learn the local ways and customs. She had spent her first six weeks in Cuttack with a group of indigenous relief workers. The six women lived in two small rooms with boxes of literature stacked everywhere, food that was incessantly yellow, water that came in buckets, and a toilet system that was nothing more than a cement slab with a hole in it. Gladys thanked God she had grown up on a farm and knew the value of hard work, but some days she became discouraged as she fought to maintain her positive "whatever-God-has-for-me" attitude.

Every day they went out in pairs and tried to sell Christian books door-to-door and talk to people about the Lord. Gladys loved visiting with the city people, but her heart longed to get out into the remote Santhal villages that peppered the mountains north and west of Baripada. They had passed by some of these villages on her first trip through the countryside. The straight, mud-walled huts with thatched roofs stood very close to the road and were surrounded by trees. A hand-dug pond was adjacent to the village homes.

She had been told of the Santhal traditions and spirit worship, how they even sacrificed people sometimes to please the spirits. Their living conditions were primitive at best, and children died at an alarming rate from illnesses that were easily preventable and curable by modern standards. Santhal families spent their money buying incense to burn and animals to sacrifice in their vain attempts to appease the spirits and save their children.

As a nurse, Gladys knew these people could be helped with a little basic education, and as a Christian, she knew Jesus could offer them even greater healing, freeing them from their terrible bondages to their spirit gods. Something powerful gripped her as she considered their plight, and she longed to get out among these villagers and bring them the good news that burned in her heart.

In January 1982 Gladys got her chance. Her next team assignment included visiting several villages, where the missionaries participated in "jungle camps" hosted by the local Christians. One of the villages they visited was a seven-mile walk through rough, mountainous terrain, but Gladys's heart was overjoyed to be there. She enthusiastically participated in all the local ways, pulling water from the well, bathing in the river, and sleeping among the bedbugs. The local women loved being with the tall, fair-skinned Australian nurse, and they eagerly taught Gladys about their simple way of life.

LOVE FOR THE LOWEST OF THE LOW

The village wasn't too far away from the Mayurbhanj Leprosy Home, and Gladys had a few opportunities to see Graham, who she learned had never been married. Most of their meetings concerned mission business, but Gladys could sense her growing attraction toward Graham, even though she tried to put her feelings aside and focus on the work at hand.

Then she was sent off to her next assignment. Gladys was thankful for the opportunity to see so much of India as she traveled from place to place with the OM teams, but seeing the leprosy home and living with the Santhal people had left a profound impact on her. Seeing the way Graham and the others cared for their patients—leprosy sufferers and outcasts from the villages—was overwhelming. Hinduism made the poor leprosy sufferers believe sins from past lives had caused them to have the disease. They'd been told they were not worthy of even a simple cup of water. As a result, those afflicted with leprosy lived out their lives in a miserable state of existence, begging on the streets and being permanently banished from their homes and families. There were none lower than those afflicted with leprosy, and no one offered them more love than Graham did.

Sufferers who came to the leprosy home were given medicines that stopped the disease from causing further damage, and they were shown love and compassion by the staff, who taught them that the disease was curable and that it was not a curse from God. Gladys was amazed at the transformation she saw in many of the patients just from feeling a compassionate human touch and hearing a few words of love. The medicine did its part to help their sores, but the staff's compassion treated their soul.

Gladys was fascinated by the work being done at the home, but she sometimes questioned her motives. Was she attracted to Graham, or to the mission there? Although she *was* developing affectionate feelings for him, she knew he was not her purpose for being in India. Besides, she had no way of knowing if Graham had any similar feelings for her. *And what if he did?* she mused. He would still have to speak to the OM leaders about it before any kind of relationship could begin. That was the rule.

By early spring, Gladys didn't have to wonder anymore about Graham's intentions. She received word that Graham had asked her OM leaders for permission to begin corresponding with her, and she was thrilled! Over the spring and summer they got to know each other as letters flew back and forth. They were amazed to learn how much they had in common. They had grown up just forty miles from each other and had similar backgrounds, and both had been called to missions at a young age. The more they corresponded, the more they realized that God was definitely bringing them together. They were married in Australia on August 6, 1983, before a delighted crowd of family and friends.

Back at the leprosy home, everyone was thrilled for Graham

and his bride. "Dada," as he was affectionately known among the locals, had served faithfully and tirelessly in Mayurbhanj for nearly twenty years, and now God had richly rewarded him with a wonderful wife who loved God with equal fervor and shared his passion for the Indian people. To the residents of the village and the patients in the compound, Graham and Gladys's marriage was an amazing testimony of God's love, and they all waited eagerly for Mr. and Mrs. Staines to return from Australia.

But it wouldn't be that easy. Gladys and Graham were to face their first trial as a couple when the Indian government refused to issue Gladys a new visa. It seemed inexplicable, but the officials simply refused to let her come back. Finally they decided Graham would return without her and attempt to work on the visa from within India.

It took several months and a lot of prayer before the government agreed to let Gladys join Graham, but still, they gave her a visa only as Graham's wife, not as a foreign aid worker. She had to promise not to proselytize or attempt to convert Hindus to Christianity. She agreed. After all, Gladys and Graham knew they could never force anyone to Christ anyway. Their main goal was to show God's love by working among the leprosy patients, and if those persons chose to respond to that love, then it was their own choice.

THE DESIRES OF THE HEART

Gladys arrived back in Baripada late in 1984 to a grateful and relieved Graham. She was excited to be back with her husband, and she quickly settled into her new role of wife and manager. She sorely missed being able to go out into the villages as she used to, but she accepted her new role with the same easygoing attitude that had seen her through so many changes in the past.

She took as her motto the Scripture verse that hung on the wall

of the beautiful old mission bungalow: "Delight yourself . . . in the
LORD, and He shall give you the desires of your heart."[1] She loved
working around her new home and helping with the leprosy
patients. She especially loved the trips she and Graham occasionally made to visit the Santhal churches, where she could enjoy a
Sunday service and encourage the women.

In 1985 Gladys and Graham welcomed their first child,
Esther Joy, who was followed by two brothers, Phillip in 1988 and
Timothy in 1992. Gladys loved mothering her little clan, and she
found it opened up a whole new area of ministry as her children
grew and played with the children in the community.

SURRENDERING EVERYTHING TO GOD

Throughout the 1990s Gladys and Graham continued to work
faithfully among the leprosy sufferers and the Santhal communities. Gladys loved taking her kids out to the villages to play with
the Santhal children, and her kids loved going with their father to
the different jungle camps, the five-day annual conferences held
by local pastors. Graham attended to assist the pastors in teaching
and preaching.

Gladys and Graham knew that many of the Santhal villagers
continually faced persecution for their Christian beliefs. They
always tried to remain sensitive to the villagers' needs, and they
prayed for wisdom in all their dealings with them. Graham never
went into the villages to convert or convince anyone to change
faiths. Instead he supported the local pastors and churches that
God had established. Nevertheless, the Santhal Christians did
face opposition, and they were often accused of converting to
Christianity because of coercion or because they accepted money
from the foreigners.

One twelve-year-old boy was attacked for being a Christian.

When he climbed a tree to look for his cattle, other boys from the villages, furious that he had converted to Christianity, surrounded the tree and wouldn't let him down. After taunting and mocking him for his faith, they drove a stick up his backside until he died. His widowed mother was devastated.

A group of Hindus stoned and then drowned another young boy because of his faith. And apart from the physical attacks, Christians had to put up with daily harassment from the locals. Their property was sometimes stolen or vandalized, or they were prevented from working their land or taking water from the village well. Year after year, the reports of persecution kept coming in, but Gladys and Graham had not received any threats themselves, and they never worried that they might be a target for the fanatics. Gladys reasoned, "We minister to people afflicted with leprosy. How threatening is that?"

On a calm Thursday morning in January 1999, Gladys was enjoying her quiet time and reading her daily devotional. The story for that day's reading was about a twelve-year-old girl who was losing her sight. When the girl's pastor came to visit her in the hospital, she told him, "Pastor, God is taking away my sight."

For a while the pastor remained silent. Then he said, "Jessie, don't let Him take it."

The girl was puzzled, and then the wise pastor continued. "*Give* it to Him," he said.

The story struck a chord in Gladys as she felt the Lord asking her whether she was willing to give up all that she loved—her husband, her children, all her possessions—for Him. As her heart wrestled with the question, tears rolled down her cheeks. She had given her heart to Christ when she was only thirteen, and from that day on she had tried to live solely for Him. She had held nothing back when she came to India, and she and Graham had poured out their lives in service and surrender. She thought she had given God everything, but in her heart she knew her temptation was to hold on tightly to the things and dear ones she loved most.

Finally she prayed, giving God the answer she knew He deserved. "Yes, Lord Jesus. Yes, I am willing. Take all that I have for Your use—my husband, my children, everything that I have. I surrender everything to You." As she said amen, she felt the comfort of the Holy Spirit surrounding and infusing her as she remembered the story of Abraham offering his son, Isaac, to God. She had no idea what lay ahead for her family, but she was confident God would be with them.

The following week, Graham was heading out to the village of Manoharpur to attend another jungle camp. He was especially excited to be taking ten-year-old Phillip and six-year-old Timothy along with him, and the boys were equally thrilled. They loved going out to the camps. It was like an adventure, camping in the Jeep and "roughing it" with no electricity or running water. But mostly they just loved spending time with their dad. The Christmas holidays had been hectic, with a constant flow of visitors, and Gladys knew it would be good for the boys to spend some one-on-one time with Graham. The four-hour drive would give them some uninterrupted time to talk.

Thirteen-year-old Esther had two girlfriends visiting her from her boarding school, so she was content to stay home and relax with her friends and with Mom.

On Wednesday, January 20, Gladys was rushing around, trying to get everyone organized and out the door. "Phil, have you finished packing?" she called to her eldest son. He was so practical and handy, just like his dad, and he was a wonderful "people person," always sensitive to others' feelings. Gladys was proud of the way he was so loving toward everyone. She could hardly believe he was going to be eleven years old in just a couple of months. They were always so busy that some days it seemed as though her children's lives were rushing past her without time to fully enjoy them.

"Boys, it's time to go," Graham called. Gladys scooted the boys out to the Jeep where their dad was now waiting. She gave both boys a kiss and a squeeze then turned to Graham for the same. They always made time for a proper good-bye because they never knew what might happen, especially in the crazy Indian traffic. Gladys knew that Tim was a little nervous about this road trip because of a car accident he'd been in last November. He had been thrown forward in the vehicle and wasn't seriously injured but was quite shaken up. Then, just a couple of weeks ago, he'd been in another close call as a big truck cut too close to the Jeep on a mountain pass. Gladys understood Tim's apprehension about the car trip, and she tried to reassure him before they took off.

"Have a great time! I'll see you on Monday," she called as they pulled away.

As she turned back toward the bungalow she remembered she hadn't checked Phil's bag. *I hope he remembered to pack his jacket,* she thought wistfully.

Then her thoughts turned to Tim. He had been suffering from a cold, and Gladys had packed a few extra clothes for him, knowing how chilly it could get in the mountains. She smiled, hoping Tim didn't strain his voice too much with all the singing. He was the singer and the preacher in the house. He loved to preach like his dad, and Gladys sometimes found him setting up the chairs in the living room to play church. It had been awhile, though, since he'd played the game. Then, on Monday, Gladys had walked by the living room, and there was Tim preaching and singing with gusto to the empty chairs lined up for his imaginary congregation.

She had intended to sit and listen to him as soon as she finished what she was doing, but when she came back, he had gone on to some other activity.

She had no way of knowing it would be the last time Tim would play church.

The phone rang at four thirty in the morning on Saturday, January 23. Stumbling out of bed through the darkness, she sleepily lifted the phone to her ear. She listened awhile, trying to calm the fear that swept down her spine like an icy spear. Esther and her friends, awakened by the telephone, appeared in the doorway as Gladys hung up.

"Mom, what's up?" asked Esther.

"Someone burned the mission Jeeps," Gladys replied. "I don't know anything else, so let's try not to worry. We'll pray, and then you girls try to get some more sleep. I'm sure everyone is fine, and you know we have a busy day ahead. I'll let you know the details when I hear them."

Those details, when they came, would be more gruesome than Gladys could ever have imagined . . .

THE SMOLDERING FURY

The tiny village of Manoharpur had been culturally divided for some time. Over the years, 22 of the village's approximately 150 families had converted to Christianity. For the most part, the two groups had lived in peaceful coexistence, but lately the tribe had become increasingly irritated with the Christians.

By summer 1998 the tension had erupted when some Christian farmers infuriated the local tribesmen by continuing to work the land during the Raja festival, the time the Santhals believe the earth is menstruating. The heated exchanges between the Christians and the traditional Santhals had eventually been quelled, but the feelings remained tense. Then, just a few weeks before the jungle camp Graham and his sons attended, another incident had occurred when the tribesmen objected to Santhali

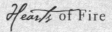

Christian music being played at a Christian marriage in the village. The tribe was known for guarding its traditions quite zealously, so this cultural separation incensed the more traditional members and fueled their smoldering fury.

Graham's arrival in the village gave the enraged Santhals the opportunity they had been waiting for. Now they could get even with those who had dared go against the traditional customs. They enlisted the help of Dara Singh, a social activist and religious zealot who was masterful at exploiting societal frustrations. His activism usually took the form of violence as he lashed out against Christians and Muslims alike.

In the early morning hours of January 23, his lurid activism reached new heights of outrage.

The previous evening, Graham and the boys had just finished eating and were saying good night to their co-workers. It was around nine thirty when the trio climbed into the back of their Jeep and settled in to sleep. The night air was frigid, and Graham had carefully placed straw mats on top of the vehicle to help keep them warm. He always tried to make the boys as comfortable as possible and always prayed with them before lying down beside them.

The Jeep was parked alongside another Jeep in front of the prayer hall, and one of Graham's friends, Dr. Ghosh, was sleeping nearby in the home of a Christian family. Around midnight, awakened by shouts and screaming, he jumped out of bed and raced to the window. He was horrified to see a large mob running across the fields—men armed with axes, sticks, and knives, and holding torches above their heads as they made a beeline for the two Jeeps. Angrily shouting, the madmen viciously attacked Graham's Jeep, slashing the tires and breaking the windows. They beat the startled occupants of the vehicle and slashed them with their weapons as Graham tried in vain to protect his two precious boys.

Dr. Ghosh ran to his door, only to find it blocked from the outside. Trapped, he could only watch in agony as the horrendous events unfolded before him.

The frenzied crowd showed no mercy for Graham and the boys. There was no escape from the brutal onslaught. The mob had also placed a number of guards at each of the huts around the complex to prevent anyone from assisting the victims, and now they screamed at the helpless villagers, "Don't come out, or we will kill you, too!"

Hasda, Graham's co-worker for more than twenty years, cried out in anguish for the ruthless attack to stop. He watched in horror as the assailants put straw under the Jeep; Dara Singh was the first to set it on fire. When Hasda rushed in to try to douse the flames with water, he was brutally beaten. The heartless mob stood and watched while Graham, Phillip, and Timothy screamed in agony until the flames ended their cries and turned their bodies into ashes.

As the violence was erupting, just one hundred yards away a group of Santhal youth performed a traditional Dangri dance to the rhythmic beating of drums, acting as though nothing out of the ordinary were happening.

After an hour, the mob disappeared back into the fields. A frantic Hasda, having been chased away earlier by the gang, had gone to the village chief for help. A messenger was sent to inform the police fifteen miles away in another village. But it was too late. When Hasda returned to the scene, he was overcome with grief as he spotted the burned-out shell of Graham's Jeep. Inside he could clearly see the three charred bodies locked tightly together in a final embrace. He knew it was an image that would remain with him for a lifetime.

As the terrified Christians emerged from their huts and gathered around the gruesome scene, they stood for a moment in shocked silence. Inwardly they all wondered the same thing. *How are we going to tell Gladys and Esther?*

A Tidal Wave of Grief

At seven Gladys was dressing and preparing for another busy day when the phone rang for the second time that morning. It was a reporter asking Graham's and the boys' ages.

"What are you talking about?" Gladys asked.

Realizing she didn't know what had happened, and not wanting to be the one who told her, the reporter said good-bye and hung up. But the phone kept ringing as questions poured in from people in neighboring villages. "Gladys, they say that Graham and the boys are missing," one friend told her.

"Missing? Oh, my God!" Gladys exclaimed. "What's happening to my precious boys? Are they out there alone?"

Finally her friend Gayathri came over and took charge of the phone. But things got progressively crazier, and Gladys still didn't really know what had happened. Her heart was in turmoil, but she expected Graham and the boys to walk through the door at any moment. Her mind simply blocked out the possibility that anything really bad could have happened, and she remained optimistic that they would be coming home soon.

Over the next couple of hours, friends started coming around, and more reporters showed up wanting to take pictures. Dozens of people were there — inside, outside, on the veranda, everywhere. It was all very chaotic, and Gladys stayed busy greeting the visitors and tending to Esther. She still didn't understand the depth of what had happened, and no one knew exactly how to tell her the terrible news.

Finally, around nine thirty, Gayathri took her hand and said, "Gladys, I need to talk to you." Clearing one of the rooms and pulling Gladys inside, Gayathri said, "Gladys, I don't want you to be like a stone, but you need to be strong for Esther."

Gladys heard the news in disbelief. Her mind wanted to deny the reality of what her friend was telling her, but there it was. The words were out, and they could never be taken back. *No!* her mind screamed. *It can't be true! They couldn't have been in the Jeep. There's been a mistake. They couldn't have been—they weren't—burned alive. How could such a thing happen? Who could possibly find it in themselves to do such an evil act?*

A tidal wave of grief threatened to swallow her up, but Gladys had to question her friend just once more. Maybe she was mistaken. Maybe the news was wrong . . .

"Gayathri . . . do you mean they are . . . dead? Graham and Phillip and Timothy—they're really gone?"

Gayathri's mournful eyes told her it was no mistake, and Gladys sat down in defeat. "How am I going to tell Esther?" she moaned.

Time stopped, but life went on. The next few minutes passed in muted misery as Gladys prepared herself to share the overwhelming news with Esther. The phone was ringing; people were calling from Australia wanting to know what had happened. More friends and neighbors came to the house to share in the grieving, flashes from the cameras of the reporters were still going off, but Gladys could think only of her daughter.

"Mommy, what is the news?" Esther asked.

Gladys took her daughter's hands in her own and looked into her innocent eyes. "It seems that we have been left alone," she gently told her daughter. Then, without a moment of fore-thought, she added, "But we will forgive them."

"Yes, Mommy, we will."

Esther's eyes glazed over as the shock settled over her. Gladys held her tight and tried to comprehend the evil deed that had changed their lives so quickly and dramatically. Emotionally, she was numbed by the reality of the situation, but the constant flow of activity helped keep her together. Finally the local doctor's son approached Gladys and quietly said, "They want to know what to do with the bodies."

The finality of his statement erased any lingering doubts that it might all be a horrible mistake.

"Bring them back to Baripada. Graham gave his life for this country. He would want to be buried here," she said.

Throughout the following week, Gladys dealt with visitors, reporters, and city officials. Finally Graham's co-workers arrived back from Manoharpur, and the details of the terrifying attack spilled out. Gladys learned that a number of the villagers had testified they saw a wide beam of bright light from above resting on the burning vehicle. She also learned of the horror of the Christians in the little encampment as they were prevented from helping, and of the bravery of their friend Hasda, who had tried to put out the fire.

She gradually realized this had not been a spontaneous incident carried out by drunken or frustrated villagers. It was, in fact, part of a larger conspiracy to strike a fatal blow to the Christian community, and the conspirators had chosen Graham as their target.

Poor Hasda was beside himself with grief. His parents had been residents of the leprosy home, and Hasda had been born there. Gladys knew he loved Graham and the boys deeply, and her heart cried out for him.

FATHER, FORGIVE THEM . . .

The funeral was held Monday morning at ten, the same time Graham and the boys were supposed to have returned home from the jungle camp. The three coffins arrived, covered with flowers, and soon it seemed as if all of Baripada had come to a halt. Stores and schools were closed, and many city officials came to pay their respects to Graham and the boys. Gladys and Esther stunned the crowd of nearly a thousand guests by choosing to sit on the grass with the leprosy home residents, who were overcome with grief for their lost "Dada." The traditional Indian service seemed to be divinely orchestrated as many mourners spontaneously shared condolences or Scripture verses. Gladys was urged to say a few words, but she wasn't prepared to stand and speak to the massive crowd. Instead, she asked Esther, "Would you be able to stand and sing with me?"

Esther agreed, and the crowd fell silent as Gladys and her daughter made their way to the platform. There they sang the song that had carried Gladys for so many years.

"Because He lives I can face tomorrow . . ." Despite her confidence as she sang the hymn with Esther, in reality Gladys was mentally singing, *Because He lives I can face today.* The truth was, she could face the future only one moment at a time. But that would be enough to carry her through so that, over time, her life became a testimony of unwavering faith in the midst of tragedy. Although she was grief stricken and emotionally exhausted, deep within herself, Gladys was at peace, and she wanted to show the world she was honored that her husband and children were martyred for Christ.

In a statement to the press, a brave Esther said, "I'm thankful that God allowed them to suffer for His sake," and Gladys reiterated Esther's sentiment with her own statement: "I truly pray, 'Father forgive them, for they know not what they are doing.' And I believe all things work together for good to them that love God, to them who are called according to His purpose. Surely, through this incident, God is going to accomplish His eternal purpose. Praise be to His name."[2]

Many friends and family members began urging Gladys to pack up and return, with Esther, to the relative safety of Australia. They assumed that work at the leprosy home would cease unless Gladys could find someone else to take Graham's place. They also asked a myriad of questions: "Are you going to take the bodies back to Australia? What will you and Esther do now? What about the leprosy home?"

She was surprised at their assumptions. She had made India her home and never considered leaving. When reporters asked her about the future, she answered, "My God is in control of all situations and circumstances. He will do only good. He is my strength and stay. He has promised 'never to leave me or forsake me.'[3] I will serve India with this hope."

FORGIVENESS BRINGS HEALING

Two months later, Gladys prepared to accept the Indo-Australian Award being presented in honor of Graham. She had been asked to speak during the ceremony, and more than three hundred people had packed the small auditorium after news went out that Gladys would be there. It was the first time she had agreed to speak publicly since Graham and the boys were martyred. A large number of police officers were also nearby for Gladys's protection.

As she prepared to address the crowd, Gladys sat silently reading over the old poem by Annie Johnson Flint that had recently given her strength:

> He giveth more grace as our burdens grow greater,
> He sendeth more strength as our labors increase;
> To added affliction He addeth His mercy,
> To multiplied trials He multiplies peace.

His love has no limits, His grace has no measure,
His power no boundary known unto men;
For out of His infinite riches in Jesus
He giveth, and giveth, and giveth again.

She finished the last line as the master of ceremonies finished her introduction.

Gladys approached the platform and simply began by noting how easily compassion had come to Graham. "If someone was sick, he was there," she said. "It might be late in the evening or early in the morning. It didn't matter. Graham didn't have to think about what to do for someone in need. He simply acted."

She finished her remarks and accepted the award, then she was invited to stay for the dinner. No one left; everyone there wanted to greet the courageous widow who didn't have an evil word to say about those who had viciously killed her husband and two boys. As they lined up for dinner, one woman said to Gladys, "I don't know how you could ever forgive."

Without thinking Gladys replied, "You have to forgive. Forgiveness brings healing."

Gladys hadn't even realized the truth until the words came out. She had forgiven her husband's and sons' murderers since the moment she heard the dreadful news. But forgiveness really had been the catalyst for healing, and she decided at that moment what her next message would be.

Speaking invitations poured in, and as Gladys was able, she accepted, always speaking of forgiveness. At each presentation she said, "Love must be sincere. We must honor one another as Romans 12 tells us: 'Bless those who persecute you; bless and do not curse. Rejoice with those who rejoice, and weep with those who weep. Be of the same mind toward one another. Do not set your mind on high things, but associate with the humble. Do not be wise in your own

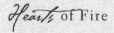

opinion. Repay no one evil for evil. Have regard for good things in the sight of all men. If it is possible, as much as depends on you, live peaceably with all men.'"[4]

Since her first public presentation at the awards ceremony, Gladys has been invited to countless schools, churches, and public events, at times speaking to as many as six meetings in a thirty-six-hour period. Today her convicting message serves as a constant reminder to a nation where violent attacks on Christians are increasing—and no one may be more qualified than Gladys Staines to deliver that message.

Epilogue

Gladys still lives at the Mayurbhanj Leprosy Home, but she has traveled around the globe speaking out about the persecutions in India and sharing her message of forgiveness. The nation of India has been shocked by the witness and the message of Christ's love coming from this most unlikely of messengers: a foreigner . . . a widow . . . a simple woman whose only goal is to serve the poor and the destitute.

It is unfortunate that it took the brutal murder of a Westerner and his two precious sons to get the nation's attention. But Gladys has faithfully served as God's mouthpiece, proving that He causes "all things to work together for good to those who love God."[5] In response to her messages, Gladys has received thousands of letters from people all over India, even Hindus, apologizing for the hateful crimes inflicted on her family.

She has learned firsthand the power of forgiveness, and she knows it remains a crucial message, even for those within the church. At a women's retreat where Gladys was speaking, she was told of a ninety-year-old man who was waiting outside, insisting on meeting this woman who could forgive those who killed her family. When he finally got to speak with Gladys, he told her his daughter had died many years ago of possible medical neglect and he had never been able to forgive the doctor. Gladys ministered to him for some time, eventually leading him in a prayer of forgiveness.

One year after the attack, Dara Singh and fourteen others were arrested and charged with the murder of Graham, Phillip, and Timothy Staines. In June 2002, Gladys was asked to testify during the trial and endured the most difficult challenge she had known since learning of her husband's and sons' murder: facing the man responsible. It was her own test of continued forgiveness.

Singh's attorney, claiming his client's innocence, attempted to discredit Graham and claimed that he had carelessly set the Jeep on fire himself with a cooking stove. As the attorney continued to talk, Gladys looked at Dara Singh and then into her own heart. She asked God to help her show love and compassion and never to look upon him with hatred. At the time this book went to press, the trial was still ongoing.

We met Gladys and Esther in Calcutta, and before departing Gladys shared another poem that had been of great encouragement to her since the death of her husband and sons. Written by the late Edgar Guest, it is called "Safely Home."

> I am home in Heaven, dear ones;
> Oh so happy and so bright!
> There is perfect joy and beauty
> In this everlasting light.
>
> All the pain and grief is over,
> Every restless tossing passed;
> I am now at peace forever,
> Safely home in heaven at last.

Did you wonder I so calmly
Trod the valley of the shade?
Oh! But Jesus' love illumined
Every dark and fearful glade.

And He came Himself to meet me
In that way so hard to tread;
And with Jesus' arm to lean on
Could I have one doubt or dread?

Then you must not grieve so sorely,
For I love you dearly still:
Try to look beyond earth's shadows,
Pray to trust our Father's Will.

There is work still waiting for you,
So you must not idly stand
Do it now while life remaineth
You shall rest in Jesus' land.

When that work is all completed,
He will gently call you Home;
Oh, the rapture of that meeting,
Oh, the joy to see you come!

Mai:
Back to Vietnam . . .
to Preach the Gospel

Vietnam
November 1989

They smelled the ocean before they could see it. Mai followed her older brother Hong, almost matching his steps along the single-file trail. One more hill to climb. The salty air swirled their hair and lifted their spirits. Mai felt the excitement rising within her. Each step brought them closer to freedom!

Finally they crested the hill, and Mai saw the boat, a platform of rough-hewn, tar-coated lumber on which a tiny bamboo lean-to served as the "bridge." The boat looked like it would splinter into matchsticks if anyone gave it a kick. She stopped walking and grabbed Hong's hand to keep him from going farther.

"I can't get on that thing!" she told him, pulling his arm until he turned to face her. "We won't make it out of the harbor, let alone all the way to Hong Kong!"

"You have to go, Mai," Hong told her, turning back toward the water and pulling her after him. Mai scanned it again, feeling fear rise up within her. Other than the bamboo hut, the deck was clear and flat. Other Vietnamese refugees were climbing on board, some cautiously looking behind them, wondering if the Chinese police would choose this moment for a raid and return them all to Vietnam.

"I . . . I can't, Hong," she stammered. "I'm . . . I'm not ready for this."

"You weren't ready to sneak across the border into China either, and we did that. Now come on. We have to go. Don't you know how much Father gave up for this?"

Hong reached deep into his pocket and pulled out the tattered handkerchief. Unfolding it carefully and checking over his shoulder, he showed her again the two gold coins. Each weighed more than half an ounce, and each would purchase one boat ride to Hong Kong, their ticket to freedom.

"Do you know how long it took Father to save up this much?" he continued. "He has been waiting and planning for this day for years. He will never taste freedom himself, but he has purchased your way. Now get on the boat!"

"He didn't purchase it for me. It was Trung's ticket," Mai responded petulantly. Mai's other older brother had been Hong's intended travel companion. Mai's father had planned to send two sons to freedom, hoping they would profit and be able to help more of their brothers and sisters get out of Vietnam.

"It *was* Trung's ticket, yes. But you know his wife just had a baby. He can't very well leave now, so you are the lucky one. You'll be free in America or in Australia. You'll be able to get a better education. And someday you'll be rich!"

He was still holding Mai's hand, part leading her and part dragging her toward the boat.

"Where will we use the bathroom?" she whined. "There's no toilet on that thing."

"The bathroom will be all around us," Hong said with a mocking laugh. Finally he stopped walking and turned toward her. "This is our chance, Mai," he said. "This is what Father wanted for us, to get out of Vietnam. To be free. To get an education. To profit from our work. It made him sick to think of all his children spending their lives in poverty. And it would make him sick to see you hesitating. Now *come on!*"

They were at the dock now, and a scowling man looked at both of them, holding out his hand. Hong knew what he wanted—the pieces of gold. Placing the handkerchief in the man's hand, Hong pulled at one corner until the two coins spilled out. The captain looked at the coins closely, putting one in his mouth and biting down to test that it was real.

"Get on," he said with a grunt.

They did as he told them. How Mai wished she had hugged her mother one more time before they left! Or talked to her father a little longer. She wondered if the boat—she'd finally allowed herself to call it that—would actually take them where they wanted to go, and she quickly prayed to the spirit of her grandfather and great-grandfather for safety on the trip.

They chose a place near the front, to get away from the noise of the engine. Mai was already sick with anxiety and the motion of the waves before the boat pulled away from the dock. She cried as she watched the shoreline slowly disappearing on the horizon.

The days on the boat became an endless exercise in boredom, and Mai and Hong realized quickly they hadn't brought enough food for the lengthy trip. After they ran out, they had to beg food from some of the forty-three other passengers. The days dragged on and on, the sands of time seeming to fall only one grain at a time.

THE STORM

Mai came up again, bursting through the surface and spitting out the bitter salt water and gasping for air.

"Help me!" she cried, desperately scanning the darkness for the boat or for Hong or for anything or anyone. Another wave came crashing over her, and she desperately tried to grab a breath before her head was once again engulfed in foamy water.

Coming up for air again, she felt an arm around her. "Swim toward shore," a man's voice yelled into her ear. Mai recognized him as one of her fellow fugitives fleeing their homeland on the rickety boat. Together they swam. She looked back toward the oncoming waves, shouting a warning each time one was about to wash over them again. He kept his eyes focused on the shore.

Finally they could stand; they walked a few more steps and then fell, exhausted, onto the sand. Others from the boat were gathering on the beach too, shivering in the strong wind sweeping in off the water. Sand coated their wet clothes. Mai cried out with relief when she found Hong, and the two embraced. In the storm there was no way to start a fire, so they huddled together, trying in vain to get warm and desperately waiting for the sun to rise.

Mai wondered at the shocking turns her life was taking. A few days ago she had been a seventeen-year-old high-school student in northern Vietnam, living happily with her father and mother in a house with a red-tile roof near the Chinese border. Now she was huddled on a wind-swept beach in China, wondering if she would ever make it to Hong Kong and freedom.

Mai's father had always wanted his seven children to have a life that was better than his. Mai had heard his education speech so many times she could recite it by heart. But the speech had never included being shipwrecked . . .

Mai thought of her mother, laughing at her husband's ambitions for his children; she thought school was a waste of time and money. She controlled the family finances and refused to give the seven children money for books or school supplies. Often,

Mai's father would sell a chicken or some other animal and then slip a few bills to his children to cover another week's schooling. Whenever his wife discovered what he had done, the two would get into explosive arguments, screaming insults and shouting curses at each other. The children tried to stay out of the way of this bickering. Most importantly, they kept going to school.

One of Mai's older brothers had left Vietnam and worked for a time as a laborer in Bulgaria. He had seen the outside world, and his tales heightened their father's desire for his children to escape.

Now Mai was out of Vietnam, but not in the place her father had envisioned. She huddled on the beach, her blanket lost somewhere in the frothing sea. The storm had forced all the passengers to swim for shore. The captain stayed with the boat, pointing its nose into the waves and trying to ride out the gale. After what seemed an eternity, the winds calmed, and the sun finally rose up out of the water. Mai had never been so thankful to see the dawning of a new day.

The refugees huddled on the beach until the captain waved for them to come back to the boat. They swam through the surf to climb back aboard their floating freedom train. The deck had been swept clean by the storm. Their extra clothing, blankets, food, and pots and pans—everything had been swept away. Mai and Hong hunkered down, hoping there were no more storms between them and Hong Kong. They wondered if the boat would still float once all the passengers were back on board.

Forty-two endless days after boarding the boat, they arrived in Hong Kong. But they were not welcome there; the police would not allow the refugees to unload. Instead, they were sent to Cow Island, an uninviting strip of land where farmers raised cows. Finally Mai, Hong, and the others could get off the boat, but what awaited them was almost as unpleasant as what they were leaving. Nearly a hundred boats like theirs unloaded every day at

Cow Island. Humanitarian aid groups handed out cans of food, but Mai wasn't used to that kind of food, and she got sick after every meal.

LIFE IN THE CAMPS

One week after they landed on Cow Island, Mai and Hong were transferred to their first refugee camp. A month later, they were transferred again, this time to Camp Nine. About a year later they were sent to Camp Three.

With their arrival at each new camp, they had to find a place to sleep and to live. Many of the camp residents were brutally territorial, and Mai and Hong had to constantly watch out for each other and guard against those who would attack them. Camp Three was especially violent, a virtual battle zone. Refugees from the same areas of Vietnam banded together and fought against those from different areas. Everything in the camp—bricks, light bulbs, electrical cables, parts of beds, and sharpened steel bars—became weapons. Sometimes the battles went on for days, with different groups trying to control the camp. The Hong Kong police couldn't control the camps, so life inside the fences was ruled by Darwinian anarchy.

During the battles, women and children hid, trying to stay out of sight while the men fought each other. Like several others, Mai huddled on her bed in the lean-to—really just a board laid across some stones—hoping the fighting would end soon. Also like the others, she longed to get out of the camps and be truly free.

"GOD SO LOVED THE WORLD"

After one particularly big fight, Hong and Mai were transferred to yet another camp, Lang Gin. The camp was a punishment camp, designed to isolate "troublemakers," and Mai didn't know why they had sent them there. There was a silver lining to the "punishment," however, because the camp had a building that served as a church—not that Mai knew what a church was. But one day she happened by the building and looked inside one of the rooms. A large white banner hung on the wall, and in the center of the banner was a red cross. Beneath the cross, she saw some words written in Vietnamese. She peered through the door so she could read them: "God so loved the world."

Intrigued, she stepped inside. The people in the room were singing a tune she'd never heard before. Then a man stood and spoke in Vietnamese, and Mai listened carefully. She liked what he said as he described a God who cared, who actually loved people instead of frightening or dominating them. She wanted to learn more about this group and their strange teachings, but she had no intention of leaving the religion she had learned from her parents. She saw the God who loved the world as one more thing she could worship, in addition to her ancestors and idols.

After more than two years in the Hong Kong refugee camps, one of Mai's friends took her to see a fortuneteller. She sat across from the woman, hoping she could tell her how soon she and her brother would get out of the camp and into a free country. The old woman stared deep into Mai's eyes then took both her hands.

"Ah, yes. I see it now. You have a boyfriend."

Mai looked confused. "No, I don't. I don't have a boyfriend."

The fortuneteller looked concerned. "Ah," she said, nodding quickly, "it must be a boyfriend from a past life who is following you to this life."

"Following me?" Mai asked, looking doubtfully from the fortuneteller to her friend. She thought the woman was telling her a demon was after her. "What does he want? How can I get him to leave me alone?"

"You must go home and worship him. Pray and ask that he will leave you alone."

It wasn't the first time Mai had been accused of having a demon. As a seven-year-old girl, Mai had been very sick. A high fever had racked her body, and she could not keep down food or drink. Her mother called in the girl's uncle, a witch doctor, to perform rituals to remove the evil spirit that was causing the sickness. Her uncle hit her with a rod, saying he would *scare* the evil spirit and the sickness out of her. Mai called out for someone to help, but the family held her down while she was beaten. Then her uncle took her by the hair and slammed her head into the iron frame of her bed, trying to *shake* the demon out of her. Sometimes the beatings lasted all night. Mai screamed in pain, but her agonized cries only reinforced her uncle's efforts as he would proudly proclaim, "Now the devil is coming out of her." He also had a small metal horse with which he would prick her skin to *lure* the evil out of her.

None of his efforts paid off; Mai continued to be sick. Finally her father took her to the hospital. After a few days of taking the medicine the doctor gave her, Mai's illness was gone. Mai wondered later why the medicine was so much more powerful than the witch doctor. Now she wondered if the fortuneteller was telling her the truth. Could *honoring* this "boyfriend" really convince the demon to leave her alone?

Mai went to the large Buddhist temple in the camp and offered worship as she had seen her parents do. She wasn't completely confident in the fortuneteller's prescription, but she didn't see any point in taking chances, especially if this "boyfriend" might keep her from getting a visa and moving on to freedom. She lit the incense and kindly asked the spirit to depart and leave her in peace.

But the more she prayed at the altar, the less peace she felt.

Deep inside, she knew her uneasy feelings didn't have anything to do with the spirit world. Mai felt trapped in the refugee camp, impatient to get out. The constant battle just to live and eat wore on her, and her natural friendliness faded into anxiety and frustration. She couldn't understand the sadness that seemed to have taken root in her heart. She longed for something different and wondered if getting to a free country would fill the void she sensed in her life.

The next day she found herself walking by the church again. Seeing the sign about God's love, she wondered again who this God really was and why He had "so loved the world." Did He "so love" *her*, too?

Stepping inside, she scanned the bookshelf and pulled down the biggest book she could find, hoping it might tell her something about this God of love. Opening it, she read, "In the beginning God created the heavens and the earth . . ."

This is a history book, she thought after reading a few more lines. She'd hated history class in school, with all those dates, people, and places to memorize. She quickly closed the book and replaced it on the shelf. Running her finger farther along the shelf, she picked out the thinnest book next, a simple volume with a handsome leather cover. She opened it and scanned the beginning—a long list of names—then she began to read more closely. It was the story of a young couple expecting a baby. But the baby was clearly special, for He had a star to mark the occasion, and great thinkers came to welcome Him to the world.

Who is this baby? she wondered. *Who is Jesus?*

RUNNING TO THE GOD THAT LOVED HER

That Sunday Mai returned to the meeting room, where a preacher was speaking about God's power. "The devil," the pastor

said, "is not afraid of anyone or anything. Except for one person. He's afraid of God. Where God is, there will be no devils."

Mai's eyes widened. She wondered if the speaker somehow knew about the alleged boyfriend from her past life who was supposedly following her. Mai wanted to believe in God as soon as she heard the message. She didn't want any part of the spirit world that had caused her so much fear and pain since her childhood. She just wanted peace.

When the pastor made a call to repentance at the end of his message, Mai ran forward. She wasn't sure of the details, but she knew she wanted to worship the God that devils run away from, the God that loved her and would set her free.

From that moment on, whenever Mai felt afraid—usually as she lay on her bed, hearing the fighting going on around her—she would read the New Testament and pray to God. The pastor had told her the devil was afraid of her reading God's Word, so she continued to read it faithfully every day!

Most people in the camp went to the Buddhist temple, and Mai went with them, even after she had gone to the front of the church and prayed. The devils might fear her when she read the Bible, she thought, but it was also smart to offer some sacrifices to them, just in case. She still had idols in her tent, and each day she prayed to the God of the Christians and to her own gods as well. If one religion was good, she thought, then two must be even better. Others in the camp did the same thing, picking and choosing the parts they liked of the different religions offered in the camp.

Then one Sunday the Christian pastor spoke about not having other gods or following other religions. He said Christians must follow only one religion and cling only to the one true God. After the service, Mai returned to her tent and threw away all her idols. Some of the Buddhists tried to stop her, but Mai insisted. If God wanted her to follow only Him, she would set aside all signs of her past religion.

"Just Use Me"

On another Sunday, shortly after she tossed away her idols, the sermon was about Jesus' death on the cross, His payment for our sins. Mai went forward again, understanding for the first time the depth of her sin and repenting for it. "Forgive me, God," she prayed. "Use me. Any way You want to, anywhere You want to. Just use me."

Though she knew very little of the Bible or of Christian teaching, she began to talk about it with everyone in the camp. She continued to read the Bible voraciously, and the Holy Spirit helped her knowledge to increase. The more she learned, the more she witnessed for Christ.

Wanting to know what his sister had gotten into, Hong went to some meetings of the camp church as well. Eventually he also accepted Christ, but his commitment was not as deep as Mai's. His focus was on liberty, on getting out of the camp and into a country where he would be free. He mapped out in his mind many plans to work and start businesses and become prosperous. He wondered if being a Christian might help him get a visa to the West faster.

In the church, Mai met a man ten years her senior, and the two began to date. He, too, was waiting for passage to the Western world, hoping to set up a business and quickly make money. As their relationship grew, Mai felt herself adopting some of his priorities. Her hunger for the Scriptures faded, and her prayer life dried up. She thought more about how she would spend her money when she was free, and she prayed only enough to feel that Jesus would accept her and let her into heaven when He returned.

The deep, heart-cry prayers that had once bubbled up from her soul had evaporated. Now she prayed mostly for God to get her out of the camp and lead her to freedom. She and her boyfriend discussed marriage, and Mai did want to marry this man. But she thought twenty was too young.

One night, as she lay in her bed, Mai heard a voice. *I won't leave you behind,* the voice told her. *When I come again, I'll take you with Me.*

Mai woke up and then seemed to hear something else: a loud, sharp, agonizing cry.

Did you hear that cry? The Holy Spirit seemed to speak directly into her heart.

"Yes," Mai answered. "What was it?"

That's the cry of those who have been left behind. That's the cry of pain and hurt.

"Let Us Go . . . Outside the Camp"

The next morning, Mai put her spiritual laziness aside. Her prayers returned to their earlier fervency, and they were for much more than prosperity and a ticket to the West. She began to pray for her family back in Vietnam and for the Christians in her homeland who were suffering for Christ.

One day as she was reading the Bible, she came to Hebrews 13:12–15:

> Therefore Jesus also, that He might sanctify the people with His own blood, suffered outside the gate. Therefore let us go forth to Him, outside the camp, bearing His reproach. For here we have no continuing city, but we seek the one to come. Therefore by Him let us continually offer the sacrifice of praise to God, that is, the fruit of our lips, giving thanks to His name.

"Let us go forth to Him, *outside the camp*." The words seemed to jump off the page and burn a hole in Mai's spirit. She was astounded at the call God put on her heart: *Go back to Vietnam. Share My Word there. Tell those who are currently left behind to call on Me.*

Mai knew that serving Christ in Vietnam would come at a great cost. She knew she would suffer if she answered God's call. But she wanted to go. She had told God she would do whatever He asked of her. If He was asking her to go back to Vietnam, then she was ready to go.

She also knew the depths of the darkness in Vietnam; she had seen it in her own family. Growing up, her family had maintained in their house a dark red alter with three vases of burning incense for the three ancestors they worshiped: Mai's grandfather, great-grandfather, and great-great-grandfather. When her father died, the family would replace the oldest incense container with one for him.

Spirits were everywhere, the Vietnamese were told, and like most Buddhists there, Mai's family tried hard to appease them. They would kill a chicken or a pig in sacrifice and then offer the food on the altar. With chanted incantations, they would invite their ancestors to come and partake of the food, hoping to garner their favor. Mai longed to share the truth of God's Word with her family and with others living in the terrible darkness in Vietnam.

The next time the Christians gathered for a meeting, Mai said she had an announcement to make. She stood up, smiling. "I have heard from the Lord," she said. "He has been speaking to me."

She looked around the room at the people who had become her friends, almost as close as a second family.

"God has called me to go back to Vietnam. He wants me to share His love with the people there, to tell them the truth."

The reaction from many of the believers was swift—but not the one Mai expected.

"This is the voice of the *devil*!" one man shouted.

"This cannot be from God," said an elderly woman, closing her Bible sharply. "God brought you to Hong Kong, and God will carry you safely into freedom. He will help you prosper so that you can help your family. God would not want you to go back to Vietnam."

"If you go back there, you will suffer," another man said. "I know. I've seen it. The suffering will probably even make you forsake God. He would *never* ask you to go back there."

Mai looked at her boyfriend, hoping to see a smile of support on his face. But there was no smile, no support. Turning away from her, he stalked out of the room.

While many in the church tried to talk Mai out of the move, her brother wasn't satisfied with merely talking about her proposal. When she mentioned the topic, Hong slapped her across the face. "How can you spit on our father's dream?" he asked. "He saved for years to get you to this point, to get you to the edge of freedom. Now you would throw it all away? You would stomp on your own parents' hearts? Don't speak of going back any longer! Not another word!"

Mai wondered how her own brother could treat her this way, and how a fellow Christian could criticize her desire to share the gospel. She prayed for wisdom and the endurance to love her brother in spite of his opposition. She was confident of God's call on her, but she prayed that others would understand the call she had as well.

Hong's physical blows were not the most painful obstacle she faced, though. The most painful blows were emotional, and they were delivered by her boyfriend.

"God brought you out of Vietnam," he told Mai. "Why would He want you to go back there? You cannot go!"

When he could not change her mind, he broke off the relationship.

"I cannot marry a woman who is giving up her dreams," he told her. "God brought you this far, and it dishonors Him, and your family, for you to turn around and go back."

"I have dreams," Mai told him with pleading in her voice and tears in her eyes. "Now God has given me new dreams. I dream of telling my countrymen about Christ's love. I want to tell them they don't have to kill any more animals, that the sacrifice has already been made for them!"

"We have different dreams, then," he said in an icy tone. "It is over for us."

Mai watched him walk away, tears streaming down her face.

With the poor nutrition and bad conditions in the camp, Mai's physical health was deteriorating. But her spiritual health had never been better. Though her boyfriend dumped her and her church doubted her, she had no reservation about what she must do. God was calling her back to Vietnam.

THE ONLY NAME ON THE LIST

Mai arranged a meeting at the camp office, where she would apply for a return trip to Vietnam. The night before the meeting, she lay awake for hours, thinking about her decision. She wondered why so few in the camp seemed to support her. She prayed, committing again to God that she would go anywhere He wanted, that she would do anything He asked. She felt complete peace and even excitement at the thought of telling people in Vietnam about the love of Jesus.

At last she fell asleep, and in her dreams she saw herself returning to Vietnam, but she was not alone. A woman was traveling with her, and a man was part of the team as well. Mai felt clearly that this was God's assurance she would not have to go back alone.

When she approached the camp office the next morning, she had no doubt she was making the right decision. She opened the door and strode to the desk.

"I want to return to Vietnam."

The man at the desk looked up at his young visitor, a combination of sympathy and confusion arranging the features of his face. "You want to go *back*?"

"Yes."

"How long have you been in Hong Kong?"

"Almost five years."

"You are close to the end of your time here. You will probably have a visa to get out of here in just a few months. Then you can go to America or to Australia. Don't give up now."

"I am not giving up," Mai answered steadily. "I no longer want to go to the West. I want to go back to my homeland."

"We don't get very many who want to do that. In fact, they just lowered the filing fee for that form, because no one is doing it. You do know what this means?"

"I know what it means," Mai said confidently. "But God has called me back."

"*God* called you?" he asked quizzically. "I see. Well, then, your visa applications will be canceled, and your file will be pulled. It will be as if you were never here . . . as if the last five years didn't happen."

"I know that. I am not going to the West."

"And you know that the government of Vietnam doesn't always welcome people back," he said, "especially people who snuck out."

"I am aware of that."

The man looked at her hard for a moment, staring into Mai's

long, narrow face. Then he reached into a drawer and pulled out a form. "I'll need your camp ID card."

Mai handed over her card then took the pen from his hand and filled out the form. A strange sense of contentment, even joy, filled her heart, and she didn't pause as she signed her name to the paper, giving up her chance to be free in the West.

The man pulled out a clipboard. At the top of the sheet were the words RETURN TO VIETNAM. He carefully wrote Mai's name on the top line. There were no other names on the list.

When Hong found out Mai had signed the repatriation forms, he beat her up again.

A Christian friend, Ms. Xuyen, told Mai she was crazy. But when Ms. Xuyen saw Mai again the next day, her story had changed. "You're not crazy," she assured Mai. "I'm sorry I told you that."

"What happened?" Mai asked her friend. "Yesterday you said I was crazy to go back to Vietnam, and today it's a perfectly rational decision?"

"The Lord spoke to me last night," Ms. Xuyen told her. "And He told me I need to return to Vietnam too, to share His message with the people there."

Mai's heart leapt in joy, knowing she would not make the trip alone. She remembered her dream in which another woman went back with her. In the dream, there had also been a man, and she began to wonder which man God was working on to go with them.

Ms. Xuyen went to the camp office and filled out the same forms Mai had completed. Her name became the second on the clipboard list.

A few days later, another member of their small church, Mr. Truong, came to Mai and said he also felt God calling him to go to Vietnam. "But it is difficult just to live in Vietnam," he said. "How can I survive there and serve God as well?"

"Don't worry," Mai told him. "God will take care of it all."

As Mai prepared for the trip back, she watched as God opened other doors and worked out the details of the trip. It was 1994, and she had been in Hong Kong almost five years. When the church members gathered to see the three believers off, many of them tearfully tried one last time to convince them to stay.

Hong walked Mai and the others to the gray metal gate of the refugee camp.

"How can you do this?" he asked Mai again. "I've written to Father and told him of your insanity. He doesn't want you to come back. He wants you to be free. Do you know how much trouble you will have in Vietnam? They do not accept Christians there. Christians are persecuted, arrested, and beaten. Mai, it isn't too late to change your mind."

"My mind is set," she told him.

"I can't believe I brought you here," he said angrily. "Who watched over you the last five years? Who protected you during the battles in the camps? Who made sure you got your share of rice when other people wanted to take it? I wish Trung had come with me instead of you. He wouldn't dishonor me and our father the way you are. Trung has respect. How can you *do* this?"

Mai looked at her brother sadly. "I can do this because God called me," she said. "You want to be free, to go to a free nation. But don't you see that there are more important things than political freedom or making money? Who will tell our family about Jesus? Who will tell them how to be free, how to go to heaven? God has asked me to do that, and I will. I may never be rich like you will be, but I am doing what God asked of me. Someday, Hong, I hope you will understand."

Her brother watched morosely as the three boarded a little white van that would take them to the airport. He didn't wave. Other Christians also peered through the gate, tears flowing

work on some craft project. As she grew bolder in her witness, she became bolder with her father: "I am going to do God's work," she told him simply.

Having her own father against her was almost more than she could bear. Her prayers became more passionate. *God,* she prayed one night, *I will do anything for You. I am ready to go to prison for You. I will even die for You, if that is Your will. But please, God, do not let my father persecute me. It is more than I can bear.*

But the persecution didn't stop. Years later, Mai understood that God had used this time as a training ground. If she could bear up under the pressure of her beloved father, there was no persecution that would keep her from doing the work God had called her to do.

DECLINING FREEDOM AGAIN

Eventually Mai met some American mission workers in Vietnam. When they saw her passion and determination, they generously offered to make arrangements for her to go to Bible school in the United States. It was an incredible opportunity. Mai had spent five years in the Hong Kong refugee camps waiting to go to the West. Now, back in Vietnam, she was being invited to go to America—all expenses paid!

When Mai told her parents about the offer, her father responded enthusiastically. "This is a great opportunity," he said. "Your 'American parents' want to arrange for you to go to America where you will have freedom and get an education. This is great news! You must go."

But Mai's vision had not changed. She re-read Hebrews 13:12–15, the verses God had used to call her back to Vietnam. Her passion for those "outside the gate" in her homeland had not lessened.

"I want to work in Vietnam," she told her parents. "God has called me to work with my own people here."

"Couldn't this be your God's way of helping you?" her father asked. "You're crazy not to go!"

But Mai chose to stay in Vietnam. Instead of going to the United States, she attended an intensive training course in Saigon. She didn't care where she received training and learned the gospel; her only desire was to serve God and see her countrymen won over to Him. The missionaries offered to help with her expenses in Saigon, but Mai graciously refused. She knew God would cover her expenses if the course was His plan.

For six months she stayed in a house in southern Vietnam, leaving only to travel on mission trips to rural areas of the country. Her northern accent would be noticeable if she went out in Saigon's streets, and she couldn't risk being asked to show her travel documents because she didn't have permission to be in the south. So she stayed out of sight for six straight months, sometimes looking out the window longingly at the passing traffic, wanting to go out for just a moment and be a part of the life that was going on around her. But she stayed put.

The days were long, the training intense, and everything had to be done in secret. They spent many hours each day in prayer and worship, studying the Scriptures, and taking pastoral training.

A Passion for the Tribes

Included in the training course was information about Vietnam's tribal peoples. Mai had been brought up to think all the ethnic minorities in Vietnam were backward, evil people who followed tribal rituals led by hocus-pocus superstitions. As she met with Christians who worked among the tribal people, though, God planted in her heart a passion to see them won over to Christ.

Vietnam has more than fifty ethnic tribal groups, and they are heavily persecuted. To homogenize the culture, the government has outlawed printing anything in any of the tribal languages: Only the Vietnamese language may be printed. The tribal people are mocked and ridiculed, and they face persecution even before they choose to follow Christ.

To reach these people, a group of pastoral training candidates would set out—sixteen of them riding on eight motorbikes—into the rural areas of the central highlands. The trips were brutal. In the dry season, the dust was so thick it was impossible to see more than five feet ahead of the handlebars. In the rainy season, the roads became like wet sheets of glass. To avoid the police, the group traveled mainly at night, and accidents were common. On one occasion, Mai's motorbike hit a dog, and she and her passenger flew up over the handlebars. Mai landed on her face, and by the time she knew what had happened, blood was pouring from her face, shoulder, knees, and head. The skinny yellow dog was dead.

Scars became badges of honor among the young leaders, and the group joked about their "trophies." They would pour salt into the wounds to kill infection, bind them up as best they could, and continue on their journey.

"You'll be fine," one of the other women told Mai as she helped clean and bandage her wounds after the accident. "Remember what the pastor said? If you don't have any scars, you're not ready to do Christian work in Vietnam. Well, Mai, you're more ready now!"

A New Creation in Christ

After six months of training, Mai returned to the north. She worked to plant churches and train leaders there, and her parents

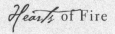

continued to pressure her to stop the work. Finally, in exaspera-
tion, Mai's father convened a meeting of the entire family,
including extended relatives.

"What do we do with Mai?" he asked, his pleading eyes going
from face to face around the room. "She continues in this foreign
superstition. We have tried to talk her out of it, to convince her to
return to our family's ways. But she will not. Shall we continue to
deal with her troublemaking, or shall we put her out of the family?"

Mai's heart broke as she listened to her father speak and
looked at the faces of her gathered relatives, people she had
known and loved her entire life. She prayed for them as they
talked, and she prayed that God would give her wisdom to answer
their questions.

And there were many of them.

She answered each one lovingly and patiently until there
were no more. The silence grew heavy in the room, and everyone
knew it was time to make a decision. Mai stepped into the center
of her family again to make one final plea, looking directly into
her father's eyes. She quickly prayed again for God to give her the
right words.

"Daddy," she began, "I will not deny Jesus. But I will not deny
you, either. You can deny my God, but even if you do, He will still
be God. You can deny me if you want to, but I will still be your
daughter. If you don't want to see me anymore, OK. But in your
heart, I am still your daughter. Even if you put me out and refuse
to acknowledge me, I will acknowledge you. You will always be
my father. And I will always love you."

When the vote was taken, Mai was still accepted in the family—
and still serving God. Later that day, Mai's father took her aside. "If
you need a place to sleep," he told her, fighting to keep the emotion
out of his voice, "you are always welcome here."

Mai thanked God that her family had accepted her, and she

continued to pray passionately that they would come to follow Christ as well.

The mission group Mai was working with continued to offer her training. She traveled back and forth to Saigon several times, receiving more training at the secret Bible school. Each trip meant long train rides, motorcycle trips, and long walks. Mai prayed before each trip, and every time she approached a checkpoint or police station. She had no government permission to travel and no legal explanation for her visits to Saigon. The lengthy train rides gave her a lot of time to think and pray, and her thoughts often turned to her father. She could do nothing but pray for his salvation, and she did so with great fervor.

On one trip, Mai received word to come home at once. "Your father is very sick," she was told. "He's in the hospital."

The diagnosis was a word that carries fear and heartache in every language: cancer. Mai went immediately to her father's bedside and became his full-time caretaker. Whatever his needs, she met them. And all the while she prayed for him and began to speak gently to him about her faith. She passed the long hours by reading the Bible aloud to her bedridden father.

Some of her fellow workers came to visit Mai's father, and he couldn't help but notice the care they showed. He found himself worrying less and less about his daughter's strange religion and more and more about his own soul. When a pastor who had helped train Mai came to visit, he stayed in the room a long time, speaking with Mai's father while other believers gathered outside the room, praying for their conversation. When the pastor left the room, Mai's father was a new creation in Christ. He immediately called for his daughter, the first true Christian he had ever known.

The two embraced tearfully as he told her of his decision to follow Christ for whatever time he had left on earth. "Now I can see that the government is persecuting the church," he told her.

"Before, I could not see. I even let them use me to persecute my daughter." His voice could not contain the regret he felt. Mai hugged her father and told him that his persecution had been a part of God's plan, a way of testing and strengthening her faith.

TAKING GREAT RISKS TO TEND THE SCATTERED SHEEP

After her father died, Mai mourned his death but celebrated the fact that she would see him again someday in heaven. And she returned to her Christian work with renewed vigor. In 1996, the mission group she worked with organized a three-day training session for Christian leaders. While Mai was praying in preparation for the meeting, the Lord spoke to her through a dream, just as He had in calling her back to Vietnam.

In the dream, Mai stood in the midst of a dense jungle.

"Where am I?" she asked.

"This is the tribal area. I have more work for you here."

"When will I go?" she asked. "And can't someone come with me to do this work?"

God answered her question with a promise: "I will send a man, a warrior, to go with you."

Many faces then flashed through her mind, a parade of people wearing colorful outfits. Each one represented a different tribe that Mai was to minister to.

After the dream and the special training that followed, Mai began to work regularly with different tribal groups. Riding her motorbike, she crisscrossed Vietnam, illegally preaching and carrying the message of salvation. In many areas, police set up checkpoints. A simple bamboo pole formed a gate in the road where police would stop travelers to ask for documentation. If everything wasn't in order, they arrested the person, or at the very least put pressure on him or her to pay a bribe before continuing on.

With no travel permissions, and carrying illegal Bibles, Mai skirted the gates, sneaking off the road and hiking through the thick forest when necessary to avoid the checkpoints. She knew the government was aware of her Christian activities and that her name had been put on a wanted list. The risks were great: Those sneaking around the checkpoints could be shot on sight. Sometimes Mai was caught and held overnight. Sometimes they confiscated the Bibles she carried. Other times the Lord miraculously hid the Bibles from their sight. Mai silently rejoiced each time they handed her bag back with the precious cargo intact.

The young evangelist saw a rapidly growing church among the tribal peoples, and she was blessed by their courage in the face of intense persecution. *The tribes are like scattered sheep,* she thought. *No one defends them but the Lord Himself.*

Mai listened to the tribe members' stories of persecution and tried to encourage them. One old man was hung in the air and beaten until the rope broke. He fell to the ground in a blood-soaked heap. Police forced Hmong Christians to move from one region of the country to another, seeking to isolate them from their own people. Christians trying to avoid the police sometimes had to leave everything behind and flee into the jungles.

In one village, Mai and other Christians were invited into the home of a tribal member who was suffering from a terrible infection, and when Mai entered the hut she had to fight to keep from vomiting, the stench was so bad. The family asked if she was a doctor or had brought any medicine. "We are not doctors," Mai told them, "and we don't have any medicine. But we know the best Doctor in the world, One who will be able to heal you."

They prayed for healing for the sick man. A month later, when she returned to the village, the man was almost healed. The following month, he was completely well. The man was eager to talk to Mai. "I want you to come with me," he said. "I will

285

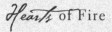

take you to my people. But it is far from here, into the jungles. It will not be easy, and it will not be quick. You must come with me for thirty days."

Mai prayed about the man's offer and felt God's confirmation. She agreed to go with him to his home village in a particularly remote corner of northern Vietnam. The villagers there were very poor and each one had only one outfit, which they wore all year. Some Christian workers had been overwhelmed by the primitive conditions and the stench of the villages. Others were turned away by the tribal culture, which spread a deep distrust of outsiders. Yet with the man who had grown up in that village to make introductions, Mai was welcomed. Soon a church was planted and began to grow. The man thanked Mai repeatedly for bringing Jesus to his village.

"When they see Christ in us," she explained later, "they accept Christ easily."

Mai sensed a special love for people of the Hmong tribe, and she began to plan additional month-long ministry trips among them. The trips were daunting, beginning with an all-night ride on a train and followed by a full day on a crowded, foul-smelling bus. Next came a half-day bus ride the next day, and the rest of the trip was made on foot. The trails in the mountains are steep, and during the rainy season they are very treacherous. One wrong step, and Mai could find herself falling into the river far below. At times, she was forced to literally crawl up the mountains on her hands and knees, fighting fiercely for each toe- and handhold.

Police gave up trying to stop the Christian meetings in these remote villages; the roads were too treacherous. In one village they *could* get to, they severely beat the fifty Christian families then forced them to move to another area of the country.

As Mai shared the gospel with the Hmong, she saw again and again the transforming power of God's Word. Many were alcoholics prior to accepting Christ while others practiced strange witchcraft rituals that included drinking animal blood. After accepting Christ, though, they gave up the rituals and were willing to face persecution for their beliefs. They believed Christ would return soon, and they wanted to be ready.

Mai sensed their hunger, and she began training Hmong Christians to be leaders. Many would travel on foot for two days to get to the training site. In some villages there were no Bibles; in others, Christians felt greatly blessed to share a Bible among forty to forty-five families. Some families sold everything they owned to go to Hanoi in search of a single copy of the Bible. But even there, they couldn't find Bibles in the Hmong language. With every visit, Mai carried more Hmong Bibles printed by her mission contacts. She was thrilled every time she saw grateful tears of joy in the eyes of the Hmong Christians as they held God's Word in their hands for the very first time.

The long trips were a drain on Mai's strength. She still suffered from motion sickness, just as she had on the boat to Hong Kong. She sometimes wondered, as she fought the nausea, why God would call her to a ministry of travel but not heal her from the miserable illness. She tried to sit near the bathrooms on the trains because she knew she would be sick. She spent countless hours balancing bags of Bibles on motorbikes while driving over the muddy roads. And she walked many miles, always carrying Bibles. She sewed the names of Christian contacts into the seams of her clothing so the police would not find them if she was arrested.

A DIFFERENT KIND OF FREEDOM

Most times her trips went without trouble, but Mai was no stranger to the police. She had been arrested ten times and usually spent from a few hours to fifteen days in police custody. Each time, the Bibles she carried were confiscated, leaving more Christians without God's Word. She often thought back to what her brother had said as she left the camp in Hong Kong. Even he hadn't known how true his words would be, how much trouble she would really face when she returned.

"You are illegally preaching!" the police told her. "Vietnam's constitution promises religious freedom, but only in government-approved worship locations and at government-approved times." One time the police gave her a confession to sign, saying she had indeed been preaching illegally.

"This report is invalid," Mai wrote across the bottom of the page, without speaking a word.

The police commander stepped forward, thinking he had broken the Christian and she had signed her name. When he read the text, he tore the paper into tiny pieces. "Do you think we are fools?" he screamed at Mai.

After another arrest, police tried to force her to sign a confession for illegally printing Scriptures and "outlaw" literature.

"God gives me this right," Mai told them. "You cannot. In Vietnam we have freedom of religion, so I can believe what I believe, whatever religion. When I walk with my Bible, that is my belief. When I talk to these people [the Christian leaders in training sessions], they are believers already, so this is not preaching. We simply share our faith together."

"There is freedom," the police told her, "but in Vietnam we keep freedom in the box. We decide who is free and who is not."

The police asked Mai to write out a report of her work and then to sign a commitment not to preach anymore. Mai agreed to write the report, and she began to write out her testimony. She wrote how she had grown up worshiping her ancestors, how she had met God in a Hong Kong refugee camp and returned to

Vietnam, and how He had changed her life. She wrote out her entire testimony.

When it came time to write out her promise not to preach, she wrote a different message instead: "The Bible is a Book the government allows to be printed (in limited quantities) and distributed. In the Bible it says we have to worship God, we have to read at home, we have to share the gospel. I do whatever the Bible says."

The police read her "confession" then miraculously decided to release her.

Each time Mai went somewhere to minister, she spent many hours in prayer to prepare for the trip. One early morning, as she was praying about an upcoming trip, she sensed there would be problems. She told her co-workers about her feeling but assured them she was in God's will whether she was in prison or on the outside. A co-worker who was scheduled to go on the trip with her cried when Mai described her feeling. "The Lord knows about this," Mai encouraged her. "He allowed this so you could come with me this time and we could encourage one another. Don't worry. I am the one who organized the meeting. You don't have to answer anything. I will carry the blame."

They set out by car, the two women and a male missionary, as well as a driver. Just as the Lord had shown Mai, the group had trouble. Police arrested them; at the station they took the two men into one room and the two women into another. In the back of the women's room was a filthy hole-in-the-ground toilet; swarms of flies covered every surface in the room. All the Bibles and Christian materials were confiscated.

After the weekend, Mai was taken to Lan Fourteen, a prison. When she got to the cell, she found several Chinese women already inside. They had escaped from China and were trying to get to Malaysia when they were arrested by the Vietnamese police. The women wanted to practice English, so Mai conversed with them in the little English she knew. The group shared one pot of rice at mealtimes, each person spooning out of the pot. Mai and her Christian friend spent much of their time in the cell in prayer, even praying for those who were there with them.

Each morning at eight o'clock a guard took Mai out for questioning. For three hours, she was interrogated. She had been labeled a "political prisoner," and the questioning was intense.

"Why do you hate the government?" one officer asked.

"I do not hate our government," she answered, always trying to remain calm and keep her voice even. "I am a follower of Jesus, and He told us to honor our government leaders. I pray for them."

"You pray for them?" the officer said with a sneer. "Where did these Bibles come from? You have been meeting with foreign spies, haven't you? Tell the truth!"

"I received the Bibles in Hanoi and Ho Chi Mihn City [Saigon]," she replied. "And I don't know any foreign spies."

"You not only *know* them," the officer said, his voice rising, "but you *work* for them! You work for foreigners against your own country!"

"I love my country," Mai insisted. "That is why I came back to it, because I love the people here."

"Who do you answer to? Who are the other Christians you work with, the leaders?"

Mai refused to name other believers. "If you want to know about them," Mai answered, "you should go ask them." She thanked the Lord silently that they hadn't discovered the names sewn into the seams of her clothes.

The questions went on like this until Mai was returned to her cell for a break. In the afternoon she was back in the interrogation room for three more hours of questioning. The pattern continued for ten days, with a new policeman coming in to question her every day. Some tried harsh tactics, screaming at her and pounding the table. Others talked very softly, telling her they knew all about the Christian meetings already, so she should just tell the truth.

On the tenth day they told her to get her belongings because she was going to a new cell. Instead, they brought her to a room where she was to sign release papers. She remembered the last time she'd signed documents to leave. It seemed a long time since she'd left Hong Kong. When the guards took her photograph to document the release, Mai was smiling. She had committed no crime, and the time in jail had only confirmed God's faithfulness to her and the ministry of reaching those "outside the gates."

I'm free, she thought to herself as she left the prison, *truly free*. She thought of her father and his many speeches about going to the West and getting freedom. *But I found a different kind of freedom. Not the freedom my father thought I would find, but a freedom far greater!*

EPILOGUE

In spite of a thriving ministry, Mai longed for companionship. She reminded God that He had promised her a warrior who would walk beside her in the battles of life. Other believers prayed with her that God would reveal this "warrior" to her—and He did.

Nam was a fellow Christian worker and a former Communist policeman. God had moved his heart with love for Mai, but he didn't tell her for many months. Instead he simply prayed that God would reveal his feeling to Mai when the time was right. And soon God made it obvious to Mai and to the leaders in the church that the two were intended for each other. They were married and continued their ministry, traveling together into rural areas to preach and train Christian leaders.

Nam's father was a high-ranking member of the Communist government and, needless to say, was not happy with his son's choice of a wife. At first he refused to speak to Mai or even to be in the same room with her. When Mai and her husband invited Christians to meet in their home, her father-in-law would stand in front of the house and chase away the arriving guests. Nam and Mai finally had to build a wall around their home so his father couldn't see when they were meeting with fellow believers.

Mai miscarried their first child during one of their ministry trips into the jungle. Doctors predicted she would never successfully deliver a child after that, but the determined newlyweds begged God to give them a family. Mai became pregnant again, but the pregnancy was very difficult. Doctors advised her to abort the baby, but Mai refused. When the time came to deliver, Mai was in labor but no progress was made. Doctors told Nam to choose whether he wanted his wife or his child to survive; they didn't think both could live. The couple prayed, asking God to spare the life of their child.

God spared both. Mai gave birth to a healthy baby girl and soon recovered her own health.

With the birth of their child, Mai's ministry has changed focus as she is now less able to travel into remote parts of Vietnam. Instead she is actively working with the local churches near her home and training rural Christian leaders who come into the city for discipleship. Nam continues the couple's rural work, traveling into the jungle villages at least once each month.

God has planted in Mai a desire to reach orphans and homeless children. She is laying the foundation for this work and envisions a day when her daughter will work side by side with her to tell these children "outside the gate" about the God who loves the world, who chases away evil, and is the only God . . . who can set us free.

Notes

ADEL:
AMID THE HORROR . . . HOPE

1. Philippians 4:13.
2. *Jihad* is Arabic for "holy war."
3. "God is great! God is great!"

PURNIMA:
A CHILD IMPRISONED, A SOUL SET FREE

1. Matthew 10:28.
2. See Matthew 5:10.

AIDA:
A VOICE FOR THE VOICELESS

1. These illegal Christian magazines were published by the underground Baptist churches in the Soviet Union. The Communists allowed only one "approved" Christian magazine to be published; it contained articles sympathetic to

the Soviet government. Underground Christians wanting to tell the real story of the church risked imprisonment to print and distribute their own publications.

2. See Philippians 3:10.
3. For further information on Aida and her trial, see Michael Bourdeaux, *The Evidence That Convicted Aida Skripnikova* (England: Centre for the Study of Religion and Communism, 1972); (American edition: Elgin, Ill.: David C. Cook Publishing Company, 1973).

SABINA: A WITNESS OF CHRIST'S LOVE

1. "The pastor! The pastor!"
2. Genesis 19:17 KJV.
3. Matthew 16:25 KJV.

LING: IN THE SCHOOL OF SUFFERING

1. Luke 10:2–3.
2. See Matthew 25:1–13.

GLADYS: A LIFELINE OF FORGIVENESS

1. Psalm 37:4.
2. See Luke 23:34 and Romans 8:28.
3. See Hebrews 13:5.
4. Romans 12:14–18.
5. Romans 8:28.

Resources

The Voice of the Martyrs has available many other books, videos, brochures, and other products to help you learn more about the persecuted church. In the U.S., to order materials or receive our free monthly newsletter, call (800) 747-0085 or write to:

The Voice of the Martyrs
P.O. Box 443
Bartlesville, OK 74005-0443
Website: www.persecution.com
Email: thevoice@vom-usa.org

If you are in Canada, England, Australia, New Zealand, or South Africa, contact:

The Voice of the Martyrs
P.O. Box 608
Streetsville, Ontario L5M 2C1
Canada
Website: www.vomcanada.org

Release International
P.O. Box 54
Orpington BR5 9RT
United Kingdom
Website: www.releaseinternational.org

The Voice of the Martyrs
P.O. Box 250
Lawson NSW 2783
Australia
Website: www.persecution.com.au

The Voice of the Martyrs
P.O. Box 5482
Papanui, Christchurch 8542
New Zealand
Website: www.persecution.co.nz

Christian Mission International
P.O. Box 7157
1417 Primrose Hill
South Africa